IT'S NOT ABOUT THE GUN

★★

LESSONS FROM MY GLOBAL CAREER AS A FEMALE FBI AGENT

KATHY STEARMAN

PEGASUS BOOKS
NEW YORK LONDON

IT'S NOT ABOUT THE GUN

Pegasus Books, Ltd.
148 West 37th Street, 13th Floor
New York, NY 10018

First Pegasus Books edition June 2021

Interior design by Maria Fernandez

Library of Congress Cataloging-in-Publication Data is available.

ISBN: 978-1-64313-730-8

10 9 8 7 6 5 4 3 2 1

Printed in the United States of America
Distributed by Simon & Schuster
www.pegasusbooks.com

For Mom,

Next time around, we'll explore the world together.

For Keith,

I chose you in the past, I choose you in the now,

I will choose you in all my futures, all my forevers, and all my eternities.

CONTENTS

AUTHOR'S NOTE

★★★

All names in my book have been changed, with six exceptions: Robert Mueller, John Pistole, Jon Huntsman Jr., Eric Holder, David Petraeus, and Louis Freeh, all men with highly public profiles.

In specific instances, I have changed physical descriptions of persons to protect their privacy, as well as details, locations, and circumstances surrounding specific meetings to protect the integrity of FBI investigations and strategies.

My work was highly classified, thus, some of my story cannot be told. As a precaution that I might have added a classified detail inadvertently, my book was reviewed and approved by the FBI's Public Relations Unit prior to publication.

Those areas deemed sensitive by the FBI's Pre-Publication Unit have been redacted for security purposes. You, the reader, will have to use your imagination to fill in those blanks. For those readers who have a deeper understanding of the inner workings of the FBI and American international diplomacy, you will, no doubt, know exactly who or what I am talking about.

The opinions expressed in this book are mine and not that of the FBI.

I hope I have been able to provide a well-rounded perspective of the life of a female FBI agent.

THE FOOT

★★★

I could not stop staring at the foot. The brownish-red henna traced along the curve of the arch was delicate, depicting what looked like some kind of vine, although the detail was too small to determine from the photo I was holding. The toenails were shiny and red, freshly painted; no scratches or scuffs marred their surfaces. This was surprising, considering the foot had been severed, blown off during a terrorist bombing committed by the foot's previous owner.

As the sweat dripped down my cleavage and into my belly button, soaking my bra and the front of my cotton shirt under my suit jacket, I felt the fatigue of the previous few days bear down on me mentally and physically. I plucked at the front of my shirt; small sucking sounds of wet fabric pulled away from drenched skin. Tiny rivulets of sweat ran down my scalp, matting my hair to my head. I asked myself why I had even bothered to blow dry my hair before leaving the Cinnamon Grand Hotel that morning. By the end of any day in Colombo, professionally dressed in my business suit, I looked like a wilted lettuce leaf, left in the sun too long. Although my counterparts dressed in cool cotton shirts and lightweight slacks, appropriate for the climate, there was no feminine equivalent for attire. I tended to dress modestly and cover as much of my figure as possible. Taking off my suit jacket to display a sweat-soaked shirt clinging to my torso would be equivalent to being in a wet T-shirt contest. I preferred to endure the heat and sweat to avoid undue attention.

I was working on a terrorism investigation in Colombo, Sri Lanka, one of the countries I was responsible for covering. I loved Sri Lanka, with its lush foliage and tropical landscape, sugary white beaches, and people who smiled more than anyone I had met in my travels. But, apart from the breezes closer to shore, the climate could be heavy and oppressive, like breathing sweltering, humid air through hot cotton balls. Sri Lanka lies 10 degrees north of the equator. For those of us who aren't ancient mariners, that is 479 miles from the exact middle of the earth, latitudinally speaking. The temperature rarely varies from a range of 82 to 90 degrees Fahrenheit on any given day. The lushness of the landscape is fed by two distinct monsoon seasons and daily afternoon showers, which means high humidity.

I had just finished having the obligatory cup of tea—*hot* tea—and cookies, while discussing the previous days' events. A team of agents from the US had accompanied me on this visit, and we had spent a couple of days at the military base, standing in the beating sun, sifting through weapons seized during a recent military raid. We were there to catalogue them as evidence in an upcoming terrorism trial. The agents and I were discussing the logistics of getting the weapons on an airplane back to the US when Mr. Weerasinghe, my main counterpart with the Sri Lankan National Police, asked me if I would take a look at some evidence from a recent terrorist bombing in Colombo. I agreed and he led us to the small windowless and airless room in which I was standing, now overly crowded with sweating FBI agents and cool-as-cucumbers Sri Lankan National Police officers.

Since the late 1970s, Sri Lanka had been embroiled in an ongoing civil war between factions of Tamils, most of whom follow the Hindu tradition and comprise the minority population, against the Sinhala, most of whom are Buddhist. The Sinhalese also happened to run the government. The US Department of State had placed the separatist group of Tamils, known as the Liberation Tigers of Tamil Eelam (LTTE), on the official Foreign Terrorist Organization list.

When a person or groups of people raise money within the United States to carry out a terrorist attack, the FBI investigates, regardless of where the terrorist attack is going to take place. It's called material support to terrorism, which is why the FBI was involved in an investigation in Sri Lanka. The FBI had been working closely with the Sri Lankan government on several investigations involving the LTTE, which had raised money in the United States to buy weapons and related components to commit terrorist attacks in Sri Lanka.

I slowly perused the contents of the room as Mr. Weerasinghe told me that a female suicide bomber, a Tamil, had entered a government official's office. While standing in front of the official's desk, she had detonated a bomb, killing the official as well as herself. Photos displayed around the room showed grisly scenes of body parts and blood and upturned furniture. Laid out on a table were the remnants of the bomber's once-vivid yellow and red sari, now covered in clots of dried brownish-red blood. As I studied the photographs, Mr. Weerasinghe led me over to a specific photo, which showed a pitted and scarred wall, faded to a dingy gray, spattered with a jellylike, yellow globular substance, streaked with blood. Mr. Weerasinghe said, "Miss Kathy, we cannot figure out what this is. We thought it might be some new bombing material, but we wanted to ask if you might know."

I inspected the details of the close-up shot, went around to all the other photos, and finally asked, "Mr. Weerasinghe, by any chance did the bomber carry the bomb on her upper body, versus in a purse or a bag she was carrying?"

"Yes, Miss Kathy." His voice lowered. "She had packed her . . . brassiere with explosive material and detonated it in front of the official who was sitting with his back against the wall."

How could I explain this one to Mr. Weerasinghe? By his reluctant utterance of the word "brassiere," I knew he was uncomfortable speaking of the subject matter with a woman. Although discussion of mutilated female body parts didn't seem to faze him, the mention of intimate female clothing flustered him. I didn't want to make him feel even more awkward or embarrassed. At the same time, I wanted him to understand the implications of what he was looking at. "Mr. Weerasinghe, the substance on the wall is breast tissue." He stared at me for a few seconds and then just nodded as if, of course, every woman knows what the inside of her breasts looks like, which, of course, most women do not know. Not like this.

I did not tell him that I had originally planned to be a surgeon. During summers and holidays, from the time I was about fifteen or sixteen until my mid-years of college, I worked in a hospital surgical department setting up instruments, collecting them post-surgery, washing them, and sterilizing them. As I became more experienced, I stood by the operating table, passed instruments, and learned suturing techniques while also learning to identify internal organs. I had seen my fair share of mastectomies and lumpectomies. The fatty, lobular tissue of a woman's breast is unmistakable.

Mr. Weerasinghe, after quietly pondering what I had just told him, gently put his hand on my arm and gestured toward his mouth as if he were harboring an embarrassing secret he didn't want the others to know. I leaned down and he said in a low, soft voice, "Miss Kathy, did you know the female suicide bomber was invented in Sri Lanka?"

"No, I didn't know that," I said, although I thought to myself that it wasn't a positive distinction to claim. I felt strangely jittery and spooked, seeing evidence of a woman who had blown herself up. At the same time, I felt a sadness wash over me, that she had felt compelled to commit such an irrevocable act. I have always felt violence belongs to men, not women. The FBI's Uniform Crime Report indicates that 88 percent of all violent crime in the United States is committed by men. Perhaps the contrast between genders can be simplified in one description: men are afraid women will laugh at them; women are afraid men will kill them. Women usually avoid the use of violence, not the other way around . . . most of the time, anyway.

I was beginning to feel the exhaustion of long days sifting through large caliber guns, rocket launchers, and other paraphernalia used to kill. As I stood staring at the carnage, that one photograph kept catching my eye, and I couldn't help but be drawn back to it . . . the photo of the foot . . . just her foot . . . the immaculate pedicure and the graceful arch of henna. Taking a closer look at the bits of sari laid out on the tables, I realized it was silk and of very good quality, not the cotton variety worn for every day.

This woman had obviously taken the time to make herself beautiful, as if dressing for a special event. Why would she do that? Why would anyone, particularly a woman, go to all that trouble when she knew she was going to die? What compelled her to present her best self, when she knew she would never walk away? I could not stop staring at the photograph. Unfortunately, our society seems to have become accustomed to seeing photos of dead men, victims of gun battles, casualties of war. Yet when I had viewed numerous photos of dead bodies during my training at Quantico, a sizable percentage of those photos were of women, victims killed at the hands of a serial killer or rapist. We have not reached the point where violence involving women has become so commonplace that we have numbed ourselves to it, at least the willful violence displayed by this woman who had chosen to take her life—and the life of another—in one of the most destructive ways possible.

Later, I was in a US embassy car that was taking me to the airport for my flight back to Delhi. The airport was only about thirty kilometers from Colombo, but the drive was always slow and could sometimes take a couple of hours. Roads were poor and filled with potholes; traffic followed no rules. Sitting in the back seat, I noticed our car was hugging the back of a public bus. Any other time I wouldn't have given it much thought. But the Tamils had started to make inroads in Colombo, which is in the south of Sri Lanka and far from the fighting in the north. Recently, a couple of buses had been bombed and several people had been blown up at a bus stop. During one of my previous visits, I had been inside the US Embassy when Diplomatic Security came around to tell everyone the embassy was on lockdown. A bicycle had been found leaning against the front wall of the embassy compound, a covered box filled with explosives strapped to the back of the seat. Everyone in the embassy had to remain inside under tight security until the police bomb squad came and removed it, allowing us to continue with our business.

Staring at the back of the bus, a feeling of alarm and panic gripped the hairs on the back of my neck. In my entire FBI career, I had felt this kind of gut-clenching fear only one other time, and that was years before while working on an investigation in the New York office.

Between the weapons at the military base, the bicycle filled with explosives, the recent bus bombings, and the photo of the foot I couldn't get out of my mind, I was becoming edgy and impatient. The ceaseless river of sweat that had drenched every inch of my clothing, now dried to an icy chill, leaving me shivering. I leaned toward the driver, tapped him on the shoulder, and snapped, "Either slow down and get a half mile away from that goddamn bus or get around it as fast as you can."

The driver was a Sri Lankan national who worked for the US embassy. He knew I was the FBI Legal Attaché. He whipped his head around to stare at me, wide-eyed. I was always kind and attentive to the local embassy staff and spent a lot of time chatting with them during each of my visits. My outburst was completely out of character. From the look on his face, I knew he was thinking I must know something that he didn't know. Not saying a word, he jerked his head back to face the traffic and swung the car around the back of the bus. Weaving in and out of traffic as best he could, swerving around tuk-tuks and bicycles and vegetable carts, he got me back to the airport in record time.

Head still on a swivel and feeling jumpy, I stood in the line for check-in to Delhi. As usual, I was at least a head taller than most people around me, so I easily scanned the array of brightly colored clothing and dark hair of the people standing patiently, inching up to the counter with bags in tow. In front of me, I saw a woman wearing a vibrant sari, swaying back and forth, restlessly touching her hair, twitching and picking at the fabric of her sari skirt. Staring at the back of her neck, I noticed she was also sweating. This might not seem to be a big detail to most, but if you're *from* Sri Lanka, or India, too, for that matter, you're accustomed to the heat and humidity. I rarely saw anyone other than westerners sporting more than a thin layer of moist "glow" on their skin. She was definitely sweating.

The more I watched her, the more nervous I became. I realized I was craning my neck over her shoulder to get a better look at her breasts. Did they look bigger than normal? Did her chest look like she had stuffed it with something other than two breasts and an ordinary cotton bra? Then I stared at her feet. They looked dusty and unkempt in a pair of cheap flip-flops. That didn't mean anything. Maybe she hadn't had time to paint her toenails. I couldn't stop staring at her. My mind fixated on the photo of that foot.

With my eyes locked onto her while I got my boarding pass, I hurried to catch up as she went through the metal detector. She sailed through. No beeps, bells, or whistles stopped her. Sitting in the waiting area, I sat several feet away from her, my agitated vigilance never wavering. I watched her every move. She sat quietly for the most part, although in my mind, she spent an inordinate amount of time assessing the passengers around her. I waited until she boarded the plane and trailed a few feet behind her. What should I do? Should I notify airport security about my "gut feeling"? Headlines scrolled through my head: "FBI Agent Profiles Innocent Woman on Airplane."

Was my paranoia simply a reaction to a dead female suicide bomber, who had perceived her situation to be so hopeless, she had willingly chosen death? Or was I paranoid because her willingness to die exposed something I didn't want to question within myself?

By the time I sat down in my seat, I was so mentally exhausted all I could think was "Fuck it. If the plane blows up, at least it'll be quick." I laid my head back against the headrest and fell immediately to sleep. The next thing I remember, I was launched face-first into the seat in front of me as the landing gear touched down onto the runway at Indira Gandhi Airport. So much for my laser-focused FBI surveillance.

After getting back to business as usual in Delhi, I dismissed my own disquiet and agitation of that day with the thought that the woman at the airport had simply been afraid of flying. Maybe, having lived in Sri Lanka—if she did live there—she had a fear of suicide bombers, too. Maybe she was just as nervous about getting blown up as I had been.

During my subsequent travels back to Sri Lanka, I never again felt the same nervousness I felt on that particular day. The woman in the airport and my own fears eventually slipped from my mind. But I never forgot about that foot. Every so often I would reflect on the woman who had blown herself up and the same old question would scroll through my mind. Why? Why? Why?

I didn't really understand why that foot meant so much to me until I woke up on the morning of November 9, 2016, the day after Trump was elected President. I had gone to bed late, after the election results were in. After crying myself to sleep, I had woken up only to cry more. I glued myself to the TV for hours, scared, unbelieving, asking myself over and over, what's going to happen to all the women in this country? Would we all become victims of "pussy grabbers"? After all the years I had worked to prove to myself and others that a woman could do the job, where would those years go? Would there be no traction for other women to gain a foothold into their own future? I felt suffocated, contemplating the loss of all those precious years of earning my own independence, moving through my life with assurance and confidence. Would I lose all joy I had felt in gaining ground for other women and the women who would come after me? A warning of what might come shriveled hard and tight inside me.

Then I thought of that foot. For the first time, I understood what it must feel like to walk out of your house, not knowing if you're going to come back, to walk out and protest and fight for what you believe, knowing you might die in the process. For the first time in my life, I understood the sacrifice women made decades ago, fighting for the right to vote. I thought of all the people who had walked into unknown situations to fight for their right to be equal, not just in the eyes of the law, but also in the eyes of every person in this country. I understood then what might drive a woman to violence.

For years, I had walked out my door carrying a gun. Though never dressing for death like the suicide bomber, I always strived to look my best, regardless what my day might bring. Business suit spotless, starched white shirt my typical "uniform." I always knew there was a possibility I might have to use my gun. I suppose, in a sense, I was willing to die for an elusive, poorly defined, patriotic sense of justice.

But, even during all those years as an FBI agent, with the inherent danger, I was rarely afraid. This was different. Now I was afraid, a terror I had never contemplated. I now knew how she felt, the woman of the foot, her suicidal violence. I knew that if I had to walk out the door for something I truly believed in, knowing without a shadow of a doubt I would not come back, I would be OK with it.

★

PART ONE

RESTLESS YEARNING

★

CHAPTER ONE

RESTLESS YEARNING

★★★

Between two worlds life hovers like a star,
'Twixt night and morn, upon the horizon's verge.
—Lord Byron, *Don Juan*

In south-central Kentucky, there is a place of rolling green hills, incredible beauty, the hum and vibration of machinery and barnyard animals. And silence. An absence of words and voices.

The year before I was born, my parents bought this place, the farm where I grew up. Three hundred acres of black dirt, the farm lay in the lush, fertile curve of the Green River, a tributary of the Ohio running four hundred miles through south-central Kentucky. A two-lane blacktopped country road bisected the farm. You could drive on that road and soon hit a dirt road leading down and down and down to the slow-moving, gray-green river itself. If you happened to make a right just before you hit the dirt road, you could cut across farms that lay in that wide curve and come out on another two-lane country road that eventually led back to the crossroad at the community of Gabe, a smattering of white clapboard houses, a red-brick Baptist church, and a country store. Across the road from the country store was a dollhouse of a post office, long shuttered after its merger with a larger crossroad about five miles away and closer to "town," the county seat called Greensburg. Greensburg,

Kentucky, in Green County on the Green River was my world, a verdant kaleidoscope, encircled and held within the confines of a cerulean sky.

Two hundred cows grazed on our dairy and tobacco farm. They needed milking twice a day, seven days a week, 365 days each year. There was no time off, no vacations. The only time I ever recall my parents taking a nap was on Sunday afternoons, after church and Sunday dinner, our midday meal. On Sundays, my father was adamant about observing the Sabbath, the holy day when God is to be respected and labor was frowned upon. I never understood how my father justified milking the cows twice on Sundays, which constituted labor in my eyes. At a young age, I hadn't yet learned to question my father. I only knew that I had to tiptoe past the open door of their bedroom between the hours of about 2:00 and 4:00 during those lazy afternoons, the only time me and my siblings were allowed to sit still and while away an afternoon in daydreams.

In our curve of the river, our farm was the most prosperous, well-tended, and cleanest of all the other farms in the area. We knew all our neighbors and they knew us. Neighbors were quick to help out if the cows got through a fence and ended up on someone else's land. To my mom's irritation, Daddy often lent his equipment to other farmers who hadn't invested back into their own property. Too often, that equipment was returned broken or in need of repair, which required cold, hard cash on our part; cash we did not have.

We were cash poor, but we had everything we needed—food, clothing, a house, and soil that sustained us. The currency on a farm is not money but hard work. All money that the farm generated was reinvested back into its success or failure. More cattle, bigger and better equipment, more modern barns, and the bulldozing of more land so that more crops could be planted, and eventually, more land purchased. More, more, more became my father's mantra. All this required an endless cycle of work generated by my family of eight.

When a car drove down our road, chances were we knew the driver. More likely than cars were tractors pulling tobacco setters or a manure spreader, or, later in the season, a wagon stacked ten feet high with sweet-smelling bales of hay to be stored in the barn loft.

I loved haying season. The green-gold rectangular bales seemed to march in parallel rows and straight lines down the field, grassy stubble mowed close to the ground already dried to a golden brown in the high heat of summer.

I would lie in bed at night with my windows open, the breeze blowing the white net curtains aside, carrying the scent of drying hay—grassy and slightly woody, mixed with sun-warmed earth. If I felt rain on that breeze, I knew the next day Daddy and my brothers would scramble to bale the hay and get it into the barn for safekeeping before it got wet.

When the hay was finally baled and put on the wagons for transport to the barn, I would stand and watch as the hay elevator trundled each bale slowly to the top of the barn, the bales placed in neat square rows, stacked one upon the other until they reached the rafters. It was there that I spent hours upon hours of my early years, climbing to the highest bales, closest to the roof of the barn, where I could peek through the crack of the loft door. From there I could see the farm, but the farm could not see me. I could listen to the sounds carried on the wind and know where everyone in the family was at any given time. The clatter of a disc and plow meant my dad was in the field, black moist earth turned to the sun, ridges drying to a light brown in the summer heat; the tap-tap-tap of a hoe meant my mom was weeding the garden; the spray of a hose meant that one of my brothers was washing out the milk barn from that morning's milking.

Nothing on a farm of that size is quiet. The chatter of the sparrows and robins and blue jays heralded the beginning of each day, followed by the singing of cardinals and the rapid-fire drumming of woodpeckers in the forest. The sharp barks of our border collie, Tootie, as she rounded up the cows for the afternoon milking. Chickens climbing down from their roost in the morning, ready for their stiff-legged stroll around the pen in search of forgotten grain or an ear of corn from last night's supper thrown across the chicken wire. The braided melody of the birds, the barnyard, and the taming of all those acres by hand and machine was as ubiquitous as wind soughing through leaves, merely a backdrop to the silence inside my head.

The house in which I grew up—two stories of white clapboard—was over a hundred years old. Sometime in the first decade of living there, my mom and dad did some renovation on the inside to upgrade the kitchen and put wall heaters in the upstairs bedrooms. Before that, I remember sleeping under an electric blanket with my oldest sister and watching my breath crystallize in the freezing air. The only stoves we had were two wood stoves, one in the kitchen and one in the den, where my dad and brothers spent their time at the end of the day: Daddy reading the newspaper, my brothers watching TV.

The girls were in the kitchen with my mom, cleaning the kitchen table and washing the dishes after supper.

My mom's days never ended. It wasn't until I had spent long years away from home that I saw her sit down at the kitchen table and take the time to eat her meal. When I was young, her normal routine was to hover around the table while doing other kitchen chores and when supper was over, she would eat quickly, and move on to the next task.

I don't really remember the first time I realized that I did not belong. I must have been around three or four. I think it was one of the times I used to sit behind the wood stove in the kitchen, petting, with a stranglehold, some scruffy animal I had rescued—a rabbit, a kitten, or a baby skunk. I watched my older brothers and sisters sitting quietly around the big table having breakfast before the school bus arrived. It was always quiet around our table. My dad did not like to hear us talk. I don't think he wanted us there at all. One untoward comment from anyone around that table could land a jaundiced eye from his direction. No one ever wanted to feel the smack of his baseball-mitt-sized hands, or be within the long, extended reach of our six-foot-six veteran of World War II dad.

As I sat and watched my mom and my siblings orbit my father's mute control, I absorbed the knowledge that silence can be a magnet, repelling and pulling at the same time. They wanted to please my father, wanted to fill the emptiness, draw him closer. At the same time, they were frightened by their failure to do so, so they circled, trying to interpret the voiceless vacuum.

At one point, I came to the realization, with the unfractured soul of a child, that not only did I not belong, I wasn't necessarily wanted. As number five of six children—number six hadn't yet come along during my quiet forays behind the stove—I was largely ignored. I wasn't particularly bothered by this. I was left to my own devices, at least for the first five years or so.

I can distinctly remember what I consider my first adventure, that first time rushing headlong into the rapturous feeling of escape, traveling beyond the edges of those safe places in my front yard and the surrounding barns. I must have been about four or five years old; I hadn't started kindergarten yet. My dad had bought a pony, solid chestnut, touched by one single slash of white between his eyes. His name was Blaze.

The first time I sat on Blaze's back, I fell in love. Blaze of the dainty ankles smelled of sweet hay and the rivulets of sweat that ran down his sun-warmed neck. I would bury my face in his thick, shaggy mane, breathing in the scent that I came to associate with freedom. Blaze didn't have a saddle. I rode him bareback, a rope halter dangling in my soft, little girl hands. I could feel the warm scratchiness of his coarse hair brushing against my bare legs, my heels lightly encouraging him to take me where I wanted to go.

Every morning before he left for school, my brother Rick tied Blaze to the front porch. I was far too young to venture out to the fields to catch Blaze and my mom and dad were too busy to bother with traipsing after a pony. Their days began well before sunrise and ended well after sunset. This one act of kindness by my otherwise grumpy and taciturn brother set me on a journey that, to this day, has never ended.

I spent countless hours riding Blaze, traveling into the forest, listening to the murmur and susurration of overhead leaves, which seemed to whisper that I would be OK. Years later, I would come to understand how the forest became my parent, the giver of refuge, my bulwark against the world.

Sitting atop Blaze, trotting along as fast as I could encourage him to go, I felt the breeze against my skin, moving past me as it came over the horizon, from a far off, mysterious place. I soon associated rapid movement forward with a movement toward where I wanted to be.

Songs and poems are written about the wind at your back, carrying you headlong into the horizon. Not me. The wind at my back spoke of someplace I had already been. The wind in my face came from a place I had not yet seen, a compass guiding me should I lose my way.

I loved Blaze, raced down the stairs every morning to make sure he was tied to the post. Mostly, I loved more what he represented, what he made me feel. On his back, I could adventure anywhere I wanted to go—the forest, the pond, the blackberry patch, the far corn field, where he often threw me off so he could eat, leisurely, the ears of corn left over from harvest. Although I never left the farm, and in reality probably never ventured more than a half-mile, I felt like I was in another place, another country.

During those early years of meandering, no one ever came for me, nor was I peppered with frantic questions about where I had been. These were the years I set my eyes on the far horizon, dreaming of the day I could walk into its endless curve. I was drawn to the singular and the extraordinary; all things that were different roused my curiosity. It became my driving force.

I was a child of no preconceptions of differentness; no racism or religious prejudice existed in my heart. I did not understand then that I craved the experience of different lands, different cultures, different people. Maybe there, I would recognize myself in others. Because as hard as I tried, I could not see my own likeness at home.

CHAPTER TWO

SCHEHERAZADE'S CARPET

★ ★ ★

*Everywhere I have sought rest and not found it, except
sitting in a corner by myself wih a little book.*
—Thomas à Kempis

My early years of freedom on the farm were short-lived. As soon as I started school, I was deemed old enough to work in the house, and later in the yard, the gardens, and the fields. On the farm, work was not only expected, it was required. Otherwise, you suffered the reach of my father and the overworked and weary wrath of my mother.

I can distill the memories from my early years on the farm into the most basic elements that would eventually carry me away from that farm in central Kentucky: the desire to travel, my love of books and music, the curiosity and need to paint a clear and vivid picture of understanding, and memories of my mom. But this last realization would take years of understanding.

❖

I don't remember a time I couldn't read. Perhaps this is because once I discovered books, the exploration that took place between the ink and paper became one of the greatest passions of my life.

My brother, Jimmie, was thirteen years older than me. Being the eldest, he had been the one to fight Daddy about going to college, paving the way for the rest of us. He also gave me the gift of books. I came home from school one day to find our back porch filled floor to ceiling with hundreds of volumes. Jimmie had purchased all the books from a local estate sale. Books were everywhere: stacked in towers of varying shades of brown and black, older volumes not yet tainted by modern standards of colorful art and design; the smell of dry paper, the dust falling in crumbs from the pages. I hid amongst the ziggurats and pyramids when I was supposed to be doing chores. Opening, closing, and sniffing out exotic, faraway places tucked behind that curve of horizon I longed to follow. I became a hummingbird in the high heat of summer, flitting from blossom to bud, sampling, sustained by the life-giving nectar of words, words that became desire and imagination entwined.

This oasis became my own personal library for a time until it departed, along with my brother, to the house he shared with his new wife. By this time, one of my older sisters had her driver's license and she deigned to drive me to the library on occasion for a supply of new books. I had been forced to flee to the local downtown library because Mrs. Caldwell, the librarian at my elementary school, had started to limit the number of books I could check out. She did not believe I could read five books in one week. She was right. I was reading ten or more, depending on the book and on how late I was able to stay awake each night after homework and chores. Mrs. Caldwell was universally disliked, and feared, by all the kids in elementary school. During "library time," she never failed to give someone a swat on the side of their leg as she roamed the room, looking for some snot-nosed kid to exhibit the tiniest iota of cheeriness, which must have been disallowed in her universe. I never saw her smile.

I won the "Bookworm of the Year" award almost every year in elementary school. Mrs. Caldwell, ever skeptical of my reading ability, would make me stand in front of her desk and provide a brief recital for each book. She was not much taller than I was, but was built like a tree stump—straight up and down, with a bosom that projected out of her polyester double-knit dress like the formidable prow of a pirate ship. A long-chained necklace snaked horizontally across the broad expanse, the locket dangling vertically just over the edge, swinging back and forth in metronomic rhythm as she stood staring at me, arms akimbo. As I described the plot of each book in the greatest detail, it crossed my mind to ask her how she would know for sure if I had read the book. I suspected Mrs. Caldwell had never ventured into the enthralling depths of a book beyond forcing it into its appropriate Dewey Decimal order, as she did with the unruly students she disliked, meant to be seen but not read.

What I did not tell Mrs. Caldwell was that elementary school reading was a piece of cake; one book per evening was my norm. By that time, my older siblings were already in college and I secretly read their textbooks. When they read the classics, I read the classics. When they learned about history, I learned about history. Later, in high school and college, I realized I had read the lion's share of the required classics between the ages of seven and twelve. The only one I ever reread later in life was *The Grapes of Wrath*. I distinctly remember where I was when I read the last scene for the first time. I was hiding behind my sister's bed. It was her book after all and I feared taking it too far from where she always left it. I instinctively felt the poverty, the despair, the sense of dislocation of the characters. Yet, I did not understand why a grown woman would nurse a grown man like a baby. I remember sitting there on the floor, in the half-darkness between the bed and the wardrobe, my back against the wall feeling a peculiar sense of . . . weirdness. I wasn't disgusted or grossed out, but knew something had been said, in the saying of nothing, something I did not understand. This was a new sensation; no matter how I pondered it, my young mind couldn't illuminate it with meaning.

Eventually books began to morph into the desire for adventure, to travel, to see faraway places. The sense of never belonging, knowing I was meant to leave one day, that other worlds were calling to me; wrapped itself around a feeling of heaviness in my chest, followed by the thickness in my throat, tears near the surface, longing to be somewhere else. Standing in front of the shelves at the library, I wanted to see the Wild West of Annie Oakley; I wanted to smell the fresh pine of the lower Sierras during the booming Gold Rush with Lola Montez and Lotta Crabtree. I wanted to feel the wind in my face while soaring the skies as Amelia Earhart. I wanted to be anywhere, as long as it was far away from Greensburg, Kentucky.

I read everything. Sitting at breakfast eating my poached egg on toast, drinking my cup of tea, I would read the box of oatmeal, the label on the Lipton tea box, the peanut butter jar.

Around the age of eleven or twelve, I had explored my way through several volumes of the new set of encyclopedias that my mom and dad had bought from a traveling salesman. I can't imagine the cost of such a luxury for our cash-strapped household, but I know my mom insisted that this window to the world outside our farm should become a part of our lives. Despite her constant weariness, Mom was curious and loved to learn new things. She would order seeds to grow asparagus and cauliflower in the garden, both exotic vegetables to our meat-and-potatoes diet. She bought a furniture restoration kit so that she could bring a renewed luster to our old furniture. Looking back now, I believe Mom wanted the encyclopedias as much for her insatiable curiosity as she wanted them for her children.

With the arrival of those encyclopedias, I immediately became an armchair traveler and fixated on Egypt and the pyramids. I decided I was going to be the next Howard Carter, sifting through dust and sand, seeking some long-lost civilization waiting to be discovered.

I took to following along behind my father's tractor as he plowed the fields in the springtime. My bare feet would sink into the moist, cool loam. When I felt a sharp prick or the pressure of a rock under my toes, I would drop to my hands and knees, digging for ancient treasure, in the process picking up arrowheads and tomahawks, pristine and intact. I would clean, then painstakingly draw each one on a sheet of paper, measuring, detailing where it was found, writing my own speculation as to how it got there and to whom it belonged. This would prove to be a harbinger for my career as an FBI agent, sifting through evidence and intelligence, documenting details of an investigation.

Mrs. Miller and the Bookmobile became my Scheherazade on a magic carpet, delivering fables and legends to my doorstep. The Bookmobile, an old box van emblazoned with bright blue letters, had probably been used by a bakery or bread company at one point. Whenever I saw it pull into the driveway of the farm, I raced across whatever field I was working in, hoping she wouldn't drive away. Mrs. Miller never minded I was usually dirty and barefoot. She let me scan the shelves as long as I wished, or until my mom came to drag me away. From June until August, Mrs. Miller arrived once a week and let me check out as many books as I wanted. She allowed me to be an armchair traveler all summer long.

Though I worked in the field by day, by night, I time-traveled to remote and alien lands. As my bare feet dug themselves into sun-warmed earth, picking tomatoes or cucumbers, hoeing row after row of newly planted tobacco, my mind strolled the streets of sixteenth-century London with Queen Elizabeth I, or struggled through the passes of the Rockies with a wagon train. My back grew strong and my imagination soared.

I longed to see the Far Pavilions of M. M. Kaye and trek the Silk Road with Marco Polo. My ears perked as I imagined the sound of a train whistling in the distance—the sound of promise, the sound of things to come, the sound of places past.

My desire to flee began to morph into an imperative.

CHAPTER THREE

MY MOTHER'S SILENCE

★ ★ ★

*Of all things upon earth that bleed and
grow, a herb most bruised is woman.*
—Euripides, *Medea*

One of my earliest memories is watching my mom pull the dry, sun-scented laundry from the clothesline. I must have been about three or four years old. It was before my little sister, the sixth and last child of our family, was born. I was standing in the grass, barefoot as usual. My mother's left arm gathered the crisp white sheet in folds, as her right hand reached up to unclip the wooden clothespins.

I loved that clothesline. Row upon row of sheets and pillowcases and towels became my own personal funhouse as I wove in and out, running my hands along the fabric, hearing the rasp of little girl fingertips against the roughened chicken feed-sack pillowcases, printed with tiny flowers and other intricate and exotic designs, none matching. Mom was thrifty and covered all our chicken-feather-stuffed pillows with feed sack pillowcases, the life of a farm-yard chicken coming full circle. I can still recall waking up in the middle of the night feeling a scratch on my face or ear, the random point of a chicken feather having worked its way out of the blue-and-white ticking. In the light of day, I would grasp the sharp, hollow point and slowly pull downy barbs of white or yellow or red. I would try to remember which chicken had given those feathers, its headless body dunked in the coal packer of steaming hot water to loosen the quills, to be plucked, then fried, ending up on our kitchen table alongside mashed potatoes, homemade biscuits, gravy, and corn on the cob.

As my mom's arm reached to pull the dry laundry to her, her hand froze in midair and I heard her gasp, a sharp intake of breath that seemed to catch in her throat, sharp as a chicken bone. I felt my own body go rigid. At a very tender age, I could absorb my mother's moods, though she held a glacial self-control over her emotions. I had already learned there would never be any hugs, never a quick kiss, never a minute to listen to my real or imagined fears. Fear was a weakness, not to be tolerated.

I was alarmed at the look of revulsion on her face. Following the path of her gaze, I saw a snake sinuously winding its way around her feet. She kicked her foot out, then stepped wide, over the snake's body. She didn't make another sound, not a shriek, not a grunt. Rooted in place, I realized it was not just one snake, but two—long and thin, black and gray—twined around each other like a serpentine yin and yang. In the middle, where they wrapped around each other, was the space, now empty of my mother's presence, leaving only the warmth of her bare feet.

I think I was too young yet to be afraid of snakes. During the few seconds I continued to watch their slow, languorous embrace, I heard Mom running back across the grass. She carried a long-handled hoe, sharp, always readied for some chore in the garden or yard. She raised the hoe over her head, the handle as long as she was tall; she had to stand some distance away from the snakes. Her lips pinched together in a white slash, eyes focused on the ground in front of her, she brought the hoe down, severing the head of the first snake. She sliced, again and again, both snakes in multiple pieces, thrashing in the grass. She continued slashing in rhythmic fury until there was no movement, not in the grass, not in her arms. Without a word or a look in my direction, she turned, dragging the hoe behind her as if too exhausted to lift it off the ground. I don't remember if *I* cried or made a sound. But I do remember *her* silence.

❖

My mom's thick, work-worn hands kneaded the dough, not with a tenderness, oblivious to the silky texture of flour melting into the buttery dough. Her movements were brisk and hurried, impatient for the ingredients to submit to the insistent will of her fingers. I watched as her left hand broadcast a light dusting of flour on the countertop, right hand slapping the ball of dough into the middle of the circle, tiny motes of flour dancing in the sunlight streaming through the window. The muscles of her forearms flexed and relaxed, the rapid movements a silent echo of the slap-slap of the rolling pin. Satisfied with her results, she used a table knife to dot pats of ice-cold butter onto the now flat circle of dough, followed by spoons full of homemade strawberry jam. With an uncharacteristic gesture of tenderness, she grasped the far side of the circle of dough in the tips of her fingers and folded it softly over the mound of buttery sweetness. Using the index and middle fingers of her right hand, she pinched the edges together in tiny, consecutive points and valleys, a crenellated half-circle, the turnover now ready for the oven. I remember standing by her side, on the braided twine stepstool. But I don't remember her voice.

❖

Flower beds skirted the four sides of my childhood home. The 1850s clapboard façade had been painted and repainted varying shades of white, layer upon countless layer. Zinnias, always my favorite, with lacy orange and yellow faces, echoed the intricacy of the doilies crocheted by my Aunt Helen. Hidden away in the cedar chest, the doilies were too delicate and fine for a practical farm wife to use. In the flower beds there were marigolds, maroon-tipped orange petals cheerfully dipping and nodding on their long stems, assured in their prescient knowledge of my future. Garlanded marigolds are ubiquitous throughout the India I would come to know and love in a future I was not yet aware of.

I can see my mother kneeling in the dirt, her fingers pinching away the dead and dried heads of each flower, encouraging their regrowth; the pinks and purples of the stately hollyhocks standing sentinel over her solicitous concern for this act of defiance, this desire to make her surroundings beautiful. I am there, kneeling by her side, her ever-present shadow, listening to her silent reverie, her escape.

❖

Mom's head bent over the sewing machine, the lamp casting the shadow of her hair over the fabric as she pushed it through the foot, needle whirring along the seam. She was teaching me to sew dresses for my Barbie, just as she taught me to sew a diaper for my cat. I remember Sourpuss, a hole cut in the back hem for his tail to wave jauntily and rebelliously, as he ran across the yard rolling and clawing to rid himself of the unwanted encumbrance.

I stood at my mom's side, our heads almost touching, watching her fingers move quickly, as her left hand pulled the fabric while her right hand held it taut. Mom did much of her sewing in the late evening, after the television had been turned off. The only two rooms heated in the wintertime were the kitchen and den, where the TV was located. So she did her sewing in a little corner of the kitchen. The antenna outside the back porch picked up the buzz of her sewing machine, causing random dots of "snow" and jagged flickers on the TV screen. My dad and brothers always complained—they were the only ones who got to watch TV—so she waited to do her sewing until after they had gone to bed. I could always sense the solitude she wrapped around herself in those evenings when the rest of the house was quiet, her exhaustion from long days and short nights softened her movements. It was during these rare moments that I was not afraid of her; her impatience from days in which she had no respite from the work of a farm wife was briefly laid aside. In these moments, she found the patience to teach me, to hold something creative in her hands and show me that I, too, could create something beautiful.

❖

I don't remember Mom speaking to me during all these times we spent together. Have I imagined her silence as my own silence, a silence I kept out of fear that I would intrude upon her exhaustion, her escapes into her own mind, her self-imposed exile from her surroundings? Surely, she must have spoken to me. How else would I know those strawberry jam and butter turnovers would need to be baked for twenty minutes in a 350-degree oven? How else would I know the trumpet blossoms of the fuchsia four o'clocks opened their timid faces to the sun only in late afternoon? How would I know to cut a pattern for my Barbie dresses, the tiny teeth of the tracing wheel leaving a lavender stain along the lines of the fabric I would later cut and piece together with my little girl fingers? Surely, my mother had a voice.

But because I perceived my mother to have no voice, she became invisible to me.

CHAPTER FOUR

MY SILENCE

★★★

"Daddy, if you don't stop hitting her, you're going to kill her." My sister Julie stood at the door between the kitchen and our back porch. She had her toddler daughter hiked up on one hip. My little sister, Rita, peeked out from behind Julie's legs, both hands with a firm grip on Julie's thighs. They were watching my father whip me.

I heard the whistle of the belt before I felt the sting on my back, the cold metal of the buckle biting into my flesh. I can't remember if I had on a tank top or a halter, but I could feel the prong of the buckle drag across my backbone as he pulled his arm back and above his head, bringing the belt down again and again and again.

I can't remember what I had done wrong, or what grievous sin I had committed, but I would have believed my sin warranted punishment. I didn't cry or scream. I didn't make a sound. That was my error. My silence only served to communicate to my father that he hadn't punished me enough, I hadn't yet learned my lesson. So, the thudding of leather against skin and bone continued for a length of time I can no longer recall.

Julie uttered not another word as she watched. I could tell she was frightened by the way she had spoken to Daddy, hesitantly, softly, sure in the knowledge that, in his frenzy, he might round on her and her baby, belt flailing blindly. Julie had moved back home for a year while her husband, Jason, was in the military. He had been deployed to South Korea and as she had just had a baby, it was agreed that Julie would move back to the farm, a move I knew she did not desire. She had gained her independence from the endless drudgery of work and silence and powerlessness. She was the one who had taught me that someday, I could leave, too. I knew she felt her place at home was tenuous at best. So, she stayed silent, her silence echoing my own, waiting for my father's arm to tire or his anger to lose steam, vented of whatever frustration he carried with him every single day of his life.

My father was a tall, lanky man, long of limb and muscle, his face chiseled from granite, prominent cheekbones jutting against the sun-browned skin, stretched leather across bony angles and hollows. His black hair was straight, thick, and shiny, and his deep-set, dark smoky gray-green eyes always had a vacancy, not of unintelligence, but of memory, seeing something only he could see. I often wondered if he was trying to pull those memories to himself or push them away. His full lips rarely parted in a smile. I rarely heard his voice directed at me, not even during those times he punished.

A few days later, I was at my sister Bev's house, mowing her yard. She had married Ben, who had come into her life when I was just eleven years old. Ben was a surgeon, "Lord and Master" of the local hospital in my small hometown. She was twenty-five years younger than he was. It was the stereo-typical relationship—operating room nurse meets surgeon, romance ensues, he's already married, town is scandalized, she's labeled with the scarlet "A" of a young temptress.

None of this mattered to me at the time. I was too young to understand why it mattered to other people, mostly to my father. When he learned of the affair, he dragged my sister away into the living room for "a talk." I knew something serious would be said, because the living room was used only on Sundays after church. Somehow, I knew "the talk" had nothing to do with God.

My sister was strong-willed, at least early in her life, and married Ben. He was always smiling and jovial and quickly became more of a father to me than my own father. He talked to me, joked with me, asked me what I studied in school, and generally acknowledged my existence . . . something my father had never done.

Ben and Bev lived in a house with a big front and backyard, so Bev had offered to pay me to mow them for her. I was thirteen or fourteen; I didn't yet have a driver's license and had no way to earn money on my own. This time away from the farm became a reprieve. In their house, I never felt the anxiety that plagued me when I was home, the worry that constantly nagged at the back of my mind, that I would get blamed for something, or not work hard enough, or bear the brunt of frustration and weariness. My sister Bev had given me the gift of a refuge.

I remember it was a hot summer day, so I had on a halter top and shorts, and raggedy sneakers sporting holes where my toes had worn through the canvas. I recall finishing the mowing and taking off my shoes only to find the tips of my toes had turned green from wet grass, the rest of my feet tanned and brown from days in the fields.

As usual when I finished mowing, I went into their house for a cold drink. As I stood in the kitchen drinking my Ski, a local soda much like Mountain Dew, except sweeter, Ben took me by the arm and steered me toward the bathroom. Ben usually had a perpetual smile on his face, with twinkling eyes that predicted mischief. As he tugged at my arm, his normal gregariousness was absent. I loved and respected Ben, so I wasn't reluctant to follow him, but I was perplexed as to why he wasn't his usual jocular self.

Inside the bathroom, he turned me so that my back was facing the large wall mirror. He pointed and asked, "Who did that to you?"

I wasn't accustomed to looking at my own back. The one bathroom we had in the house where I grew up had only a small mirror over the sink, certainly not large enough to see my back after a bath. I craned my neck to look at myself and saw dark blue and purple bruises crisscrossing the expanse from neck to waist, the U-shape outline of a belt buckle clearly delineated in darker blue-black. I had felt the soreness in my back but put it down to the ache and tenderness of the daily farm chores. Now I stared at myself. Then I remembered. Until that moment, I had forgotten.

I have been told that Daddy frequently hit me, although very few times have surfaced in my memories. Other incidents were relayed to me through exchanges that my husband, Keith, had with my siblings and other family members. Once, my older brother, who had married and moved up the road, was driving past our house when he saw my dad beating me. My brother did not stop to ask questions. Keith was told by other family members that they, too, had witnessed Daddy hitting me. I don't recall the punishment, nor do I recall anyone intervening on my behalf. Those siblings who left our hometown had decided to leave it all behind. Those siblings who remained close perhaps retreated into the silence of their condemnation of his actions, if they had any at all.

One memory was dredged to the surface many years later by a visit to my dentist in San Francisco.

"Kathy, have you ever been in a car accident where you might have hit your face or the side of your head?" the dentist asked. My mouth was completely open while he examined my teeth, all I could manage was a slight shake of my head. I had never been in a car accident.

"Hmmm, odd, all the teeth in your left bottom jaw are cracked down the middle." Still unable to speak, I shrugged. As I lay back in his chair, I sifted through my memories trying to come up with an explanation as to why my teeth were cracked. Thanks to a childhood of fresh milk growing up on a dairy farm, I had always had strong, straight teeth, and never needed braces. The blow must have been pretty hard to crack teeth. Then I remembered. But it was a memory I was unwilling to share with my dentist.

Daddy had slapped me hard across the face, in the process dragging an earring out of my ear, a deep gouge scratched into the side of my cheek. I don't remember why he hit me. I only remember looking down at the gravel of the road I was standing on, searching for my earring, a cheap little green and brass car. I had recently had my ears pierced and had amassed a small collection of earrings I hung from a plastic earring stand that looked like a pink and orange carrot, covered in tiny holes just large enough to insert the wire of an earring. I fiercely guarded those earrings, making sure each one was placed in its hole every night, proud of my meager collection. Looking down, I couldn't see it amongst the dirt and pebbles. My regret at losing that earring far outweighed what Daddy had just done. I dared not move lest he strike me again, so I stayed quiet until I heard his long strides carry him away. I carried that tiny white scar on my face for years.

"Kitten, if he ever does that to you again, you'll come tell me, won't you?" Ben's voice was kind and it brought tears to my eyes, the tears I had not shed in front of my father. I nodded and looked down at the floor, ashamed of my own display of weakness.

Ben, a tall, thickset, muscular man, formidable in his own right, must have said something to my father because he never hit me again. My father would later express his disdain for me through words.

CHAPTER FIVE

SUNDAY MORNINGS

★★★

My father rarely participated in the lives of us kids or my mom. In school, we were not allowed to participate in ballgames or band practices or after-school activities. We all had work to be done once the school bus delivered us back home. It would be many years later, after I got my driver's license, that Daddy would relent and allow me to be a part of my school's community. He showed little interest as each of my older siblings graduated from high school, attending the ceremonies only after being shamed and harangued by my mom.

Daddy did, however, spend a great deal of his time preparing for an afterlife. He was steadfast in his belief that St. Peter already has his name in the "good book" and that his entrance through the gates of heaven was guaranteed. When I was older and brave enough to challenge my father, I asked him why he was so sure he was going to heaven. "Because I've already talked to St. Peter and I'm in." This statement was punctuated by a brisk nod of his head, which I knew brooked no argument. I remember thinking, hopefully, St. Peter wouldn't ask any questions about how Daddy treated his wife and kids.

Because of his unshakable faith in his own heavenly fate, Daddy set himself the task of saving the rest of our souls. Every Sunday morning, we were forced to attend Sunday school, followed by the sermon, which could last an hour or longer, depending on how well the preacher could rouse the guilty and distraught congregation with his fire and brimstone warnings, entreating all to walk the aisle and declare themselves a sinner or go to hell and suffer the wrath of a vengeful God who deemed them unworthy of being saved.

I hated those Sunday mornings. When my mom would come upstairs to wake me, I knew not to complain; otherwise, I garnered her wrath as well as my father's. I didn't understand why my mom never complained about what I considered to be wasted hours. Mom was stingy with her time, as she had none to spare in her sunrise to midnight days of backbreaking work. She did not seem to experience joy in listening to the sermons. Every time I would look over at her, her head was lowered against her chest, eyes closed as if in silent prayer.

As much as I hated church, I decided I should spend the time reading the Bible while the minister droned on about sin, hell, and damnation. At one point, having read enough of the Bible to take note of contradictions and parables that defied belief, I ventured to ask my dad why Abraham was allowed to have Sarah *and* Hagar and how Methuselah could live to be almost a thousand years old. "You don't question the Bible, things were different back then!" roared my father, eyes daring me to question his unyielding faith that everything in the Bible was an edict, not to be disputed or challenged by the likes of a sinner such as lowly little me.

After my father's death, and shortly before her own, I gave my mom the gift DVD called *Walking the Bible*. My mom loved to listen to me talk about all the foreign countries I had lived in and visited. In my naivete, I thought this gift would combine two things that seemed important to her, travel and religion. Several weeks after I had given it to her, I found it, still in its cellophane wrapper, tossed under a pile of newspapers.

"Mom, why haven't you watched your DVD?"

Her blue eyes tight with scorn, she said, "Because I don't believe in any of that *shit*!" The last word was spat in obvious contempt. From my years of quiet observation of her, I had learned to interpret my mom's facial expressions. Her lips pinched in a tight circle meant harsh words were headed my way. More often, I had learned to search her face for those rare declarations of love and support, which I yearned for but seldom received. Her face now said she was finished with the subject at hand. Mom was sphinxlike in sharing her most deeply held feelings. I can count on one hand the number of times I ever saw her cry. I suppose in her mind, why bother, there was no one to listen.

Caught off guard at her vehemence, I said, "Whaaat?" In all the years of my life, I had believed that my mom followed the same moral principles and dictates as almost everyone who lived in central Kentucky, the rigid Baptist doctrine of hard work, which eschewed happiness, providing a guarantee for the gold-paved streets of heaven waiting to greet them upon their last breath, finally allowing a much-needed rest.

As I stared at her, speechless, I tried but failed to recall a conversation I had had with my mom about religion, about the Bible, or about God. Not a single one came to mind. I had painted her with the same overzealous brush that I had painted my father. I had been blind to her beliefs my whole life.

"Then why did you make us all get up every Sunday morning and go to church?"

"That was your daddy. If I hadn't made you all get up, he would have beat me." Then she went back to staring at the TV, totally absorbed in *Gunsmoke* or *Mayberry RFD* or whatever show she had already seen a hundred times.

I watched her eyes close in what was now one of her many daily naps and realized all those hours in church were a respite for her, a time when she could drowse, retreat to a meditative place where there were no demands upon her body, her mind, or her emotions. She probably looked forward to it, although I doubt this realization had ever crossed her mind.

As I watched her lined face in repose, I wished I had spent more time talking to my mom not just about the places I had traveled, but the religions and customs and superstitions I had encountered in my life traveling with Keith and working overseas with the FBI. She knew I wasn't religious, but she never chastised me for not attending church. Once when she called me in San Francisco on a Sunday morning, she teased me by asking, "Did you go to church today?"

"Yep, Mom, I did. I went and sat on the edge of a cliff overlooking the Pacific Ocean. Because, if there is a god who can create something so beautiful, then she's bound to be there." Mom laughed. As the years progressed, and I grew into myself, I started to refer to God as a "she" whenever Daddy would bring up religion.

I knew it pissed Daddy off, but not nearly as much as our doomed discussion about reincarnation. I had told my father I didn't believe in the Bible but thought it an interesting series of myths and metaphors to help people explain their lives. Reincarnation was something I had believed in since I was ten years old, having discovered Edgar Cayce in one of my oldest sister's books. Daddy rarely spoke to me after that conversation. Shortly before he died, he barked, "I'm going to die knowing one of my children is going to hell. I feel sad about that."

Although accustomed to a lifetime of my father's wrath, I felt a tight fist curl inside my chest. Too proud to let him see the impact of his words, I mustered a smile and said, "Well, unfortunately, Daddy, I have a feeling we'll be seeing each other again." An unsmiling, green-eyed glare was his only response.

Now that I can look back at my father with the knowledge I've gained in my training and experience with the FBI, I can see that he probably had PTSD. His silence, pain, and inner turmoil were born of many things. The horror of the war in which he had fought; the holiness in which he beheld his much-loved mother who had died while he was miles away, fighting that same war. I wish I could tell him there is no shame in survival. I wish I could tell him I forgive.

CHAPTER SIX

THE WHITE WOLF

One never reaches home, but wherever
friendly paths intersect, the whole
world looks like home, for a time.
—Hermann Hesse

"How can you hear a song, sing along to the words, tell me the name of the band and the exact year the song came out, but you can only recall a few memories from your teenage years?"

Keith's curiosity wouldn't be the last time someone would ask me that very same question.

I began to consider this absence and the reasons I had forgotten or denied those years existed. By the time I was twelve, my four older siblings—two brothers and two sisters—had gone away to college, moved out of the house, and married, leaving only me and my little sister, who was four years younger. I don't remember my dad's anger and violence toward me before this time. He rarely spoke to me and, if I had to venture a guess, he probably didn't even notice me. While I still had siblings who lived at home, getting lost in the litter was easy. By the time I moved into my teenage years, however, I became the brunt of his discontent.

With the absence of my siblings, our house became even quieter, my days filled with long periods of silence. It was during these years I began to retreat inside myself.

As I entered my teens, I was transferred from the tiny elementary school at the nearest crossroads to the middle school in town. It was there I learned the difference between the "country" kids and the "townie" kids. Greensburg, at the time, was a thriving personification of what a small, rural American town should look like—town square lined with stores and shops, a corner drugstore with a soda fountain, a hardware store, a diner, a town library, all surrounding an old courthouse. Kids who lived in town could walk or ride their bikes everywhere—the public park, the swimming pool, the soda fountain. They lived a life I glimpsed only briefly on TV shows.

I, on the other hand, was from the population that surrounded the county seat. We children of the farms were separated from town by no more than five miles but were five thousand miles apart in social standing.

While summer was a welcome break from school for most kids, I hated when the school year ended. My summers began on the tobacco setter, hands repetitively placing a young tobacco shoot into a mechanical arm to be rooted in the ground. A month or so after this planting, I would be back in the same field with a hoe, chopping weeds from between the plants to prevent them from overtaking the delicate green stalk that would bring in the "green" at the end of harvest.

I wasn't really bothered by the differences that existed between my world and the kids who lived in town. In school, I was always at the top of my class and had reached the height of almost five-foot-nine by the time I was eleven, which earned me the nickname, "Stick Stearman." Somewhere in my young soul, I already possessed the congenital conviction that I would leave someday.

An unfortunate circumstance of being tall at such a young age is that I was perceived as being much older as I entered high school, particularly when I didn't behave like most young girls. I was quiet and shy and carried myself differently, cautiously. Because I looked older, I was frequently asked out by older guys. My mom and dad rarely let me go out, so I didn't date much.

When Bryan, one of the most popular guys in high school, asked me for a date, I was reluctant but curious. He was a townie kid and was friends with a circle of popular girls who placed me in the bull's-eye of their townie cabal after one of their ex-boyfriends asked me on a date. Apparently, dating a member of this clique was like being in the mob; you weren't allowed to date anyone else without their express approval.

Bryan was sweet and friendly, not what I had expected. He said he asked me out because he liked the way I walked around school. When I asked him what he meant, he said I held my head high, I never looked at anyone, nor did I talk to anyone when I was in the hallway. He said I walked like I owned the world. But he had guessed I was shy and wanted to know why I seemed afraid.

I was surprised by this conversation, which was far more insightful than any conversation I had had with a boy up to that point. Most times, boys at that age were interested only in kissing, getting to first base, and the sex they hoped might follow. In spite of the "talk" I had gotten from my mom, "You know boys won't buy the cow if they can get the milk for free," I wasn't going to have sex with anyone until I was ready.

During what I now call my quiet years, music joined books as a favorite escape. I would stay awake deep into the night, crouched on the windowsill of my bedroom window, stereo headphones on, riding on the waves of sound to places I had read about in books brought to me by the Bookmobile. Music and words allowed me to escape the discord of my home and travel to a place where the silence in my head was replaced with visions conjured by words and composition, written just for me. Time would cease to exist, and the vibration of the music became a recognition of my own longing to be far, far away.

After he left home, my brother Rick had gifted me with a stereo. Although Rick and I were close for a time when we were kids, he was prone to mood swings. He slept like the living dead and when my mom would send me to wake him up, he was like a bear wrenched out of hibernation before springtime. I found a long stick and would stand several feet away from him, while I poked and prodded him awake, well clear of a random fist. I realize now that his gift was instrumental in providing an escape, although at the time I was confused by his generosity.

For Christmas one year, when I was about five years old, I received a child-size set of bagpipes, the ivory chanter and red, blue, and black plaid bag all made of cheap plastic. I loved those bagpipes and played them every day, all day long. It should not have been a complete surprise when I found my little plastic bagpipes under the bed one day, the bag neatly slit open, completely ruined. I remember crying for what seemed like days. I always felt Rick was responsible, because he complained the loudest about the noise I generated with my new toy. When he bought me the stereo, I thought perhaps it was because he felt guilty for slashing my bagpipes all those years ago.

My senior year of high school, knowing the time for me to leave for college was drawing nigh, I began to come out of my shell and outwardly display aspects of my inner self. I painted my jeans with rainbows, wore my hair in multiple plaits, polished my nails with black and silver stripes, pierced my ears multiple times, tried pot, had sex for the first time, got drunk on gin and Sprite, all the while making As, reading everything I could get my hands on, and listening to Gino Vannelli and Barry White, the Eagles and Journey, castoff records donated by Rick.

At some point during my middle-of-the-night music sessions and surreptitious reading, I happened upon a story about a pack of wolves that had shunned one of their own because she was all white, unlike the grays and blacks of her tribe. The story was told from the perspective of the white wolf, her longing as she stood on the outside, her circle of security and protection closing ranks against her because she was different. I felt like that wolf. And like the white wolf, I knew someday I would have to turn from everything I knew, everything that was familiar, and walk into an unknown future.

★★★

PART TWO

THE FBI WANTS YOU!

★★★

CHAPTER SEVEN

BEAUTIFUL HORSES
AND FAST WOMEN

★★★

*You must give up the life you planned in order
to have the life that is waiting for you.*
—Joseph Campbell

I did not grow up dreaming of becoming an FBI agent. Television programs depicting the drama and adventure of the FBI were not on my radar. When my father wasn't watching the news, my two older brothers dominated the TV.

At the age of twenty-four, I was still naive about the FBI. I had no idea the words "This is the FBI," could cause some people to seize up in fear, while sending others running in the opposite direction to avoid arrest, interrogation, or punishment. So, when I picked up the phone and heard a voice say, "Good morning, Kathy, this is the Louisville FBI office," I didn't feel fear. There was no *What the hell have I done?* The voice continued, "We received your letter to the Secret Service. We're obviously not the Secret Service, but if you want to apply to the FBI, we would like to send you an application." My only thought was, *Had I sent my letter to the wrong address?*

After I changed my major in college, from premed with plans to go to medical school to international business, I started working on my MBA, my eyes, as always, looking toward the horizon. At one point, while spending a weekend in my hometown, I was having a conversation with a family friend, Rob, who knew I craved something different, wanted to do things that most women do not do. Rob suggested that I might want to look at government agencies, such as the FBI, Secret Service, CIA, and State Department. As a Kentucky state trooper, he knew each of these agencies hired women and had offices all over the world. But more importantly, they would provide the adventure I craved. He knew a Secret Service agent he could introduce me to, so I started with the Secret Service.

Just a few days prior to receiving the phone call from the FBI, I had sent a letter of introduction to the Secret Service office in Louisville, a copy of my résumé, and a request for an application to their Special Agent program. So, how did the FBI get my letter? I had no idea, but I was not about to let this opportunity slip through my fingers. I couldn't say "Yes!" quickly enough.

A few days later, I received the preliminary application from the FBI, which screens applicants for citizenship, education background—all agents must have at least an undergraduate degree—and three years of work experience. I passed the first step, piece of cake. The next phase was an in-person, written test to assess the applicant for logic, reason, judgment, and personality. The test took place at the field office and lasted for several hours. I can't recall if the test had an actual score, all I cared about was the letter I received that said, "You pass!"

I returned to the field office a couple of weeks later for the panel interview, the next phase during which several agents would interview me, asking a series of questions for which I couldn't study. I was told only that I would be judged on my responses, my poise, and my ability to counter any argument or discussion the questions might engender.

In the Louisville field office, I sat on one side of a long conference table while three Special Agents, all men, perused me from the other side. I sat, back straight, hands in my lap, willing myself to smile but not too much in case they might conclude my levity was an indication of stupidity. I never gave a second thought that no female agents were part of the interview. I had no idea I was applying to a bastion of male testosterone, good old boy networks, and water cooler hijinks. I can't recall a single question asked, but I do remember walking out at the end of the interview, my face hurting from forced half-smiles. I didn't know if I had done well or not; I was just glad it was over. As

I walked out of the room, I glimpsed silent smirks and grins passed from face to face on the other side of that table.

Around the same time, I had continued to pursue the Secret Service by sending another application to their office in Louisville. This time, it got to the right place. I received a preliminary application in the mail and I met with Rob's Secret Service friend in a restaurant close to his work in Lexington. He was friendly and open to all my questions, but professional to the point of being aloof.

I was afraid I had made a bad impression until he asked if I would like to meet with a female Secret Service agent, Gerri. Hearing the words "female Secret Service agent" was like hearing the words "there's a unicorn in the forest." I couldn't imagine such a creature, but I was pretty sure meeting her would be both intimidating and enlightening.

The timing was perfect as my brother-in-law Ben was traveling to Washington, DC, for a medical conference, so I accompanied him and my sister on the trip. I had made arrangements to meet Gerri in Alexandria, Virginia, at Joe Theismann's Restaurant, just a short walk from the Metro station. I had told Gerri I would be wearing a dark red coat and that I was tall with long, brown hair. I stepped inside the restaurant, and the cold air of the door closing behind me blew hair in my face. I stopped to take a breath, calm my nerves, and swipe my hair out of my eyes, while scanning the tables for someone who might resemble a Secret Service agent.

A woman sitting at a table against the window stood and waved. "Kathy?"

This woman could *not* be a Secret Service agent. She was tall, blond, curvy, and downright gorgeous. I don't know what I was expecting, but she wasn't it.

Gerri was open and friendly, with a broad grin that stretched from ear to ear. We spent the next couple of hours talking about her experiences in the Secret Service, traveling the world. She was one of very few women in the agency and warned me that sexism was rampant, especially at the training academy in Georgia. Gerri had an easygoing manner and treated male chauvinism as if it was a nuisance. I had never considered I might be treated differently because I was a woman, so I laughed along with Gerri when she regaled me with stories of men behaving badly. I left my meeting totally in awe of this independent, smart, and beautiful woman. Those hours spent with her solidified my decision to do something unique with my life. A couple of years later, Gerri and I would end up as roommates in Alexandria, Virginia.

By the time I met Gerri, I had learned that I had passed the FBI's panel interview and had a multipage application to fill out for my background investigation, accounting for every single day of my life since the day I was born. As part of the background process, friends, family, and neighbors would be interviewed about my competency to serve as a Special Agent of the FBI. This process can take weeks if not months, so while the investigation was humming along, I continued with the Secret Service process, which included a polygraph. I had never even seen a polygraph being conducted on TV, so I didn't know what to expect.

I was seated in a straight-backed, wooden chair, a blood pressure cuff around my arm, sensors attached to my fingers, and multiple tubes and sensors strapped to my chest, all of which were, in turn, attached to the polygraph machine sitting on a table to my left. After a few test questions, the polygrapher, an attractive thirtyish male, indicated that the next questions would be "for real" and I needed to answer them honestly with a simple "yes" or "no." *Piece of cake, I have nothing to hide.*

After about a dozen or so questions about my life, like where I lived and what I had studied in college, the polygrapher said he was going to take a break while he reviewed my results. I was to sit quietly. After a few minutes, he continued asking questions of a more serious nature, questions about drug use, criminal activity, and false statements on documents. My answers came easily, so I didn't think too much about it when he said he would take another break to study my results. Once again, I sat quietly while he stared at the long roll of paper in front of him, making pen marks on the lines and squiggles zigzagging up and down on the graph paper. After several minutes, he met my gaze with a solemn glance. He then got up and walked into another room. Having no other choice, I continued to wait quietly. He finally came back with no explanation other than, "OK, let's continue."

He began with more in-depth questions about drug use and other criminal behavior, specifically the forging of documents. Again, I didn't hesitate in my answers. I had tried pot in high school, but it never appealed to me, so I hadn't made it a habit. In truth, I found it a waste of time, and I didn't have the money nor the inclination to try it again. Plus, my dad—and my mom—would have beat the shit out of me. I had already told the polygrapher all this when I filled out the questionnaire in advance. There was nothing more to tell.

After this series of questions, he repeated the process by appearing to study my results then disappearing into another room for an even longer period of time. The only thing I was beginning to worry about was whether I would need to pee before the whole thing was over. The polygrapher returned, a worried look on his face, although so far, he had engaged me in no conversation other than to ask questions. This time, in a more forceful voice, he asked me again if I had ever falsified a document. "No." Related questions followed. "Have you ever falsified a paper, a bank check, or an application?" Each time I answered with a firm "no," but I was getting pissed off. Finally, the polygrapher got up and stood in front of my chair and started yelling at me, "Your polygraph tells me you're lying! Why are you lying? We know you've falsified some document in your past, you just need to admit to it!"

Not sure what to say or how to react, I looked at him and said, "I don't know what to say to you. I'm being honest. I have never falsified a document in my life."

"Not even in college? Didn't you ever copy someone else's report or take someone else's words as your own?"

"No, never." I wasn't afraid of failing the polygraph. I was more confused about what I might have done that I couldn't remember. I couldn't think of a single time I had written something that wasn't my own. As he continued to stand in front of my chair, silently glaring at me, my mind was sifting back through my essays and papers and school loans and applications on which I might not have been completely honest. Absolutely nothing came to mind. I shook my head again and said, "I'm not lying."

After one more round of the same questions asked in a dozen different ways, about my so-called criminal activity in forgery and false documentation and lying, the polygrapher indicated the test was over and walked out of the room.

By this time, about three hours had passed without a break and I seriously had to pee. As much as I might want the job, I wasn't willing to pee in my pantyhose for the sake of proving to the Secret Service I wasn't a criminal. The polygrapher finally came back in and, without saying a word, began to remove the sensors and cuffs from my fingers, arm, and chest. As I stood up, he asked, "How do you think you did?"

I had already concluded I was not going to become a Secret Service agent, so I didn't bother to hide the fact that I was pissed off and anxious to find a toilet.

"Obviously I failed and frankly, right now, I don't care. I just need to find a bathroom." He threw back his head and started laughing. "You passed it."

The polygraph experience turned me off to the Secret Service. Years later, I would experience other polygraphs while working for the FBI, yet none were as overtly aggressive as this one.

By this time, I had passed the physical fitness test, which was the FBI's last phase. The Secret Service faded further into the background after I received a letter from the FBI offering me the opportunity to attend New Agents Class (NAC) at the FBI's training facility on the Marine Corps Base in Quantico, Virginia. Serendipitously, the day before I was planning to leave for Quantico, I received a phone call from the Secret Service letting me know I had been chosen to attend their training academy in Glynco, Georgia. I was happy to say, "Sorry, I leave for the FBI Academy tomorrow."

Two days later I found myself in a modern tiered classroom, long white tables placed one behind the next, where thirty-nine men and ten women, including myself, sat quietly in business attire, anticipation and anxiety palpable. None of us moved or chatted. Our seats, permanently assigned to us during our time at the academy, were in alphabetical order, which meant I was in the last row at the back of the classroom. From my vantage point, I could see everything and everyone in the room. After we were asked to stand and introduce ourselves, I watched with a combination of nerves, excitement, and naivete, as each one of my future classmates stood and revealed a slice of their personality. Some were serious, others were funny, a few were shy.

Then it was my turn.

"Hi, my name is Kathy Stearman. I grew up in Kentucky, where the horses are beautiful, and the women are fast."

I never figured out how my letter to the Secret Service made it to the FBI office, but it no longer mattered. I had made it to the FBI Academy, and I was ready for the challenge. Or so I thought.

CHAPTER EIGHT

THE GERBIL TUBES

★★★

"You're crushing my balls!" Jared whispered hoarsely into my ear as he clung to my back, my right arm between his legs, my left hand gripping his right arm, his torso draped across my neck in the classic fireman's carry. I sensed he was gritting his teeth while trying not to let anyone else overhear. Jared was a two-hundred-pound Navy SEAL not wanting to advertise his discomfort at having his gonads flattened against the shoulder of a female, fifty pounds lighter, who was struggling to hang on to him.

"Shut the fuck up! What do you think you're doing to me?" I spat. I was hot, I was sweaty, and I wanted to get him off my back. But I was determined to make it down the field toward the finish line, where I could see all my other classmates had finished and lined up to watch me stumble toward my goal, to dump Jared as unceremoniously as possible at their feet. We were told to run the distance of a football field with our partners on our backs. But there was no way I could have even broken into a trot with the solid muscular hulk of a Navy SEAL clinging to me. I was happy to get one foot in front of the other without my right knee giving way. I knew I still needed to make it through the last physical fitness test, which involved a two-mile run.

The fireman's carry would culminate the hardest day in the latter half of training. It had started with a long run up Radar Hill. I can't remember if the run was five miles or ten miles. Distance does not matter when carrying a medicine ball held out to either side, in front, or over our heads as the instructor yells out commands. By the time we made it to the top of Radar

Hill, and headed down the other side, it was all I could do to grip the ball against my chest without dropping it. My delts and traps were on fire, my hands slippery with sweat. Just when I thought I couldn't take another step, we arrived at an ops training course.

We were allowed to rest for only a few minutes, but I don't remember being allowed to have water. Maybe my memory of water was superseded by the fact that all my clothing—navy nylon shorts, a workout bra, and a gray short-sleeved T-shirt, class emblem on the front and our last name handwritten in black marker on the back—were soaked with sweat. The mid-July summer heat and humidity of the Virginia countryside sapped every ounce of water from an already overheated and overtaxed system. My tongue stuck to the gluey roof of my mouth as I fought the urge to wipe the sticky residue of saliva from the corners of my lips. I wished more than anything in the world to bury my head, neck deep, in an ice-cold tub of water.

The ops training course consisted of several room-like sections barricaded from each other with plywood walls at least eight to ten feet tall. Within each "room" was a mishmash of loose boards, sawhorses, wooden platforms, rope and pulleys, some stretched over small water-filled ponds. We were divided into groups of six or seven and told that each "room" presented a task to be completed, working together as a team. While we talked and evaluated how best to accomplish each exercise, we were judged by an instructor standing off to the side, clipboard in hand. In between each room, we had to do a physical activity such as run the obstacle course across a gravel road from the ops training facility, drop and do sit-ups and push-ups, or run laps around the field. The point of the exercise was to judge our ability to make critical decisions while exhausted, thirsty, and stressed.

It was during one of these "breaks" from our ops training when I found myself carrying Jared on my back. When instructed to find a partner to practice the fireman's carry, all the women in the class picked another female. I was the odd one out as there were nine remaining females in the class.

As I reached the instructors all standing at the finish line, I let Jared slither onto the ground. I didn't care if his balls were intact or not. All I cared about was getting his weight off my back so I could breathe. As I bent over with hands placed on my knees, trying to catch my breath without vomiting first, the instructors started to clap. One of them came up to me with a grin ear to ear, and said, "Kathy, I can't believe you just did that."

My mind said, *Fuck off before I puke on your shoes.* Instead, I just looked up at him and nodded, taking the water bottle he held out to me. Not a bad prize for crushing the ballsack of an aloof, arrogant, albeit friendly in his own condescending way, Navy SEAL.

❖

The FBI Training Academy had turned out to be, surprisingly, not too dissimilar from what you would expect, including the extracurricular activities that are going to ensue when men and women, anxious, stressed, and in phenomenal physical condition, are locked down in the same location for weeks. The running joke was that every person of the opposite sex started to look good after traipsing back and forth through the hallways, called gerbil tubes because they were encased in glass and connected all the buildings. There was no relief in sight for all the pent-up hormones until curfew was lifted and we were allowed a weekend away from the academy. I soon learned quite a few people hadn't bothered to wait for that weekend away.

Every now and then I would go running with some of the girls in my class over to the Marine Corps officers' training school. There is nothing finer than a shirtless, young, exceedingly fit Marine glistening with sweat, red nylon running shorts clinging to every muscle and curve. It was incentive to work out as often as possible.

Training at the FBI Academy involved long days filled with physical fitness classes; running, boxing, self-defense; long hours of shooting on the firearms range; classroom work; and practical exercises in Hogan's Alley, the small fake town located on the academy grounds.

Toward the end of our fourteen-week training, we spent more time at Hogan's Alley, practicing various scenarios for arrests, conducting searches of homes and businesses, interviews, and surveillances. The FBI Academy hired several local actors and actresses to take part in our exercises so we could get a feel for what it was like to interact with the general population once we graduated and went off to our assigned field offices.

On one particularly hot day, we had just finished with an arrest scenario and were taking a water break while waiting for the next to begin. Instead of our usual training gear—navy pants and light blue polo shirts—we were wearing business attire. That meant suits and ties for the men and skirts, blouses, and jackets for the women. I had on a melon-colored jacket and beige skirt, beige pantyhose, and beige high heels. I thought lighter colors would give me some relief from the sun. I was wrong.

I was standing on a sidewalk, trying to find some shade in the overhang of a building when Jim, who sat next to me in class, started laughing and pointing, "Stearman pissed herself, Stearman pissed herself!" Jim and I had become buddies. I truly liked him, even if he had been a state trooper and thought he knew everything already. He was funny and irreverent and had a jokester streak in him that bordered on cruel and heartless. I didn't necessarily like his mean streak, but he could always find a way to make me laugh. Being his buddy also meant I was the butt of his jokes. Most days I took it in stride and gave back as good as I got. But today I had had enough of his buzzing in my ear like a mosquito, tutoring me on what I was doing wrong.

I looked down at the front of my skirt where Jim was pointing. Streaks of sweat were running down from my knees into my shoes. Maybe I'm an anomaly, but my armpits don't sweat. My back sweats, my cleavage sweats, my scalp sweats, but not my armpits. Perhaps as comeuppance, though, my kneecaps sweat like a fireman's hose on full blast.

"I didn't piss myself, Jim."

"Yeah, you did, you pissed yourself. Everybody, look, Stearman pissed herself." He rotated a gapped-tooth grin, wanting to make sure everyone heard, "Stearman pissed herself, Stearman pissed herself." At that moment, he was the chanting bully on a playground.

"My knees are sweating. Don't your knees sweat?" My classmates, following this exchange, shook their heads.

"See, you pissed yourself," Jim jeered as he continued to point.

Hot and annoyed, I said, "Fuck you, Jim, if you had to wear pantyhose in ninety-five-degree heat your knees would sweat too. Just. Go. Fuck. Yourself. OK?"

At the FBI Academy, I never showed my anger or irritation, no matter what I was feeling on the inside. I had been doing it my entire life; I had learned the art of accommodation. I wanted to fit in, so I had adapted my personality to be fun and outgoing, laughing off jokes and ribbing, shooting off ribald comments in exchange. I wanted to be part of the team and the hazing was part of the process. Being in the FBI was a huge responsibility, and I wanted that burden. I wanted to be part of this family.

So, when I yelled at Jim, his taunting stopped abruptly, his eyes wide. This was a Kathy he hadn't seen before and he didn't know what to say.

The next day in the classroom, he leaned over, touched his shoulder to mine, and said, "You OK?"

"I'm fine, just don't fuck with me anymore or I'll fuck you up. OK?" I knew Jim meant no harm. He had helped me in ways I could never repay. I also knew he felt that helping me allowed him a certain leeway to use me as his punching bag. But I had been punched enough. I was learning to fight back.

CHAPTER NINE

KENTUCKY WINDAGE

★★★

"Face it, Stearman, you can't shoot. You're going to wash out so you might as well quit now!"

The voice in my right ear was muffled by my shooting "ears," the earmuff protection worn during firearms training. But I could still hear every single hateful word.

Tommy showed up on the shooting range every day, joking and laughing with the male agent trainees. When he looked at one of the females, his upper lip curled away from his teeth, an alpha dog growling his dislike at a mongrel cur. It didn't take me long to recognize that Tommy was a misogynist son of a bitch. It took me less time to decide I needed to avoid him at all costs. That effort proved to be futile. Tommy was the supervisory firearms instructor for New Agents Training class (NAC) 87-12 (the twelfth class to pass through the FBI Academy in 1987). I was Tommy's new pet project.

At the time I entered the FBI Academy, approximately 600 of 10,000 agents in the organization were women, having been allowed to join only in 1972. This was just two short months after the death of the legendary and infamous FBI Director J. Edgar Hoover, who quickly began rolling in his grave. Today, with over 13,000 agents, the FBI's female population still counts approximately 2,600 agents, only 20 percent of the total force.

Of the ten women who started in my class, one female agent trainee had already been told to leave because of her lack of firearms skill. Her dismissal came early in our training, so I knew that if I didn't pass muster, I might be next. I hadn't given it much thought when she was asked to leave. The class was told she had hurt her ankle and as a result, would not be able to pass firearms training. I thought it was odd a minor injury would have prevented her from being "recycled" to the class behind us after a short recovery period. Now, having to endure Tommy's sarcastic harangue in my ear every firearms session, I was beginning to wonder if she had indeed hurt her ankle or if she had been Tommy's first victim. All I knew was that he had now set his sights on *me*.

Every time I stepped up to the firing line and waited for the signal to start shooting, Tommy positioned himself directly behind me, slightly to my right. I could feel his breath on the back of my neck. Goosebumps shivered across my shoulders and my muscles clenched involuntarily, waiting for the first insult of the day. Every now and then I would glance back at his pale, nondescript face, balding head covered by a baseball cap, arms crossed over his wiry little chest. His cold, unsmiling eyes would narrow as they looked into mine; his lips would press together in a nasty smirk. I would turn around without comment, trying my best to tune him out so I could focus on my target.

I had grown up on a farm in Kentucky, so I wasn't a stranger to guns. I had occasionally been allowed to shoot a "critter" gun, which in Kentucky parlance is a shotgun or rifle used to rid the farm of groundhogs or moles that invaded the yard and fields. My childhood had afforded me more experience than a lot of people in my training class and certainly more than most of the other female trainees. On our first day at the firearms range, I shot pretty well. At least I hit the target. But, after the first day, something changed. Every time I fired a round from my Smith & Wesson Model 13 revolver, nothing happened on the target in front of me. Literally, nothing. No bullet holes appeared even though I was aiming center mass. What if Tommy was right? Maybe I couldn't shoot after all. Maybe that first day had been an anomaly and I was going to wash out of Quantico, a girl from Kentucky who couldn't shoot a freakin' gun. I would never hear the end of this back home.

During every firearms session, I stood in the long line of my forty-seven other classmates and stared down range at the paper target. Theoretically, it's supposed to be shaped like a man, but it actually looks like an oversize bowling pin. A thin black line divided the no-man's-land—the section around the edges that does not count in scoring—from the middle part of the target that actually counted. I needed to get my bullets *inside* that black line. Squaring my shoulders and gritting my teeth, the twinge of hot tears behind my eyeballs,

I doggedly kept shooting. Every now and then, a pitiful little hole would appear somewhere in the corners of the rectangular cardboard, but never inside the lines where it counted. I had already told Tommy multiple times I thought there was something wrong with the sights on my gun. His response was always, "There's nothing wrong with the gun, Stearman. The only thing wrong here is that you just can't shoot. Give it up and walk away."

Other than Tommy, the rest of the firearms instructors were pleasant, if not overly friendly. At least they weren't actively trying to get anyone booted out. Tommy held that distinction. Although I was pretty sure some of the other male instructors knew it, they couldn't really say anything. Tommy was senior, and as I found out during subsequent years of my career, male agents stick together, no matter what.

Joe, another firearm's instructor, tried to be helpful whenever he could. I think he was aware of Tommy's attempts to demean me and he tried to put me at ease with a bit of humor.

"Stearman, now just relax. Pretend like you're shooting around the toilet sitting on your front porch back in Kentucky," he would say in my ear, as I took aim at whatever target was in front of me. I would turn and give him a little smile to acknowledge that I knew what he was doing. He had started kidding around with me that everyone in Kentucky was barefoot, toothless, and had various nonfunctional items of indoor furniture and appliances on their front porches. I was too new and too nervous to joke back, so I just accepted his ribbing with a grin and a shrug of the shoulders.

I started to dread firearms even more than I had learned to dread my father's wrath. I didn't really mind all the other training, but firearms was my nemesis and as soon as I received the new weekly schedule, I would scan it, seeing nothing but those half-day chunks of time at the shooting range. My stomach would churn, and a funk would settle in as each firearms day approached.

Several weeks into training, I found myself in the athletic trainer's office, lying on an examination table. My right knee had started to grind painfully every time I went running. Not passing the physical fitness test was a no-no and if I blew my knee out, firearms would be the least of my worries. The physical fitness trainer had a quiet, no-nonsense demeanor. I hadn't really dealt with him prior to my knee injury, so I didn't invite any extraneous chatter. As he iced down my knee and secured it with an ace bandage, he looked up at my face and asked me if I had cried since arriving at Quantico. I don't know what prompted the question, but I am certain I didn't look like I was about to cry.

I looked up at him and said matter-of-factly, "I grew up with a six-foot-six father with hands like baseball mitts, who fought on Okinawa in World War Two. I can take anything anyone dishes out here."

He cast his eyes down, then looked up at me with a little Mona Lisa smile and said, "OK, but if you need to, don't cry here at the academy. Go off to Lake Lunga, you know where that is, right?"

Lake Lunga, the largest lake on the Marine Corps Base and located behind the main FBI Academy, was a quiet retreat where trainees often walked on the weekends. It was surrounded by back roads I had occasionally run with other female trainees. Despite my own anxiety, I briefly wondered if the trainer had ever asked a male trainee if he had cried and offered the advice, "Don't show your misery and insecurities around here. Go someplace else." For a split second, I felt a tiny flicker of sensitivity and empathy coming from the trainer. In the next second, I thought to myself, "Don't be stupid, Stearman, he's just another guy. He's not here to offer you sympathy." I never went to Lake Lunga, nor did I cry.

Although my creaky knee had not completely healed, I started to worry less about it as the second firearms test quickly approached. I had passed the first firearms test, barely squeaking by, but my shooting hadn't improved. I knew I could easily fail this second test. Tommy hadn't tired of standing sentry near my right ear, berating me, sarcasm lacing every disparaging comment. I knew I wouldn't get a second chance if I didn't pass. I needed to change my strategy.

Jim, the former West Virginia State trooper who sat next to me in class, came to my rescue. We had struck up a teasing friendship—he liked to razz me about being from Kentucky, which I thought ironic since he was the embodiment of a good old boy and loved nothing more than to encourage that stereotype. Jim routinely showed up for class seconds before the bell rang, hair smeared into buttery cowlicks, unbrushed morning breath wafting in my direction. I would ask him if no one from West Virginia owned a toothbrush. His response was always a wide grin, totally unfazed that I could see he had just rolled out of bed.

But Jim had a sharp mind and experience as a police officer. So, I recruited him to help me out. As luck would have it, Jim not only sat next to me in class, he stood next to me on the firing line at the range. He could not help but hear

Tommy's verbal abuse. Although respectful of all our training supervisors, Jim loved a challenge, which is when his wicked, rebellious streak shined. There was no need to cajole him; he agreed to help me immediately.

During regular firearms sessions, all trainees were lined up, side by side on the firing line. However, during certain exercises, only a few trainees at a time stood on the line to shoot. The rest of the class stood to the back and waited their turn. On one of these particular days, I asked Jim to stand behind me and tell me exactly where all my bullets were going when I fired at the target. While I was shooting, Jim stood to my right, just as close to me as Tommy did. As quietly as possible, so as not to alert the attention of the firearms instructors, he located every single bullet.

"Lower right. Lower right. Lower right." I heard Jim's calm voice in my right ear. My center mass aim resulted in all my bullets landing off target to the lower right, somewhere in the dirt of the berm. Finally! I knew what I needed to do. I already envisioned myself flashing a smug smile in Tommy's direction, with a "Take that, you asshole!" under my breath.

Being from Kentucky, I knew all about Kentucky "windage," which means adjusting your aim to account for wind or other factors in order to be able to hit your target rather than adjusting the physical sights on the gun. If all my bullets were hitting lower right, I needed to aim upper left in order to hit center mass.

From that point on, every time I stood at the firing line, I aimed upper left on my targets. This really worked only for targets that were stationary. My shooting still sucked when it came to the pop-up targets or any other moving targets used for tactical training. But our final firearms test was on a stationary target, so I needed to improve, and I needed to improve fast. I still felt like I had swallowed a brick every time I stepped onto the range, but by aiming upper left versus center mass, which felt counterintuitive, my scores began to improve.

Finally, our months of training were coming to an end and the last firearms test loomed. Waiting on the range with everyone else that morning, I felt like I was going to vomit, although there was nothing but roiling bile in my stomach. I had eaten nothing for breakfast. All I could think was that I hadn't come this far only to be kicked out. Instead of laughing and joking with my classmates as they stood around in clusters, chattering away in happy anticipation of being finished with firearms, I stood off to the side, shoulders hunched against failure, trying to calm my nerves and my shaking hands.

All at once, the range tower microphone clicked on and I heard Tommy's voice say, "Today we'll see the last of Stearman. She's not going to make it." Cold, icy prickles shivered across my skin as if someone had thrown a bucket of frigid water over my head. Every head on the range turned to look at me, some with pity, some wide-eyed, not knowing how I would react. I knew instinctively Tommy had done it on purpose to psyche me out. So far, he had been winning that game of warfare.

Jim grabbed my arm and whispered, "Don't let that asshole get to you. You know how to pass this."

"Yep."

"You know where to aim on the target, so just do it."

"Yep, upper left."

"I'll be right behind you, counting every bullet hole."

"OK, thanks."

In spite of Jim's encouraging words, I could hardly respond. I could barely breathe. The next ninety seconds would decide if I would have a career with the FBI.

For our last firearms test, only a handful of trainees were on the line at a time. When my turn came to step up, Jim walked up behind me and stayed just far enough to my right so as not to draw attention from the supervisors, but like before, close enough for me to hear. He gave me a "fuck 'em" grin, followed by a thumbs-up before I turned and faced my target. After each shot, I could hear Jim say quietly, "That one's in. That one's in. That one's in." Although a few stray shots landed outside that much-hated little black line, I knew as the clock ticked down, as Jim confirmed each shot, that I was going to make it. Tommy did not speak to me the rest of the day. His game of warfare had just been won . . . by ME!

Just a couple of days before graduation, the class was headed out to the gun range for some final drills when I stopped by the gun safe to pick up my weapon. The agent in charge of the safe came back to the counter and told me he couldn't find my gun. *Shit, do they think I stole my own gun or something?* This was a ridiculous thought, since the massive safe was either locked up or manned at all times. But the ongoing paranoia of firearms had taken its toll on me. As I stood staring at the agent, speechless, Tommy came up behind me and said to the agent, "Her gun's on the repair rack." The agent, looking confused, walked over to a special section of the safe where repairs were done, read a tag tied to the trigger guard of a gun, snapped it off, and handed the gun over to me, butt first. He didn't say a word.

A few minutes later on the range, we stepped up to the line for the last time. Now accustomed to my Kentucky windage aim, I fired away. The target remained a pristine white blank space.

"*What the fuck?*" I continued to stare down range a few seconds, my mind as numb and blank as the cardboard target in front of me. Then I put two and two together. During the next volley of shots, I aimed center mass. A neat tidy circle of holes appeared on my target. I was both pissed off and ecstatic. The sights of my gun had been manipulated all along. I hated Tommy more than I had ever hated anyone in my life.

As I headed back into the gun cleaning room later on, Tommy sidled up to me and said, "You know, Stearman, I did my best to get you kicked out, but you made it anyway. Congratulations." He turned and trotted away on his little cloven hoofs.

CHAPTER TEN

SMITH & WESSON GAMS

★ ★ ★

Despite Tommy's efforts to get me kicked out, the FBI Academy was an experience I quickly grew to love. For the first time in my life, I felt I was part of a "team." Little did I know, I was making friends who would be part of my life for decades to come.

Our days were divided up into three main categories—physical fitness, classroom work, and firearms. I was in good shape, but I wanted to improve my time in the two-mile run, a required part of the physical fitness tests. Darren, one of my classmates who had attended college on a track scholarship, always finished his two miles about the time I finished my first mile. He would then pace me through my second mile, talking to me, encouraging me, urging me toward the finish line. At the time, I did not realize I was anemic. My heartbeat would flutter like a bird's, and when running, I could never find a comfortable rhythm to my breathing. It would be a couple of years of iron tablets and a steady diet of steak before I really started to like running. Meanwhile, I spent afternoons after class running extra laps and lifting weights in the gym to improve the strength in my legs.

One day, about six weeks into training, my class was on the firearms range running through some exercises. These targets were beige cardboard overlaid with the silhouette in the shape of a man in black. They were attached to a metal frame which could be flipped to the left by the instructor in the range tower, so the shooter could see their target only when the frame was facing them.

As I recall, we were doing timed exercises where we shot from behind wooden barricades to simulate shooting from behind a place of cover, while still engaging the suspect represented by the target. Once the target was flipped away, we would holster our guns and run to the next barricade. We would then wait until the target flipped into view, never knowing if it was going to be a couple of seconds or the space of a heartbeat, and then shoot the specified number of bullets. The point of the exercise was to unholster our guns and get bullets inside the silhouette within a few seconds.

Tommy told us today's exercise wasn't an "official" test. He also said whether we passed would determine if we were going to get washed out of the program. I suspected Tommy was trying to psyche us out, and it worked. Hearing this set my gut churning. The sights on my gun were still out of line. Jim had helped me perfect my Kentucky windage aim but I wasn't sure how I was going to fare in this exercise, with targets flipping back and forth and only seconds to aim high-left to hit center-target.

The barricades were set up at staggered intervals, so only a few trainees were shooting at any given time. The rest of the class stood, as usual, to the back of the range waiting their turn. When it came my turn to shoot, I stepped up to the barricade, trembling hand cupping the grip of my revolver. Something happened to me once the clock started. I forgot everything and everyone; I saw nothing but the target and heard nothing but the sound of the buzzer signaling me to run, stop, holster, or draw my weapon. When it was over, adrenaline rushed through my system, my heartbeat elevated as if I had just finished a two-mile run. I had no idea if my bullets had hit their intended target.

Each group of shooters was assigned an instructor who would check the targets and record scores passed along to Tommy at the end of the session.

On this day, my firearms instructor was a DEA agent, Hispanic, short, and muscular, solid as a tree stump, legs splayed as he watched the exercise behind sunglasses, clipboard clasped against his chest. He was rumored to have been part of the DEA operation that hunted down the killers of DEA Special Agent Kiki Camarena, who had been kidnapped and murdered by drug traffickers while working in Mexico. I had already seen a few of these agents on campus, some with obvious wounds and injuries. At the time I attended the Academy, the FBI shared the training facility with the DEA. It was common to have lunch in the cafeteria when the DEA trainees were eating. It was also common for DEA instructors to help when additional instructors were required for certain training exercises to ensure the safety of the group.

To a man—and they were all men—these seasoned DEA agents were physical specimens of solid muscle, stretched tight over bone, eyes that stared into the distance seeing everything and nothing. I always gave a wide berth when I met one passing through the gerbil tubes. Their features set in glacial stoicism were all too familiar to me. It was the same look I always saw on my father's face.

I watched as the DEA instructor walked downrange to peruse my target. His pen moved as he marked my score on his clipboard. His face impassive, he walked back to where I was standing, stood close to my side, and said under his breath, "You missed by one point."

I would have vomited if the contents of my stomach could have passed through the knot in my throat. All I could think was *I just washed out. What am I going to do now?*

He then turned his face to me and said in the same slightly accented undertone, "But I know what *he's* trying to do to you. I won't let that happen. I gave you that extra point."

I could not see behind his sunglasses to judge what he was thinking or why he would do such a thing to help me. I didn't ask who *he* was, I guessed he meant Tommy, since Tommy made it clear he hated my guts every time I was on the range. I didn't know what to say, so I said nothing as he turned and walked away.

A few weeks later, I was in the gym after class going through my normal routine of leg exercises, when I saw the DEA agent who had given me the extra point, also working out. I had seen him a few times in the hallways and on the range, but he had never said anything else to me nor I to him. Subconsciously, I feared he might still somehow take that point away from me or admit he had cheated on my behalf.

As I was getting up from the leg curl machine, he walked over to me and said, "Your legs are like a Smith & Wesson. They're both deadly." This time, though, I could see his eyes. His face still held that stoic, don't-fuck-with-me look, but his eyes had squinted in the tiniest of smiles, as if he knew a secret, which I suppose he did. Then he walked away without saying another word, just as he had on the range.

Because our training was coming to a close and graduation was only a couple of weeks away, I saw him only a couple more times in the cafeteria or in the hallways. He never spoke another word to me, nor did he make any untoward movements in my direction.

I have thought of him often since then and wondered why he felt compelled to help me. I never got the impression he expected some reciprocity for his actions. Quite the opposite; he seemed to go out of his way to avoid me, never smiled in greeting, when we saw each other in passing.

I hadn't felt offended when he had commented about my legs. I hadn't felt anything really. It happened so fast I just shrugged my shoulders and went back to my exercises. I was so focused on graduating that nothing else mattered. Plus, it was pretty common for female trainees, FBI and DEA alike, to be the recipient of comments from the profusion of males that swarmed the academy campus. With multiple FBI, DEA, and National Academy (US and international police officers) classes running at the same time, men far outnumbered the women, and it was always open season on sexist comments. Some female agents invited them, others ignored them; most of us kept right on doing what we were doing and considered sexist remarks business as usual.

I have wondered if my mysterious DEA agent would have given me that extra point if I hadn't had legs like a Smith & Wesson. If not for his help, would I have become an FBI Special Agent? Or would I have been another victim in Tommy's war against women?

CHAPTER ELEVEN

FOLLOW THE YELLOW BRICK ROAD

★ ★ ★

"Goddamn you, fucking asshole. That hurt."

I didn't have time to look down at the paint splotch on the front of my T-shirt. I didn't need to; I could feel the sting in my nipple. Resisting the urge to rub my boob to ease the pain, I straddled the wooden beam, placed my foot carefully on the rope ladder trailing down the other side, and jumped to the ground.

Today was the Yellow Brick Road, a fun run through an obstacle course deep in the woods of the Marine Corps base. Everyone remaining in the class had passed the final physical fitness test, firearms test, and classroom tests. We were all set to graduate. Today wasn't going to be timed; nor was it meant to be stressful or intimidating. It was the last time we would run as a class; one unit that had spent months together laughing, arguing, bonding, and now saying goodbye.

Running the Yellow Brick Road had become a rite of passage for every FBI graduating class. I looked forward to it, feeling the weight of a thousand Smith & Wessons lifted from my shoulders after passing my final firearms test. Tommy's sabotage made me feel smug in the deep-seated loathing I still harbored for him. But nothing was going to ruin my mood. It was a sunny, hot summer day and I was going to graduate the FBI Academy and head off to my first field office in Alexandria, Virginia.

The obstacle course was comprised of tall wooden barriers, some with ropes, others bare wood. Some barriers were rope ladders suspended from a wooden beam ten feet or more in the air, to be climbed up, and down the other side. We crawled through mud, underneath barbed wire, tiptoed along narrow boards stretched across mud holes of indeterminate depth. Along the way, our class instructors had run alongside us, cheering us on, laughing and making jokes. What I hadn't bargained for were the other instructors hiding in the bushes and trees along the way, shooting at us with paintballs.

It seemed like every time I reached the top of an obstacle or barrier, pausing to assess the climb down the other side, I would feel a sharp zing in my breast or crotch. At first, I didn't understand what was happening. I initially thought I had pulled a muscle or caught my skin on a splinter. I just kept moving forward on the course, yelling out and joking with my classmates. It took a while to figure out what was going on.

As I was climbing the last barrier, I felt multiple stings in my nipples. They really hurt by now and when I looked down, I could see red paint splotches covering both breasts on my white T-shirt and a paint stain near my crotch. Sitting astride the barricade, I looked off into the woods and saw an unfamiliar instructor grinning from the shrubs, a paint gun pointed straight at me. I stared at him and shook my head, knowing he and his buddies had had great fun using breasts and crotches as target practice. He barely registered in my thought process. I was about to graduate and there was nothing he or his misogynist buddies could do to dissipate the heady rush of elation I was feeling.

Anticipating another volley of stings, I hurried down the other side of the barricade and ran off into the woods toward the end of the course, which turned out to be a huge mud hole. Hot, sweaty, and exhilarated to have the last physical challenge behind us, we all jumped in and started smearing each other with yellow-brown muck. Who knew how many countless Marines had pissed in that very hole? But we didn't care. Our time at Quantico would soon be over.

❖

The day I carried that Navy SEAL on my back, I'll never forget the return bus ride to the Academy. Everyone was as quiet as I had ever seen them. We were drenched with sweat and there was no chatting, no laughter; even jokester Jim was quiet. Everyone was either looking out the bus windows or leaning over, elbows on knees, staring at their feet. As exhausted as I was, for the first time, I felt a sense of my own strength, both physical and mental.

Before going to the FBI Academy, I had been unaware how strong my back was, how sturdy my legs, all forged in the years of backbreaking work on a dairy and tobacco farm. I had become proud of my strength. I could shimmy up a thirty-foot rope and carry a Navy SEAL on my back. My body became confident in its ability to be agile and lean and I knew without a doubt that if I needed to fight off another person, I could do it.

It would take me years to ask myself the question, if I was physically strong, why had I felt like I couldn't fight back against my father and men who would try to stand in my way? I had yet to learn that the power of my words and actions could carry more weight.

l

PART THREE

GUNS, BADGES, AND GRIT

CHAPTER TWELVE

BUCHICKS

★ ★ ★

*Whatever you choose, however many roads you travel,
I hope that you choose not to be a lady. I hope you will
find some way to break the rules and make a little
trouble out there. And I also hope that you will choose
to make some of that trouble on behalf of women.*
—Nora Ephron

"What are you all going to talk about?" Matt asked peevishly, lips pursed, eyes squinted. "Are you going to talk about us? Why can't we go?"

"Us, who?" I asked, forcing my face into innocent blandness. I enjoyed teasing Matt. And I knew who the *who* was in his question; I just wanted to hear him say it.

Matt was a young, fairly new agent like me and we had become friends while partnering on an investigation. He loved nothing more than to be in the middle of the female agents when we talked. He routinely scoffed at some of the things we discussed, but whenever there was a crowd of women, which in an FBI office was more than two, he was there with ears perked for some juicy tidbit he might pick up about the female psyche.

"You know! Us *guys*?" the last word squeaked out in a fit of pique.

"Contrary to popular belief, Matt, we have better things to talk about than you guys. And besides, this is just girls, no guys allowed," I said, as I rolled my eyes and left him staring after me like a puppy who had been smacked on the behind with a newspaper.

Back in the late 1980s, the FBI's Alexandria, Virginia, field office was small by bureau standards, with only about eighty agents, as compared to the Washington, DC, field office, our neighbor across the Potomac, which had almost six hundred agents. For such a small office, Alexandria had an inordinately high number of female agents, all of whom seemed to be the focus of never-ending fascination for the male agents.

Even my training agent, Don, who had graduated only six months ahead of me, was fascinated by all things female. He told me I cursed too much and drove my bureau car too fast. He edited my paperwork with red ink. And he asked me endless questions about what it was like to be a female FBI agent. Once, when I saw Don's apartment with walls covered in prints by Patrick Nagel, all depicting the female form, I began to see his fascination with women in a different light. I wasn't sure if he truly appreciated women or if he was someone I should be slightly afraid of. Given the fact that he was a brilliant nerd, I suspected he had never been exposed to so many women in his life. And women who carried a gun and handcuffs might be a source of education he wasn't about to squander.

One day, several of us girls were catching up, no doubt in the bathroom, and decided we should start a monthly lunch get-together, all girls, no guys. We wanted to be able to talk about "girl" things without the guys around. Contrary to what I had just told Matt, though, we were most assuredly going to be talking about the guys. Not all the time, and not exclusively, but we weren't going to pass up a chance to gossip and laugh about them while they weren't around.

The Alexandria field office was located on a side street in Old Town, so there were plenty of good restaurants within walking distance. Since most of the guys were too cheap to go to a "nicer" restaurant, we knew we would be pretty safe from their prying eyes and ears. I don't really remember how many of us gathered for that first lunch, but I recall several women crowded around women crowded around a long rectangular table, lively chatter raised in the camaraderie of a sisterhood. We commiserated on wardrobe malfunctions, such as the fact that wearing a skirt with a gun and holster on the hip creates a lopsided look with one side of the skirt hanging at least three to four inches lower than the other. It became a running joke that if you were walking behind a woman on the streets of Alexandria and saw their skirt hanging several inches lower on one side, she was sure to be an FBI agent.

We also told stories about dating while carrying the accoutrement of an FBI agent. Men we dated inevitably wanted to know if our handcuffs were fur lined. This interesting quirk of the male gender led to stories of men who had been given the "honor" of being cuffed to a headboard. Usually, these men understood quickly that being the submissive party of a gun-toting woman wasn't as thrilling as they might have thought.

We laughed about starting a business to invent a thigh holster for our guns, the act of raising our skirts up to our crotches would be enough to distract while arresting a criminal at gun point.

"If we're going to do this on a regular basis," I inserted into the chitchat, "we should give ourselves a name."

"How about G-women?" someone suggested.

"No, too much like G-men," came a reply.

Assenting voices could be heard around the table, silverware clicking on salad plates—salad, of course, being the food of choice for a group of athletic women who worked out regularly and sported guns on their hips.

"How about BuChick?" came a voice across the table. "You know, for Bureau Chicks."

"Perfect!" voices raised in unison.

I didn't know it at the time, but I was incredibly lucky to have been assigned to Alexandria as my first field office. The circle of women I got to know, some of whom became mentors and lifelong friends, was the polar opposite of the experience other new female agents had in their first offices, where they were often the lone female, or close to it. This became my first lesson in how women can empower each other in the midst of a testosterone-filled organization.

I would learn later in my career how important female empowerment could be when I found myself the only woman in the room.

CHAPTER THIRTEEN

FULL FRONTAL

★★★

My handsome Iraqi. I don't remember his name, nor do I remember the position he held at the Iraqi Embassy in Washington, DC. But he certainly left me with some memories.

It was August of 1990, and Iraq had just invaded Kuwait, which would eventually lead to the Gulf War in early 1991. Because of Iraq's attempts to try to close the US embassy in Kuwait City, Iraqi diplomats stationed at the Embassy of Iraq in Washington, DC, were told they had to return home. In other words, they were being diplomatically expelled. A specific date and time for their departure was set, and the FBI supervised the task of ensuring all diplomats would be aboard a special flight. FBI agents were deployed to surveil the Iraqis around the clock so they wouldn't try to remain in the United States illegally by disappearing into America's hinterlands.

My assignee, a young male, proved to have a mischievous sense of humor. He and all the other soon-to-be-expelled diplomats knew they were being surveilled. He decided he would have a little fun before heading back into what would soon become a war zone.

As a diplomat, he was allowed to drive an official vehicle assigned to the Iraqi embassy, displaying a red and blue diplomatic license plate, with the letters BZ, the State Department designator for Iraq. In any other city, these unusual license plates would set him apart. But in Washington, DC, diplomatic tags are as ubiquitous as the daily intersection closures ahead of a presidential movement—those times when the President was hurried to and from the

White House in his bullet-proof limousine. I had to stick very close to the rear of his vehicle in order to prevent losing him in traffic.

I soon learned my Iraqi considered himself a bit of a hotshot. He would slow down or even come to a full stop at an intersection with a green light, only to speed through as soon as it turned red, leaving me to rush through oncoming traffic to catch up. Infuriated, I would then watch him give me a wave and grin in his rearview mirror. At other times, he would drive himself to a restaurant or grocery store and park his car illegally on the street, leaving me to block traffic and endure curses, middle fingers, and horn-blowing while I waited for him to return. Other agents on the same detail were assigned to follow him into whatever establishment he entered to make sure he didn't try to slip out the back door or have an accomplice on the inside who would help him escape, so I was always given a heads-up before he got back into his car. He would usually walk by my driver's side window and give me a wink, a smile, and a finger waggle before driving away at top speed.

After several days of his nonstop antics, I was thoroughly pissed off, and more than ready to put him on a plane. On the last day of my assignment, I was to accompany him to his apartment so he could pick up his luggage, and then follow him to the airport so he could make his flight.

After following him to his apartment building and accompanying him to his door, I stood outside and waited in the hallway while he fetched his suitcases. I waited several minutes and after checking my watch, I realized the time for getting my unwanted protégée out to the airport was closing in. Not bothering to disguise my impatience and annoyance, I started banging on his door. I was *not* going to be responsible for the illegal overstay of an Iraqi diplomat.

The object of my irritation opened the door immediately, as if anticipating that my frustration would soon spew to the surface. There he was, framed in the doorway, wearing not a stitch of clothing other than a pair of white athletic socks and plastic sandals, his nakedness incongruous against the footwear, which had blue and white horizontal stripes across the top. With a proud grin, white teeth shining against his warm, brown skin, he struck a pose—arms spread slightly away from his sides, palms turned outwardly toward me as if to say, "Here it is, go for it."

If I hadn't been so annoyed, I might have flinched in surprise. However, his hijinks from the previous days had set my teeth on edge. Not cracking a smile, and with my best stone face, as slowly as I could I allowed my eyes to travel down the length of his face. Mustering my best cold, hard stare, I met his eyes briefly and continued down his chest and stomach. By the time I got to his groin, his penis had started to retreat into the forest of black pubic hair, much like the Iraqi troops would retreat back into the desert in the coming months. But neither of us knew that then.

As gratingly as I could muster, I said, "You have ten minutes to get dressed *or* you can go like you are, I don't really care. We're leaving." I reached in, grabbed the door handle, and shut the door in his face. A few minutes later, fully clothed, he sheepishly appeared in the hallway, trailing his suitcases behind.

I'm not sure what he was thinking. Maybe he had been watching old TV reruns from the mid-seventies when streaking was all the rage, something certain to be censored from Iraqi pop culture. Or he figured, what the hell, I'm going back to a war zone and she might be interested if I show her the goods. Maybe that's how he thought it worked in America—the man struts around like a peacock, but instead of showing his feathers, he gives his potential mate a gander at his goose.

I haven't given much thought as to what happened to him upon his return. Being a diplomat in a country such as Iraq meant he was educated, from a wealthy, upper-crust family. I suspect he didn't suffer during the Gulf War and may have even been hailed as a hero. Nor do I know what might have happened to him during the subsequent Iraq War, post 9/11. However, I hope he didn't lose his cheekiness, as irritating as it could sometimes be. Maybe that quality helped him survive. Despite my stone face at his naked display, what I had really wanted to do was laugh. His arrogance and pride in himself was childlike and audacious. And I must admit, he was quite handsome, with black curly hair, smooth brown skin, and long-lashed amber-brown eyes.

I later wondered why I found his brash display of nakedness amusing, whereas if one of my fellow male agents had done the same, I would have been pissed off. But then, I didn't have to work with my handsome Iraqi full time. I suspect Iraqi women don't have the freedom to put similar masculine displays on a long airplane ride as I was able to do.

CHAPTER FOURTEEN

FUMU

★★★

"Good morning, Kathy, this is Amanda. Could you please come up to the ASAC[Assistant Special Agent in Charge]'s office as soon as possible?"

The ASAC? My mind started down the list of things that might have gotten me into trouble. I hadn't wrecked my Bureau car, nor had I been driving it while drinking. Any misuse of a Bureau car will either get you fired or land you on the bricks—sent home without pay for a specified amount of time; neither was a good option. Louis Freeh hadn't yet been appointed FBI Director, but his "Bright Line" policy would end any and all drinking and driving when operating your Bucar, should one be so inclined. The Bright Line would be the end of a lot of careers for those old-timers who made a habit of keeping a bottle of alcohol in their lower desk drawer.

My next train of thought went to any recent interviews I had conducted. Had I pissed anyone off? Had someone complained about me? No, I couldn't think of any situation I had gotten myself into that might have been misconstrued as abusing my position as an FBI agent. You never knew when someone would take offense to the fact that I was female, something that had caused a few doors to be slammed in my face.

As my mind cataloged all I might have done wrong in the past few days, I walked to my supervisor's office on shaky legs, my sphincter resisting the urge to slam shut with the iron clang of an Alcatraz prison door. The ASAC is the person second in command of a field division and any communication with his office should have been handled according to chain of command.

This meant the ASAC's secretary should have contacted my supervisor first, and then we both would have been summoned to his office for a face-to-face discussion of my transgressions.

I was still a fairly new agent with only about three years on the job, so I was loath to tell my supervisor I might be in trouble. Maybe she already knew and was just waiting for the wolves to circle. No, Kate, my supervisor—tall and slim, with a short, swingy flapper-girl haircut—was one of the only female supervisors in the field division. She didn't take shit from anybody. With her athletic build, she ran a 10K in her ninth month of pregnancy. I also knew she wasn't about to cut me any slack just because I was another female. If anything, she expected more from me than from the guys. But she wouldn't sell me out, either.

I stood in the doorway of her office and said, "Kate, I just got a call from the ASAC's office. He wants to see me right away."

She looked up from what she was reading, raised her eyebrows, and asked, "Do you know what it's about?" There was no expression on her face other than confusion. *OK, she's just as much in the dark as I am.*

"No, I was just told to come to his office." I hesitated. "What should I do?"

"Go see what he wants. But let me know as soon as you get finished, OK?"

As I stepped into the ASAC's reception area, Amanda smiled from behind her desk. "You can go ahead and go in, Kathy."

I could see Vince sitting behind his desk, stocky but with a muscular build, thick black hair combed straight back from a tanned, olive-skinned complexion. Vince was known around the office as being a dapper dresser, suits immaculately tailored, shoes shined to a spit-polish. Though on the short side, rumor was he considered himself to be quite the ladies' man. I avoided him simply because he was the ASAC. Best not to land in the sights of the head of the office in case shit needed to flow downhill to some agent who was easy to blame for a screwup.

I stepped into his office and Vince stood up, flashed his shiny, white, I'm-so-cute smile and said, "Close the door and then come sit in front of me."

It didn't occur to me to be concerned. Maybe he just wanted to chew my ass out in private without Amanda overhearing. Word would get around the office anyway, it always did, so I don't know why he would bother. But I did as he requested.

"Kathy, I have a friend who needs a date. I want you to canvass all your little friends in the female ranks and find someone for him to go out with."

At first, I couldn't believe what I was hearing. *He wanted me to play matchmaker? What the fuck?*

"I'm sorry. What?" I stared at him with my mouth half open, still not sure I had heard him correctly.

"Yes, his name is Scott, and he needs someone to go out with. I told him I would find someone from the office."

It just so happened that I had received a phone call from Scott several evenings previously. Most FBI agents have unlisted home phone numbers. Any calls to the office switchboard by an outside party must be patched through only if the agent gives permission. Somehow Scott, who was the ASAC of another section of our field division, had used his position to get the switchboard to patch him through to my number without my permission.

Scott, with all the charm of an Irish setter, had informed me he was getting a divorce and wanted to know if I would go out with him.

"No, I don't date agents," I responded. This was the truth. I had had one relationship with another agent and swore I would never do it again. I had learned that when you date someone you work with, everyone in the office considers *your* relationship *their* business, which is especially galling when the relationship starts to unravel in front of everyone.

"Oh, OK, do you know anyone else I could go out with?"

Are you fucking kidding me? What the fuck is wrong with this guy?

Scott, as an ASAC, was positioned a long way up the chain of command from where I stood. If he wanted to, he could have screwed my career a thousand ways from Sunday. Still, I wasn't about to give him what he wanted, least of all the phone numbers of my female agent friends. I opted for politeness, and said, "No, sorry, I don't know anyone."

I stared at Vince as the phone call replayed in my head. *What a couple of fucking losers!* Not heeding my own common sense, I leaned forward toward his desk, hands on the arms of the chair, elbows cocked out, and said, "Your friend Scott called me the other night for a date. I told him I didn't want to date him. I heard he also called some of my other 'little friends' and they don't want to go out with him either. First of all, he's old enough to be our father; second of all, he's still married. So, no, none of us want to go out with your friend."

At that point, I pushed myself out of the chair, walked out the door, and headed straight for Kate's office.

I told Kate word-for-word what had happened. By this time, I was angry, the sting of tears I refused to shed making me angrier. One of the traits I dislike about myself is when I'm angry, I spew a volley of venom, tears to follow when I'm finally alone. I always tried to punch down my anger or keep it at a low simmer so as not to ruin any emotional capital by devolving into tears in front of other people.

While I was telling her my tale, Kate sat back in her chair, hands laid flat on the desk in front of her. She hadn't said a word during my whole diatribe. Now she jerked herself forward, hands clasped in front of her, and said, "You have two choices. You can go to OPR [Office of Professional Responsibility, the unit responsible for investigating FBI employee misconduct] or you can do nothing."

"What would you do?" I asked.

"I'll back you up no matter what you decide. But I'm going to tell you something. If you go to OPR, he will win, and you'll wear it for the rest of your career. He won't."

I nodded my head, knowing she wouldn't steer me wrong. She had been an agent far longer than I and had surely had her own experiences dealing with these sorts of male agents.

"OK, I'm just going to let it go."

A few months later, Vince was caught having sex in the back seat of his Bureau car with one of the office secretaries. She was fired. He was promoted out of our field division and into a higher position in another city.

It was then I coined FUMU—Fuck Up, Move Up—the path to promotion I would, unfortunately, see time and time again.

CHAPTER FIFTEEN

SLEEPING WITH THE INFORMANT

★★★

Sleeping with an informant will get you fired, unless you're a male agent and you decide to kill your informant after you sleep with her or him. Then you go to prison. This actually happened once in a small town in eastern Kentucky. I've heard many stories about male agents who have slept with their informants, but I've never heard one about a female agent sleeping with hers. So, unless there are women out there harboring a deep, dark secret, I'm a party of one.

It wasn't a long-term affair; it was only for two nights. I didn't make it a habit. And I didn't kill him afterward, although the thought did cross my mind while I was sharing a bed with him.

It all began one Friday morning when Sue called me from FBI headquarters (FBIHQ) where she had taken a position as a supervisor in the Undercover Unit. Sue, my friend and mentor, was a feisty, assertive, and outspoken female agent. Her favorite expletive when she was pissed or just needed to blow off steam was "Fucka, damna, shitta, hella!" bellowed at the top of her lungs. One of the guys on our squad brought a broom into the office one day and mockingly presented it to her by saying, "Sue, if your Bureau car doesn't start one morning, you can just fly this into work." She thought this was hilarious and laughed for hours over her "gift." When she was promoted to FBIHQ, Sue passed the broom to me in an office "ceremony" that involved earsplitting hoots, whistles, and catcalls. In today's FBI, the gift of a broom to a female agent by a male agent would be grounds for a trip to the sexual harassment counselor. In the early 1990s FBI, you laughed, shrugged it off, and got back to work.

Sue had been influential in my acceptance to the FBI's undercover program a couple of years before. There were older female agents who felt other young women, fresh out of training, needed to have their backbones forged into the finest steel by the same searing fires they had experienced. They rarely offered advice as a result. Sue, however, was very generous with her hard-won knowledge of the Bureau, and often mentored other female agents, me included.

Very few female agents wanted to work undercover and an even smaller number wanted to slog through the rigors of a predominantly male-attended and male-run undercover school. This left the FBI with a shortage of female role-players. I happened to be young and eager and, at the time, particularly inexperienced about the roles I would be asked to play. After passing undercover school, I ended up on the FBI's list of female undercover agents qualified to go out and show some ass, cleavage, leg, or whatever the current role for female sidekick required.

When I picked up the phone that morning, I had been thinking not so much about work, but about the weekend ahead with the guy I had been dating for several months. Keith was from New York City and I lived in Washington, DC. We were taking turns commuting in order to spend time with each other. I was thinking of his visit when I heard Sue's voice. At first, her question didn't quite register; all I heard was "yacht," "stripper," and "leave tonight." I pushed images of Keith out of my mind and focused on what she was saying. Sue wanted me to go out on a weekend undercover assignment that involved hanging out on a yacht on the Gulf of Mexico. My attire for the weekend would be a bikini; I would be posing as the stripper girlfriend of an FBI informant. These details slowly slammed into my brain, one at a time. Two years before, it would have seemed like a fun, new adventure. Today, it was one more assignment where I had to act like a dimwitted twit. My weekend curled up in bed with Keith was far more appealing than spending a weekend undercover, even if it *was* on a yacht on the Gulf of Mexico.

Working undercover is strictly voluntary in the FBI and an agent cannot be compelled to take on a role they don't want. Sue knew I had been dating Keith, so I was honest with her when I confessed my reluctance to take this assignment. I knew I was taking a risk; turning down assignments meant I might not get offered as many in the future. But I didn't care; I was getting tired of the same old roles. Sue, being Sue, cheerfully said she would just find someone else.

A few hours later, I looked up from my computer to see my supervisor, Kate, standing on the other side of my pod staring at me. Our office space was brand new and we were all separated by modular cubicles decorated in varying shades of beige and gray, meant, no doubt, to corral a roomful of rowdy agents. Frankly, I liked the bullpen style of working together, where we had a wide-open space to fling insults and paper wads at each other while brainstorming a case. I missed the lunchtime play of musical chairs in our old squad area. There had been only a couple of desk chairs that didn't have at least one wheel missing, or a seat cushion that didn't leave your ass numb from being pinched in the cracked leather upholstery. If you were lucky enough to arrive early in the morning and snag a good one, you'd find it missing after chasing down a lead or going out for lunch. It made for a room full of light-hearted fun. Now the only time we saw each other was when we popped our heads, like gophers, above the chest-high walls.

The carpet and sound-deafening fabric had prevented me from hearing Kate until she appeared in the empty cubicle opposite mine. I could tell from the serious look on her face and the wrinkle between her eyebrows that something was up. I stopped my typing and looked at her expectantly, knowing she would spit it out in her own good time.

"I got a call from the Undercover Unit's Unit Chief [Sue's boss]. He said the unit called you earlier and you turned down an undercover assignment for this weekend."

"Yep, they want me to be a stripper and drool all over some informant on a white-collar crime case. I'm not interested."

"Yeah, I know, but they can't find anyone else to do it. They asked me to talk you into it. So, can I talk you into it?"

I sighed, knowing Kate wouldn't be asking me unless she was getting pressure herself. "Kate, you know I've gone out and done just about everything I've been asked to do, and it was fun. I don't regret a *thing*. But now I'm tired of being a bimbo."

She nodded her head, her mouth curled up in a wry sympathetic smile and said, "I knew you would get sick of it at some point. But what if this could be your last role? Would you do it then? They apparently really need someone for this case because one of the key players will be on the boat."

In my head I heard myself saying, *Shitta, fucka, damna, hella*. I knew Sue wouldn't have handed me up, which is why the Unit Chief had called Kate.

They were obviously desperate to get someone on board that yacht. I was really grateful to Sue for helping me all these years, and I felt I owed her. Seeing my weekend with Keith slipping away, I found myself saying, "OK, but this is the last one."

Several hours later, I walked out of a small airport on the Gulf Coast of Florida, carry-on bag in hand; a bikini doesn't take up much room. I had called Keith before my flight to tell him I had to cancel our weekend. He knew better than to ask where I was going or how long I would be gone. That was information I was unable to share. He also knew he would have no way to contact me nor would I contact him while I was on assignment.

I had been told there would be two other undercover agents on the boat for the weekend; Ben, whom I was acquainted with from a previous case, and another female agent, Christy, whom I hadn't met. As I watched Ben walk toward me, I felt the warm, humid Florida breeze on my face, melting the tension and disappointment of the past few hours. I knew Ben was a solid guy, married with a couple of kids. He was the lead agent on this assignment; he would keep things moving smoothly. *OK, piece of cake . . . I can get through the next couple of days.*

Our launching point for the weekend and our home-away-from-home each night after coming off the yacht was a two-bedroom condo set on a narrow waterway leading to the Gulf. Through the sliding glass doors that led to a large deck, I could see sunlight glinting off the water. To my right was a first-floor bedroom and up a short flight of stairs was what I assumed to be another bedroom. Already seated in the living room, decorated in the typical tropical motif of pastels and palm trees, was Christy—short, pretty, smiling, and bouncy, with a head full of dark curls. I disliked her immediately. Christy stood to greet us alongside a tall, very thin man with pomade-slicked hair, wearing polyester pants and a Hawaiian shirt opened to mid-chest. He had a smarmy, used-car-salesman smile on his face. He swaggered over to me, arms outstretched as if he were about to sell me a souped-up 1968 Camaro with polished chrome mag wheels. *This is the asshole I have to pretend to like for a whole weekend? I am NEVER fucking doing this again!* Just as his arms wrapped around me, I shoved him away, stuck out my hand, and introduced myself with my undercover name. *Time for hugs later, asshole!* He stepped back, smile gone, but politely put his hand out and told me his name was Vinnie. *Seriously? Could he be any more cliché?* He looked like he had stepped right out of central casting for *The Godfather.* The thought of the flirtatious friendliness, handholding, and hugging required to make the relationship with Vinnie believable made me slightly nauseated. *Oh god, I just want to vomit and get away from this place as quickly as I can run!* As always, when I found myself in a bad situation, I straightened my spine and arranged my best stone face.

After "pleasantries" were exchanged, we spent an hour or so talking about our roles for the next couple of days. Ben told us the main goal of this undercover operation was to find out if Joey, the owner of a famous "gentleman's club," aka strip joint, would be a credible witness in the eventual trial of Walter, the main subject of a major money laundering investigation. My role was to act as Vinnie's girlfriend, while Christy would be Ben's girlfriend. The plan was to schmooze Joey all weekend with sunshine, booze, and the trappings of the rich, hence the yacht. Ben would elicit information while Joey was in an inebriated and carefree state of mind.

The informant, Vinnie, knew Joey from some shady business dealings and had issued the invite to hang out on "Ben's yacht." Vinnie briefed us on Joey's personality, his likes and dislikes, as well as the fact that Joey would be bringing his girlfriend, Sara, who happened to be one of his "girls" at the strip club he owned. In spite of being one of Joey's stable of regulars, Sara would have very little information on Joey's activities. My job, along with Christy, was simply to be flirtatious and entertaining arm candy for the men. As undercover roles go, this one had no heavy lifting—just hang out on the yacht in a bikini and have some fun.

During our planning session, I politely chatted with Vinnie but kept a physical distance. As I was to be his stripper girlfriend, we had come up with our back story, how we had met, and how long we had known each other. Throughout our planning session, Vinnie had continued to eye me warily. My indifference to his attempts to be overly friendly with me let him know without my having to say it aloud; I was an undercover agent, and he was the informant. I was not about to invite his displays of affection until we assumed our respective roles.

Details ironed out and our covers established, we left the condo to get an early dinner. We would be meeting Joey and Sara early the next morning for a full day of fun-in-the-sun sport fishing on the yacht.

After feigning amorous feelings for Vinnie over dinner in a public restaurant—on an undercover operation, you never knew who was going to be watching—we arrived back at the condo. I turned to Christy to ask which bedroom she and I would be sleeping in. Inside the condo and away from prying eyes, I assumed we would split up, so Christy and I could share a room while Vinnie and Ben shared the other. Before I could utter a single word, I watched Ben and Christy lock lips, hands flailing on hips and ass, while crab-walking sideways into the nearest bedroom. As the door slammed in my face, all I could do was stare. My brain, fuzzy and tired from not wanting this assignment in the first place, could not grasp what I had just witnessed.

In undercover school, there are a few do-not-do rules that are drilled into your training. Sleeping with your fellow undercover agent was one of them. I felt disappointed in Ben. I had thought he was a standup family man and I wondered how long this fling with Christy had been going on. Did it start during the undercover operation or had it started before?

I shouldn't have been surprised. Working undercover is stressful and when a male agent and female agent are working together as a couple, the real world sometimes feels a long way off. The constant secretiveness and need to trust only each other starts to seem as if it's just the two of you against the rest of the world. People being people, undercover life begins to imitate real life and hormones take over. I had felt it myself on a couple of occasions. But I had never acted on it.

I turned to find Vinnie, who was smiling like he had just ordered a platter of fried chicken and was about to tear into it. *Fuck! There just aren't enough fucks in the world for this shit show! Could this weekend get any worse?* I felt the beginnings of hot tears pricking the backs of my eyeballs and I wished with all my heart that I had never agreed to this assignment. Determined not to cry and angry at my own feelings of vulnerability, I realized with dismay that I was about to break another rule drilled into my head at undercover school—never sleep with your informant.

I crooked a finger at Vinnie and headed up the stairs toward the second bedroom. He followed like a puppy headed to the dog bowl. Once inside, I slammed the door, jammed my finger into his chest, and snarled, "We'll sleep in the same bed, but you *will* stay on your side, and I'll stay on mine. If you touch me once in the middle of the night, I will fucking fuck you up. I will break your fucking arms and then I'll break your fucking face. If I even feel your little pinky toe on my side of the bed, you will regret it for the rest of your life. And don't think I can't do it because I can, and I will! Do you understand me?" Vinnie nodded, eyes wide. He didn't say a word. *Good boy!* We climbed into bed, thankfully king-sized, fully clothed. I lay facing the opposite wall and he did the same on his side, barely breathing. After a few minutes of no movement from Vinnie's side of the bed, I knew I had sufficiently intimidated him into submission for the evening. I finally fell into a fitful sleep, fully cognizant of his every little movement. The next morning when I got out of bed, he had not moved from the exact spot I had left him the night before. I smiled to myself, satisfied I had not been forced to deal with his middle-of-the-night groping. *He takes orders well. Nice puppy . . .*

The yacht was small, as yachts go, with a third platform called a tuna tower. In the back of the boat were two large chairs, which looked like a cross between a comfortable dentist chair and a La-Z-Boy with fishing poles attached. Joey was sitting in one chair, tanned and handsome, with Sara, a striking long-haired brunette, sitting in his lap. Sara had a habit of pulling one side of her long hair across her face while looking down. Her body would have played well in a *Playboy* centerfold, perfectly proportioned and stunning. I could see why she was one of Joey's favorite girls at the club. Although in great shape with 14 percent body fat and muscles that could have fulfilled my promise to fuck Vinnie up the night before, I was not centerfold material. I stared at Sara, feeling a little envious of her fantastic body. Then, I mentally smacked myself for the envy and then smacked myself again for feeling arrogant and judgmental over the fact that she was a stripper. I could not know who she was or why she was a stripper. Later, I noticed a long, jagged scar on the side of her face that she hid with her hair. I suspected there was more to her than just a great body. I sensed a sadness about her and a story she might not want to tell. Maybe she felt her body was all she had, all she was worth. I wanted to ask her questions but knew that wasn't my role on this operation. I might draw suspicion by being too inquisitive. *Stick to the plan, Stearman, you're just a vapid bimbo in this scenario.*

A little later, after smiles and handshakes and a friendly exchange of names, our yacht headed out to deeper water. I was sitting in a chair on the side of the deck in my bikini, legs propped up on the railing, when one of the two yacht "staff" walked over to me holding a tray of margaritas. A fit woman in her thirties, dressed in shorts and a polo shirt with the name of the yacht embroidered on the pocket, looked down at me comfortably ensconced in my cushy chair.

"Would you like a drink?" she asked. Then she looked directly at my crotch and added softly, "Didn't have much time to prepare, huh?"

"What do you mean?" I craned my neck to look down at my crotch, frantically thinking of all the things that could be wrong with my tiny bikini bottom. Had I started my period? Was there a hole in it? Confused for a split second, it hit me. My "landing strip" had way too much grass on the field. Any stripper worth her G-string would never allow something resembling a chia pet to grow out the sides of her bikini bottom. My throat constricted in panic. *Fuck, is my cover blown? Surely someone who owns and works at a strip club will guess I'm not really a stripper.*

My panic morphed into annoyance. This whole undercover operation was starting to piss me off. *The nerve of this bitch, pointing out my other than well-coiffed nether region.* Bent out of shape at her, but more annoyed with myself, I knew she was trying to do me a favor. "Thanks," I whispered. Not saying a word, she curled her upper lip in disdain and turned away. *Yep, still a bitch.*

Both staffers were FBI undercover agents, along with the "captain" of the boat, ███████████████████████. I knew the yacht had living quarters so, thighs pressed together, I minced down to the small bathroom in search of a razor. After rifling under the sink cabinet, I finally found a razor abandoned in a dusty corner. With a few dried hairs stuck to the blade, it was, thankfully, rust free. I didn't care who had owned it or how long it had been there. It was most likely left over from another undercover operation. I pushed aside thoughts of hepatitis and rare flesh-eating bacteria; all I cared about was trimming the garden and getting back to pretending to be a brainless twit and sprawling all over Vinnie without gagging. A word to the wise: Never try to shave your pubic hair on a boat . . . while the boat is moving up and down. With a few strokes of the dry blade, my mission was accomplished with only a raw scrape here and there. Making a mental note to slather tanning oil on my tender, newly exposed skin, I headed back up to the deck, desperately needing a whole pitcher of margaritas.

Later in the afternoon, faintly nauseous after letting Vinnie fawn all over me, I climbed the ladder to the tuna tower to get some fresher air and have a few minutes of quiet time. I found "Captain" Mike smoking a cigarette. We chatted about innocuous things as we stared out over the water, the smell of fish, saltwater, and coconut suntan oil mingled to create the unique scent of vacation. After a few minutes, I started to relax. Mike was another undercover agent, although we had never met prior to this operation. He was older than I, in his mid-to-late forties, short and stocky with a leathery face that fit his role, crinkled eyes that had seen a lot of sea and sun. As Mike and I stood under the tower awning, listening to the drunken laughter down below, I felt his right hand slide into the back of my bikini bottom, grip my left butt cheek, and squeeze. Completely caught off guard, I lashed out at him in panic and knocked his arm away with my elbow. I stood as tall as I could—which was considerably taller than he was—looked down my nose, and with gritted teeth whispered in tiny gasping breaths so that I wouldn't be overheard down below, "Touch me again and I'll fucking break your arm. Then I'll throw you overboard and feed you to the sharks!" I wasn't sure if the Gulf of Mexico had sharks but the look on his stunned face was sufficient evidence that he did *not* want to become chum for some man-behaving-badly-eating fish, lurking under the waters to mete out the punishment he deserved.

I turned around to climb down the ladder and felt my stomach contract. A quake, the tiniest shift in the tectonic plates of my own abilities to protect myself, rippled through me. Gripping the metal railing, I climbed shakily down the ladder as fast as I could go. My feet touched the main deck and I stood still for a few seconds to refocus my eyes and breath. For some reason, a fleeting thought crashed into my psyche: "Is this what Sara's life is like?"

Did Mike think he could touch me as part of his role as "captain" of the ship? Did my role as a stripper make me a piece of meat, literally up for grabs? I had been dropped into several undercover operations and done a lot of role-playing at the undercover school. Not one single guy had touched me in an improper manner, knowing, and hopefully respecting, the fact that I was a fellow FBI agent. Actually, most of the guys I had worked with on undercover operations had appreciated having someone they could really talk to, especially those in deep, long-term roles. They rarely had the opportunity to be them-selves and my presence seemed to give them permission to let go of the mental pressure, if just for a little while. I had held more than a few male agents in my arms while they cried away their stress and fears, long days and weeks away from family and friends. The first few times after this happened, I started to think I had a "you can confess anything to me" sign on my forehead. When I told the Undercover Unit about this phenomenon, they realized how a female agent could actually complement the required psychological assessments. They began to ask for my opinion on the mental well-being of some of the agents who had been deep undercover for long periods of time. I had learned that agents who were in long-term undercover roles could sometimes start to think the role was "real" versus their FBI life as an agent. One agent, who was deep undercover in a drug case, drove a Ferrari and lived the expensive, high life of a drug dealer. He had admitted that when his role was finished, he didn't want to go back to living the lifestyle afforded by an FBI agent salary.

Mike probably treated all women with disdain, which shouldn't have surprised me. Even Vinnie, with whom I had slept in the same bed the previous night, had the good sense to stay on his side without touching me in a sexually provocative manner. But *this* asshole, one of my own peers, felt he had the right to feel me up on an official assignment. If my undercover career wasn't going to finish on an all-time high by sleeping with an informant, it just might end on an even higher high by feeding one of my own to the fish.

Later that evening, after a drunken and sunburned but uneventful dinner with the cabal of strippers, informants, and cheating undercover agents, I slept one last time with my informant. Vinnie didn't budge all night and I didn't have to threaten him once. I think he was too exhausted from lack of sleep the night before, too much sunshine, too many margaritas, and hours-long nervous vigilance to not touch me overly much during the day.

The next afternoon, I deplaned at Washington Reagan, feeling raw dismay about Ben's, Christy's, and Mike's behaviors, which made my decision easier. I realized undercover work was no longer fun for me. I did not want to be touched by men who felt my undercover status afforded free reign over my body.

I recall the moment vividly. Still dressed in undercover mode, looking fresh from a sun-filled vacation, I had on a skin-tight white tank top, short denim miniskirt, sky-high white cowboy boots, and a dark summer tan. I didn't look like an FBI agent. I knew I was good at undercover work. No one ever suspected me of being who I was or what I did. I had an uncanny ability to elicit information from people without their noticing. But I was done with pretending to be someone else.

Keith was waiting for me out there somewhere. I wanted to learn to be myself with him.

CHAPTER SIXTEEN

GREEN EYES

★ ★ ★

It is that moment that divides the
intoxication of Life from the awakening
—Kahlil Gibran, "Of the First Look"

I felt the cold swoosh of wind against my calves as the heavy wood-and-glass door closed slowly behind me. I had arrived at Boxers, a bar and grill in Greenwich Village, New York City, with my two friends, CJ and Rayna.

A scarred and scratched wooden bar, polished to a shine, stretched away to my left. A row of barstools marched along its front edge, each occupied by a chattering customer, others crowding behind, two and three deep, drinks in hand, laughing and conversing loudly. I saw all this through my periphery. The pull of eyes, wide and green, fringed by dark lashes, had narrowed my vision to a single face in the crowd. All I registered was the slow quaking that erupted in the vicinity of my heart, traveling down my arms to my fingers, my stomach, my legs. Everything else fell away: my friends, the bar, the sounds of this October Saturday night.

"It's him," said a voice in my head.

I walked past him, following my friends, paralleling the line of barstools filled with rowdy customers. But my eyes never left his.

At some point, I caught up with CJ and Rayna, both oblivious to what had just happened. Could anyone have noticed? Needing to do something, anything, to still the trembling I felt must be obvious to everyone in the room, I asked my friends what they wanted to drink and headed to the closest bartender. While the bartender mixed our vodka tonics, I turned around, my back to the bar. There he was. The man with the green eyes. He stood not three feet from me. I could have reached out and touched him, but I didn't. I simply stood, a stillness replacing the quake, and stared into his eyes. He didn't say a word. He looked back at me, his face solemn, contemplative as if he were trying to unravel a mystery. I knew without a single doubt he had felt the same eruption, the same bone-deep quiver of recognition.

❖

Almost two years later, I stood inside a set of glass double doors that opened onto a deep covered balcony.

"Are you ready?" CJ's voice, low and solemn.

I turned to my friend, her face a mask of anxiety and disquiet, an echo of the uncertainty thrumming through my veins.

I knew without a doubt this was one walk CJ was never going to take. She was happy for me, but as hard as she was trying, her inclination to jump on her motorcycle and ride hard down an endless highway was far preferable to wedded bliss.

I could hear Chris and Laurie strumming their guitars, Laurie's voice, husky and low and hypnotic. Chris and Laurie had first met in college in Tennessee. The first time Chris saw her, she was sitting on a stage, her acoustic guitar resting on her lap as she sang. Her voice could tear away all defenses. Chris fell in love with her immediately.

Through the windows, I could see Mom and Dad, Mom wearing the dress I had bought for her. When she had opened the box, a look of delighted surprise had suffused her face. It was cream silk, with a pink and light blue jacket, the same blue of her eyes. It was pretty and feminine and totally unlike anything she had ever worn. But a mask fell across that joy and wonderment as I heard my dad say, "That's too pretty for her. She's never had anything like it." Not wanting Mom to change her mind about wearing the dress, I said quietly, "Well, that doesn't say a lot about you now, does it, Daddy?"

I had not asked my father to take this walk with me. I had never belonged to him and I wasn't about to continue the illusion that he was in any way happy for me, much less happy to be here. I had written a letter to my family members with an ultimatum—you come, or I never speak to you again. I meant it. My two brothers and one sister who had taken the time to be here shifted impatiently, already itching to make the return trip home.

Keith's parents were sitting next to my mom and dad; Keith's father, Ted, happily chatted to my dad about some military issue. He had found a kindred spirit. Ted had been in the Navy and he and my father had gotten along immediately. My dad, although forever reluctant to talk about his time on Okinawa during World War II, was more than willing to listen to Ted provide a long dissertation on the current state of the US military.

Louisa, Keith's mom, was sitting quietly, unusual for her. Tall and statuesque in a bright red dress, she was determined to be seen, center stage her preferred habitat. She was studiously ignoring my mom, knowing she was not going to dazzle in that direction. My mom never suffered fools gladly. At dinner the evening before, Mom had shut Louisa down with one sentence: "I can't understand a word you're saying." No one had ever dared to interrupt Louisa's look-at-me chatter.

As CJ, a tall redhead, dressed in a pink leather miniskirt, strolled through the open French doors, all eyes turned. Unlike most Leos, I don't like to be the center of attention. The thought of all that scrutiny filled me with an aversion that shivered down my skin. My friends and colleagues had gotten up at an early hour to arrive by 10:00 A.M. I could see that most of them were cold and desperately needed a drink . . . another reason I wanted this to be quick. I needed a drink, too.

Stepping toward the open doorway of the Officer's Club on the Marine Corps base at Quantico, I could sense, but not see, the Potomac River in the distance. Beyond the balcony's edge, a heavy mist left drops of moisture that clung to the treetops, and a low-lying fog obscured everything beyond. I couldn't see the familiar horizon, that place I always looked to for direction.

This wasn't a long walk, as walks go; perhaps thirty feet. Maybe I had subconsciously chosen this place for that reason. I had wanted to get married at the top of a mountain in Europe, no one around, just the trees and the grass and the sun to witness our being there. I had wanted to stand on the edge of a valley and fling my arms high as I whirled, miles and miles of possibility stretching into the distance. Not today. Today, I tilted on the edge of a precipice, everything in front of me and the path below shrouded.

The day Keith asked me to take this walk with him, I had cried for a full five minutes, not uttering a word. Keith later told me those five minutes had felt like a lifetime. I was afraid, afraid to lose my independence, afraid of being controlled by a man, afraid I would lose the *me* I had discovered within myself, finally, after almost thirty-one years. Who would I become if I had to share, for a lifetime, that fresh and raw knowledge of who I am? Would there be anything left I could call my own?

I had had relationships with men who were going my way, if just for a short period of time. When I had dated other men, I would run their police record to determine if they were safe for me to date. I had to digest the fact that the insidiousness of men can be hidden by a mask of civility that no police record can reveal. These men had one thing in common; they were all as emotionally unavailable to me as I was to them. Keith had changed all that. Keith had taught me it was OK to cry. He had taught me that happiness and hope could be wrapped up in a future I had thought would be solitary.

Hesitating, I stepped through the door and there was Keith, standing against the balcony railing, tall, long dark curly hair pulled back into a ponytail. His square jaw was clenched, his hands held in front of him, long fingers loosely entwined. This man had taught me to love, had cleaved me senseless with his raw unapologetic emotion, had broken through my brittle I-need-no-one-but-myself veneer.

Laurie's voice began to sing, "I don't know what brought us here . . ." my cue to move forward. Keith's green eyes, luminous with tears, locked onto mine. Answering tears blurred my own.

CHAPTER SEVENTEEN

KEEP YOUR MOP OUT OF MY BUCKET

★★★

About five years into my FBI career, I was ready for a change. I had been working white-collar crime, beginning with governmental fraud and later healthcare fraud. I had no interest in either, even though my medical background was relevant to the FBI's interest in a healthcare fraud initiative, dictated by the Department of Justice. As far as I was concerned, fraud was dry as a dog biscuit. As hard as I tried, I could not conjure an interest in people stealing money from other people, corporations, or other government agencies. Hats off to those agents who love it and do a great job, landing well-deserved jail sentences for the criminal element. I was not good at fraud investigations because I wasn't interested. I didn't want to be a failure, not to myself, and not in the eyes of my fellow agents.

I decided to pursue one area I had been interested in since joining the FBI, counterintelligence and espionage. The FBI had a program through which they sent agents to the Defense Language Institute (DLI) in Monterey, California, to learn foreign languages. Those agents were then placed on a counterintelligence or espionage squad in a field office that had investigative need of that language. Because I had studied Russian in college, I wanted to apply for one of the slots at DLI, improve my Russian speaking ability, and get assigned to a counterintelligence or espionage squad.

When applying to DLI, the applicant first must take the Defense Language Aptitude Battery (DLAB) test—an invented language, with an accompanying set of grammar and vocabulary rules—meant to test one's aptitude for learning a foreign language.

I scored in the highest bracket on the DLAB, which earned me one of the coveted slots at DLI. I was told by the Language Unit at FBI headquarters that upon graduation from the language school, I could choose to transfer to one of five field offices: San Francisco, Los Angeles, Chicago, New York City, or Washington, DC. I had no real preference, but Keith, who had moved to Washington, DC, to be with me, had decided he wanted to move back to New York. My choice was easy. We were moving to New York City after I graduated DLI.

A few weeks before Keith and I left for DLI, a call from the Language Unit informed me the slot I had been chosen for, to study Russian, had been canceled. The FBI had decided, shortsightedly as it turns out, there was no more pressing need for Russian linguists since the Cold War was over. However, since I had scored so highly on the DLAB, I could choose another language. My choices were Mandarin Chinese, Korean, or Arabic, all Category IV languages, meaning they were the most difficult of all foreign languages. When I asked which of the Category IV was the most difficult, I was told Mandarin Chinese. "That's the one I want," I said.

Two and a half years later, having graduated from DLI's Basic and Intermediate language courses in Mandarin Chinese, I was transferred to the New York field office. The New York office is one of those places most FBI agents avoid, unless they are natives. The city is so expensive, they have to live two hours away in order to afford even the smallest of houses. To those agents who did everything they could to avoid being transferred to New York City, it was known as the "black hole," like the Hotel California. You can check in any time you like, but you can never leave.

On my first day, I was introduced to Don, the agent assigned to acclimate newly arrived transferees to the division. New York City, the FBI's largest field division, with an agent population easily doubling any other office, and including hundreds of administrative and support personnel, found it necessary to assign one agent, full-time, to handle administrative issues for all agents arriving for duty.

Don, nearing the end of his career, most of which he had spent in New York, had been assigned to give me a tour of the office. After first introducing me to the SAC—Special Agent in Charge, head of the field office—Don squired me up and down hallways, moving from floor to floor since the New York office took up a lot of space at One Federal Plaza. He walked me through every squad, introducing me to people we encountered along the way. I knew I would never remember their names, but I nodded and listened as he chatted about office shenanigans.

As we were walking down a hallway, he stopped in front of an unmarked door. Don looked at me and said, "Don't ever open this door unless you knock first."

I nodded in agreement. "OK, no problem. What's in there?"

"It's the broom closet. It's where people go to have sex." We continued down the hallway.

I was surprised and not surprised. I had learned early on, starting at the FBI's training academy at Quantico, people find ways to hook up and have sex—married, not married, looking for love, bored—it didn't matter. Human nature and hormones prevailed over common sense.

I never had reason to knock on that door, nor did I ever open it to see who might be inside. But if I were so inclined, I certainly wouldn't have sex in a closet full of dirty mops and brooms. Only a desperate libido sought out the smell of Lysol and mold as an aphrodisiac.

Don's tour proved to be a foreshadowing of my time in New York City. While I was at DLI, I had fallen in love with California. Although I had very little time outside class and studying, Keith and I used our spare time to explore—camping along the coast, visiting national parks, driving remote winding roads through rolling golden hills. The more I saw, the more I yearned to explore the incredible beauty of America's west. Arriving in New York City after living in Monterey, California, was like falling into a cacophony of 24/7 nonstop clamor. Skyscrapers blocked the sun, creating shadowed canyons where people moved down sidewalks, across streets, up and down subway steps. Even the interesting work I was doing on a counterintelligence squad, monitoring the activities of foreign spies and protecting US critical national assets, could not persuade me I wanted to stay. Keith had also decided that Thomas Wolfe was correct. You can't go home again.

Transfer papers in hand, we headed west once again, this time to the San Francisco Division.

CHAPTER EIGHTEEN

BEHIND THE GLASS

★★★

"It's the only time in my life I ever considered committing suicide."

Jess and I had known each other for more than twenty years. Jess, a beautiful African American woman, had a wide smile, easy laughter, and a calmness capable of drawing you into her circle, an orbit of warmth and kindness.

We had met when we both attended DLI in Monterey, California, to learn Mandarin Chinese. I had heard many of her stories, but never this one heart-wrenching admission.

Jess was born in Alabama to a large family of seven. She was the baby girl and grew up knowing she was loved in a close-knit household. Jess's father was a warm and loving man who enjoyed a good laugh. But Jess's mother was her strongest influence who instilled into her daughters the importance of independence. She wanted her daughters to pursue a future without fear, earning for themselves a freedom from the influence of men by making their own money and getting an education. Growing up under the sphere of her mother's teachings, Jess knew she could go out into the world on her own terms, a supportive family at her back.

Jess didn't grow up wanting to be an FBI agent. She attended the University of Alabama, where she majored in communications, and upon graduation, joined the military. While in the military, she fulfilled a dream of learning a foreign language, German, followed by years stationed in Germany. Once she had fulfilled her military obligation, Jess knew she wanted to continue to serve her country, preferably working at a federal government agency. On the day she approached the FBI at a job fair, Jess knew little about the FBI but found the recruiter to be persuasive. He told Jess her military background and language ability would be useful in a career as an FBI agent. A few months later, Jess was invited to attend FBI New Agent's Training Class.

Jess told me she had gotten lucky at Quantico. Her instructors treated her with respect, though she was the only Black female of eight female trainees in her class. She was also the only Black female to pass through the FBI Academy that year. On the evening transfer orders were passed out, Jess learned she was being sent to Memphis, Tennessee. Jess's future was set.

The FBI's Memphis office was considered small, with only about seventy-five agents spread throughout the state of Tennessee. Memphis, division headquarters, had about thirty-five agents assigned to three squads. There were three Black male agents with Jess again the only Black female.

Shortly after Jess's arrival, a set of circumstances placed Jess in the eye of a storm. A group of Black agents nationwide had filed a discrimination law-suit citing complaints regarding lack of career development and promotion amongst the Black agent population, which at the time numbered almost five hundred. Although Jess, newly arrived from the training academy, was not part of the lawsuit, she nonetheless became the target of racism in reaction to the lawsuit, which permeated the office. The racism and sexism, allowed to run rampant and unchecked, rose to a boil. Jess became the object of prejudice and misogyny amongst the male agents.

Jess's training agent, Harry, made no bones about despising her. A training agent assigned to a new agent is meant to be a mentor and instruct on the daily duties of an FBI agent. Jess soon learned that Harry did not plan to teach her anything, so she set her sights on office personnel who would be willing to give her tips on how to navigate the mine field in which she found herself.

Assigned to the criminal squad, Jess soon learned that her supervisor was not going to be an ally, either. He happened to be the leader of the office clique that was vehemently opposed to minorities in the Bureau and hated the discrimination lawsuit brought by the Black agents. He refused to speak to Jess for three weeks, after which time Jess worked up the nerve to enter his office and say, "I know you don't want me here, but you've got to give me some work to do."

Jess also realized the agents on her squad were unwilling to partner with her while hunting fugitives. She went into dangerous neighborhoods alone with no backup, conducting surveillances and interviews by herself. However, when she tracked down her first fugitive, she was not allowed to make the arrest herself, nor was she allowed to put handcuffs on the suspect. The male agents on her squad received the credit for the arrest.

Working alone, Jess soon developed a trust and collaboration with the professional support people in the office. The women in the typing pool, most of whom were Black, took Jess under their wing and taught her the complexities of processing paperwork. But there is a pecking order in an FBI office and although these women wanted to see Jess succeed, they held no position of power, had no means to help Jess fight against the discrimination she was receiving from the men. Jess learned to function in an office where she was not welcomed as a colleague. She existed in a shadow zone, where agents commented without a care and within hearing distance—"I didn't want these bitches on my squad" and "The bureau is just fucking up by bringing in all these minorities and women."

One day she was sitting at her desk when her beeper vibrated, displaying a number she wasn't familiar with. When she called the number, she was directed to a recording that spouted racist dogma, likening Black people to monkeys. Jess knew she had been beeped while at her desk so squad members could watch her reaction. She didn't give them the satisfaction.

Jess felt she had no one to talk to about the multitude of small incidents that occurred daily. She knew no one in Memphis and had no social network. Other Black professionals in Memphis were from the region and did not readily make friends with strangers. Being an FBI agent is isolating in the best of circumstances and making new friends in a racially divided city was not an easy prospect.

Jess's only outlet was a periodic meeting of the eight female agents in the office, which always took place at one of their homes, away from the prying eyes of the men. This secret circle of women was the only place Jess felt free from the racism and misogyny she experienced every single day. The furtive meetings the Memphis female agents organized were radically different from my first office experience where the female agents openly met as a group, bonding over shared experiences. I have often asked myself if I would have stayed in the FBI had I experienced Jess's isolation.

In the Memphis office, all agents working on criminal matters were required to respond to bank robberies. One day, a call came over the radio that a bank robbery was in progress. Jess immediately radioed dispatch to let them know she was on her way to the scene, following protocol to let other arriving investigators know she was available for the investigation.

Arriving at the bank, Jess realized she was not the first agent at the scene and could see her training agent, Harry, already inside with other agents. Harry was the senior bank robbery investigator placed in charge whenever there was a robbery. Protocol dictates that the doors to the bank are to be locked while attending agents go about their investigation without the intrusion of the public.

Jess walked up to the door, peered inside, and knocked. As she held her face to the glass, Harry looked up and locked eyes with her. He paused and continued to stare at her, then turned and walked away. Jess was confused as to why he didn't open the doors for her. On a bank robbery investigation, it's important to wrap it up quickly, to limit disruption to the bank's daily business.

Jess knocked on the door again and another agent started walking towards the door in a gesture to unlock it. About that time, Harry called the agent back and said something to him, after which the agent hung his head and looked at his feet. He didn't look at Jess behind the glass, nor did he make a move to unlock the door.

After standing there a few minutes longer, Jess finally realized her efforts were futile. Harry wanted to humiliate her in front of her peers and let her know he was in charge, not only of the investigation, but of the other agents who were too cowed to break through Harry's circle of control. Jess drove away from the crime scene knowing she was never going to break through that circle. As long as she stayed in Memphis, Harry would do his best to keep her on the outside of that door, looking in.

Jess began to have headaches from the stress and dreaded coming to work each day. She finally decided to find a way to transfer out of Memphis or leave the FBI altogether. She applied to the Secret Service in St. Louis so no one in Memphis would know what she was doing as the Memphis Secret Service office was right next door to the FBI. Knowledge that she was planning to resign would have brought even more wrath upon her head. Simultaneously, Jess knew that if she stayed in the FBI, a change of office was needed. Knowing she could utilize her language capability, Jess applied to the FBI's foreign language training at the DLI in Monterey, California. When Jess was accepted to DLI, she opted to stay with the FBI and pursue her love of languages.

I had first heard Jess's stories at DLI, where we had become friends and classmates. Jess was one of the most calm, poised, and caring people I had ever met. I liked to tease her by calling her Mother Earth. So when Jess confessed she had once considered suicide, I was rocked. But like Mother Earth, underneath Jess's unruffled exterior, she had a seething layer of magma, hot and unsettled, smoldering just beneath the surface. She had endured where others might have given up, justifiably so. Perhaps Jess's Mother Earth persona was similar to the Stargate shield I had learned to use to protect myself.

During her time in Memphis, Jess had gone from having headaches and not being able to sleep to feeling that being dead would be better than the hell she was living through. "I never really wanted to die, I just wanted to change my circumstances somehow. I had to get out of there, but I wasn't so desperate that I actually made a plan to kill myself. I would have resigned before committing suicide," Jess told me in the same calm and composed voice I was familiar with.

When I asked Jess what had kept her from taking her own life, she said she had gone through the FBI Academy just like everyone else in the Memphis office. She deserved to be there just as much as they. She wasn't about to let someone run her off and get the best of her.

After Jess retired, she felt she should have fought harder against the racism and sexism she experienced in Memphis. But she also knew that if she had taken the step to file a formal complaint, she would have been vilified for the rest of her career, just like the other Black agents were who had filed that class action lawsuit. Women and minorities didn't have a way out then. Although mechanisms were technically in place for employees to report discrimination or harassment, the reality was completely different. It was common knowledge that those women who took this path became objects of contempt. Although Jess feels racism and sexism still exists in the FBI, female agents now have more protected avenues to bring their complaints forward, to be judged by the events that have occurred and not the fact that they have been brought to light by a woman.

Jess feels her experiences in the FBI changed her. She had been warm and friendly prior to joining the FBI. Now she is harder, more unwilling to take anyone's shit, with an anger that never seems to dissipate, which has rendered her personality into something new, intractable, unbending. Feeling helpless to punish those who had caused her pain affected how she carries herself and how she views others. It is difficult to find her true self, the self that could never have anticipated the level of hatred she has since learned to deal with.

When Jess looks at the FBI now, occasionally demonized in the press, she still feels a level of protectiveness toward the organization. Much as her patriotism for the United States has been steadfast, she understands that people in the FBI, for the most part, want to do the best for their country. They are hardworking, from the agents to the analysts to the professional staff, who, day and night, bust their asses to protect those who cannot protect themselves.

CHAPTER NINETEEN

RATCLAW

★★★

"Do you know where Chad is?" Diane, a fellow squad mate, asked as she walked in the squad area.

"I think I heard him scurry down the hall on his little rat claws about an hour ago," I responded sarcastically. Hands paused over my computer keyboard, I looked over at Diane with my front teeth lapping over my bottom lip, mimicking the sound of a chittering rodent. Diane belted out laughing and as she left the squad area to hunt for Chad, I could hear her chuckling down the hallway, "Ratclaw, yeah, that's a good one."

Some agents should never be supervisors, and Chad was one of them. Chad was universally hated on our squad. To use an old adage, "shit floats" would make Chad a giant turd in the punchbowl that everyone was doing their best to pretend wasn't there.

At that time, I was stationed in the San Francisco Field Division on a counterintelligence squad of about twelve agents, five of whom were female. Having so many females on one squad was unusual. I'm not sure how it happened, but I think the universe had finally decided that Chad needed to be dealt with, even if Chad hadn't yet received that particular newsflash.

Chad had no knowledge of counterintelligence and was constantly running to either Diane or me to ask the simplest, most mundane questions that even a new agent could have answered. Afterward, he would scurry back to his desk to continue his phone conversation and pretend to demonstrate his newfound knowledge with whoever was questioning his "expertise." Diane and I would look at each other and just shake our heads. We had work to do and, for the most part, we could do it without his input, so he was largely ignored by most everyone on the squad. Until he couldn't be ignored.

Diane was the first one to leave and go to another squad. She was the senior agent and tired of Chad's micromanagement and lack of knowledge, which led to a lack of support for the work the squad was supposed to do. When we needed resources or permission to carry out a classified, clandestine operation, it was Chad's job to be our advocate. Oftentimes these operations were time sensitive. We ended up wasting valuable time explaining to Chad the who, what, where, and why of what our operations would entail. Sometimes he was so confused, he refused to back us up and several investigations of vital intelligence importance fell by the wayside.

After Diane transferred to another squad, Chad seemed to take this as an insult to his leadership skills and he set his sights on another female agent, Sherry. Sherry was smart, thorough, and hardworking. His constant implications that her work was unsatisfactory started to take an angry turn and became more frequent as weeks went by. One time I found her in tears. She had worked long hours on a particular case and Chad had, with a few barbed insults and criticisms, told her she didn't know what she was doing. Inevitably, Sherry decided she, too, needed to get away from Chad.

I had been sorry to see both Diane and Sherry leave the squad, but Diane was a senior agent, and I knew she could take care of herself. Sherry had a lot of confidence in spite of Chad's harassment and I knew she, too, would land on her feet. But the two other female agents left on the squad had me worried.

One agent, Natalie, despite having several years on the job, was a vulnerable soul. She lacked confidence, even though she was smart, funny, and attractive. Sometimes I wondered what had happened in her life to make her feel so insecure. I wanted her to believe in herself, while at the same time, I wanted to shake her silly and scream at her to buck up and grow a backbone. She was a tiny thing, and although women of smaller stature were not uncommon in the FBI, she had a fragility about her that made me frightened for her. Little did I know this would bring out the predator in Chad.

One late afternoon, I had been away from our squad area and had just walked in the door when I saw Chad's back, his hand held up and away from his body, as if ready to strike. Cowering against the wall in front of him was Natalie, several inches shorter and half-hidden by his considerable bulk. When he heard my footsteps, he stepped back, turned on his heel, and walked out of the room.

I strode over to Natalie as quickly as I could, asking, "Did he hurt you? What happened? What's going on?" Natalie was in tears. She said he had come in and starting yelling questions at her about one of her cases. When she stood up to talk to him, he backed her against the wall, and it was about that time I walked in. I gave her a hug and told her I would take care of Chad. What I didn't say was that it might take some time and we would all have to endure more of his incompetence and wrath for a while longer. I was determined to put a stop to his misogynist behavior.

Right after this event I started to "keep book" on Chad, something I had never done in my entire career. "Keeping book" on someone in the FBI means you are secretly documenting their transgressions. Every time Chad made a disparaging remark to one of the females or gave them a bad review—while the guys always got the good ones—I would write it down. I started my record-keeping revisiting the incompetence he displayed when he first arrived, documenting his harassment of the two females who had already left the squad. I made copies of anything disparaging or harassing he put in writing and kept it locked in my office safe, hidden in the middle of my investigative files.

Natalie's file review was the next point of contention. When an agent is assigned an investigation, they are called the "case agent." A file review is a regularly scheduled meeting with the supervisor to review all work the case agent has accomplished in the previous quarter. I knew Natalie was traumatized when she came to me and asked if I would sit in on her file review with Chad. When I asked her why, her reply was simply, "I'm afraid of him."

I told her I would be willing to, but when I walked into his office with Natalie, Chad told me Natalie's file review was none of my business and ordered me to leave. I did leave, but I stayed just outside the door, making enough noise pacing back and forth so that he would know I was there. He was civil with Natalie although abrupt in his speech. I think because he knew I was there, he kept the meeting short. Natalie's fear of Chad and his refusal to let me sit in on the file review also went into my "book." I knew it was a matter of time before Natalie, too, would leave the squad.

After Natalie's departure, I waited to see who Chad's next victim would be. Unsurprisingly, he chose the most recent graduate from the FBI's training academy, Ellen. Ellen and I were in the Bureau car one day, returning to the field office after she had picked me up at the airport from an official travel assignment. It is standard protocol for agents to pick up a fellow agent at the airport, so the traveling agent won't have to take a taxi, at government expense, to the office. Ellen's Blackberry rang and I could hear Chad screaming at her at the top of his lungs. In his diatribe, Chad screamed that Ellen had no business picking me up and that the both of us needed to get back to the office as soon as possible. Ellen told him we were on our way and asked if there was an emergency. No, there was no emergency, he just wanted to know where we were.

Ellen's hands were shaking, knuckles white, as she gripped the steering wheel. Ellen looked at me, eyes wide, and said, "What should I do?" Ellen was still on probation, a period of two years when a new agent is reviewed and evaluated on a regular basis. If the agent is found wanting, they can be dismissed. Ellen had wanted nothing more in her life than to become an FBI agent. She was terrified that Chad was going to be the instrument to bring about the end of her dream, all for picking a fellow agent up at the airport.

I kept trying to reassure Ellen that everything was going to be OK. On the drive back to the office, I laid out my plan for her, a plan in which she might need to play a part.

As soon as we arrived, I called the secretary of the ASAC to request an immediate appointment. The ASAC, Frank, was available and after swinging by my desk to pick up all the evidence against Chad, I headed up to Frank's office.

I walked in, closed the door behind me, and sat in the chair in front of Frank's desk. Frank was all smiles. "What can I help you with today, Kathy?"

I verbally summarized my case against Chad, my documented evidence laid on Frank's desk, my hand resting on top of it. I didn't want to show it to him until I gauged his first reaction, which didn't take long.

Frank's smile immediately disappeared, and he got a look on his face like that of a stubborn child who refuses to eat his lima beans. I could tell he wanted nothing to do with my allegations of sexual harassment and gender discrimination, although at that time, I believe I couched it in terms of "Chad hates women." Frank hemmed and hawed and finally said there was nothing he could do about it. Hoping the look of disgust I was feeling on the inside was clearly displayed on my face as I stared at him across his desk, I said, "Or you just *won't* do anything." It wasn't a question; it was simply a statement.

From Frank's office, I headed directly to the office responsible for handling all employee complaints, including sexual harassment, gender discrimination, allegations of fraud, and other misconduct. I wanted to know what my options were in filing an official complaint to the OPR at FBI Headquarters. Once a complaint was filed, there was no turning back. An investigation into my allegations against Chad would be launched. Although the investigation itself would be private, or as private as an accusation can be in the FBI, word would get out that I was "complaining" about another agent. Unfortunately, in the FBI, when a female agent files a complaint against a male agent, particularly if that male agent is her superior, blowback most always falls on the one making the accusation. Sometimes this blowback would simply be to gain a "hallway file" for having a chip on your shoulder or worse, being a "man-hater."

Armed with the knowledge of what I needed to do should my last resort prove to be unhelpful, I took my documentation and went to the office of the Special Agent in Charge (SAC), the highest-ranking agent in the division.

Normally I would have made an appointment with Greg, the SAC, in advance. But I didn't want Frank to head me off at the pass. I told Greg's secretary I needed to speak to him urgently.

Greg happened to be in his office. When I told him briefly why I wanted to speak with him, he asked me why I hadn't gone to Frank first, rather than go outside the chain of command. I explained that I had spoken to Frank earlier; however, Frank said there was nothing he could do. Greg then asked his secretary to have Frank report to Greg's office immediately.

When Frank saw me sitting in Greg's office, his face dropped. From that point forward, Frank didn't say a word. He sat in his chair with a hangdog look while I verbally laid out the allegations against Chad. Then I handed Greg the folder that contained my written observations, signed and dated by me, stretching back for months.

Greg looked up at me and said, "Kathy, you're a senior agent and you have a good reputation. Plus, you've documented everything I need to know. If it were someone else and not you, I wouldn't do what I'm going to do."

Greg then picked up his phone and called another supervisor, who happened to be female, and told her she would be acting supervisor of my squad from that point forward. I don't know what he said to Ratclaw; that conversation was held behind closed doors. However, that afternoon, Ratclaw cleaned out his desk.

At the time Ratclaw abused his position as a supervisor and agent, the FBI provided mandatory sensitivity training, which included sexual harassment and discrimination. I'm pretty sure Ratclaw missed that class. Although mandatory implies participation, it can't force a person to think a certain way. But it can make that person aware that perhaps his—or her—way of thinking and acting is unacceptable, hurtful, and, in some cases, illegal.

But what can the FBI do in the face of a September 22, 2020, presidential directive that all federal government agencies suspend diversity training until further notice? Do we want the FBI to move backward, where a Ratclaw can once again belittle women, behave with impunity, and damage the mission we've all fought to be a part of?

CHAPTER TWENTY

THE SILENT TERRORIST

★★★

One afternoon, when I was stationed in New York, I was walking back to the office from Little Italy, after lunch with two female colleagues from my squad. We had cut through a park in Chinatown, a green space in lower Manhattan where dozens of people gather early in the morning to practice Tai Chi.

When I was at DLI, my Chinese teachers had not just taught us their language, but also their history, their food, their literature, and the art of Tai Chi, a series of slow martial arts movements meant to be both meditative and beneficial for keeping the body supple and strong. I had forgotten most of the Tai Chi movements. When I was out and about during those early morning sessions, I loved to stop and watch what appeared to be a choreographed dance, silent and sinuous.

The park that afternoon was devoid of the Tai Chi practitioners, so we stepped lively to get back to work. Standing just off the sidewalk, a slim Chinese man, in his late thirties or early forties, stepped up to me, a tentative smile on his face. "Would you like to have your fortune told?"

"No, thank you." I politely returned his smile and kept walking. It's not that I don't believe in fortune-telling. I'm convinced some people have the ability to see into the future, to know where you've been and where you're going. As a believer in reincarnation, I had read extensively on the subject and studied religions built upon the basic tenets of reincarnation. Any other day, I would have been eager to match wits against a fortune-teller to see if he or she was for real. But on that day, I was in a hurry to get back to work.

I had not moved three steps forward when I felt something akin to a giant hand reach out of the sky and turn me around. The next thing I said was "Yes, I would like to have my fortune told."

The man, who didn't give me his name, led me over to an ancient woman, skin creased into a million minuscule wrinkles, as if someone had crumpled a piece of tin foil and tried to smooth it out. Beneath the wrinkles, her skin was flawless; no moles, freckles or sunspots marred the surface, which was the color of old parchment. Her hair, tucked back over her shoulders, was wispy and white. Her name was Aunty Tam.

I sat down in a chair in front of her and sat quietly as she placed a hand on either side of my face. Her eyes, though dark, were slightly opaque, as if she were in the early stages of developing cataracts. I couldn't tell if she could see me because her eyes seemed to look beyond my shoulder, far off into some distant place only she could see.

Aunty Tam told me many things that day, some of which I have never revealed to another living soul. My two friends stood behind me and I could hear them scoffing at some of the things she told me of my past, things I knew to be true, but they did not. She also told me that most men would be afraid of me because they sense I am stronger than them. She told me I have three children allotted to me, should I choose to have them. Then she told me I would become extremely ill. If I survived to the age of forty-three, I would live to be eighty-six.

That day, I did not give her prophecy much thought. But I never forgot.

❖

I sat on the edge of the hot tub in our backyard in San Francisco, the letter I had just received lying on the outdoor table. The letter, from the Women's Breast Health Center, asked me to come back to the center as soon as possible for another mammogram.

I wasn't surprised for a number of reasons. My paternal grandmother had died of breast cancer. My maternal grandmother had died of breast cancer, along with two of my mother's sisters. I had a history of breast cancer on both sides of my family, so I had been getting mammograms every couple of years for over a decade. But this wasn't my first thought as I read the letter. My first thought was Aunty Tam's prediction. I was thirty-eight years old.

❖

I can still picture Dr. Freeman sitting in front of me, his round bright purple glasses magnifying his kind, compassionate, gray eyes, his curly gray and black mop of hair flopping over his forehead; he looked like he had combed it with an eggbeater. Dr. Freeman was my oncologist, a short, wiry banty rooster of a man who high-stepped his way around the office, head jerking to and fro while chatting with the staff, patients, and, quite often, himself. During our first meeting, he spent almost two hours going over my treatment plan—six months of chemo accompanied by loss of hair, eyelashes, eyebrows, and every hair on my body. I later learned my particular chemo treatment was called the "fat plan." My guess is that Dr. Freeman did not want to add insult to injury by informing me, along with a diagnosis of breast cancer, I would soon morph into a bald butterball.

In his thin, high-pitched voice, he slid his rolling chair closer to where Keith and I were sitting and said, "Now I'm going to tell you what I've seen happen to my patients during cancer treatment. You'll find some of your best friends will disappear, while people you never in a million years considered will climb out of the woodwork to help you." With a long but kind stare at Keith, who was quietly but rigidly taking in every word, he added, "I've also seen marriages break up under the pressure of this kind of treatment."

Dr. Freeman's comment about friends disappearing did not register, because my mind focused on getting through surgery, six months of chemo, and two months of radiation. But his words came back to me, as I watched women who had been my best friends disappear over the horizon, no goodbyes, no apologies, just an empty space where our friendship used to exist.

The FBI had become my surrogate family early in my career. But I did not realize how quickly they would rally to my side after my breast cancer diagnosis. I hadn't expected the outpouring of love, support, and encouragement I received from the San Francisco office—from the female ASAC to one of the guys on my squad who waltzed into the office one day, head shaved down to his scalp in support of my own baldness. I developed friendships and relationships during those months of treatment that have never wavered in all the years since.

❖

On the morning of September 11, 2001, with only about a month left in my chemo treatment, I was getting ready to drive across the Bay Bridge to my acupuncture appointment. Dr. Wilson, a former emergency room physician who had transitioned to acupuncture, was treating me for nausea from the chemo. After more than five months of chemo, there were days when I couldn't keep anything in my stomach other than water. The phone rang and Keith, in a frantic voice, said, "Don't cross the bridge! There's been some kind of attack! Don't go across the bridge!"

My brain was fogged from chemo, so I didn't register what he was saying. "What? What are you talking about?"

"Just turn on the TV, but don't go across that bridge! I gotta go, I'll be home soon."

I watched on TV, as much of the rest of the world did that day, as the World Trade Center slowly fell into a massive heap of twisted steel, burning ash, and crushed bodies. I felt a regret deep in my bones that I was not there with my squad mates. I was not with my FBI family. I knew they would be scattered to the winds, as the search for the terrorists would get underway immediately. I would be stuck in a chemo chair, IV snaking out of my right arm, my own silent terrorist invading every cell of my body, destroying the good along with the bad in order to keep me alive. My terrorist was loyal to no country, knew no borders, and was indiscriminate in what it destroyed in its path.

❖

Doctors told me if I survived for five years after the initial diagnosis, my survival rate would be approximately 86 percent. After the fourth year, and multiple tests every six months to monitor reoccurrence, I realized I had been holding my breath, looking over my shoulder, waiting for death to sneak up on me. I wasn't living my life. I was simply going through the motions. Just as I had not been immune to my own terrorist, the cancer that had invaded my body, 9/11 had proven America was also not immune to an attack.

The events of 9/11 revived a dream I had long held of working in the Legal Attaché Program—the cadre of FBI employees who are stationed overseas in US embassies. It had been one of the driving forces in attending DLI to learn Mandarin Chinese, with the hopes I would be able to utilize my language skills in an international capacity. After my cancer diagnosis, I had put that dream aside, believing it was a goal that I would no longer be able to achieve. I sat down with Keith and asked him if he would be willing to move with me to FBIHQ in Washington, DC, the first step to getting a position in the Legal Attaché Program.

Keith had moved from New York City, where he lived when we first met, to where I had lived in Washington, DC. Then he had been willing to move to Monterey, California, so that I could attend DLI to learn Mandarin Chinese. He had left New York City again to move to San Francisco. Now this incredible man was willing to move to Washington, DC, so I could pursue a dream.

★★★

PART FOUR

OVER THE HORIZON

★★★

CHAPTER TWENTY-ONE

LOBSTERS IN THE BOX

★★★

Two years later, after a stint at FBI Headquarters in Washington, DC, as a supervisor, I arrived in New Delhi, India, my first Legat assignment. A few days after I arrived, I found myself sitting around a small table at the headquarters of the Intelligence Bureau (IB), the Indian equivalent to the CIA, drinking tea and eating almond cookies.

It was my first introductory meeting with them, and they were congratulating me on my posting as the head of the FBI office in India.

One of the gentlemen laughingly said, "Miss Kathy, here in India it is very difficult to be promoted and rise in the ranks like you have done in the FBI."

"I find that hard to believe," I said. "After all, you are all in the highest ranks of your agency."

"Miss Kathy, have you ever heard about the box of Indian lobsters?"'

Curious and looking forward to a tale, I said, "No, but I would love to hear it."

"In India, you can leave a box of lobsters unattended with no lid. None of the lobsters will escape. Do you know why?" he asked with a slight grin on his face.

Following along, knowing he was enjoying this anecdote he had surely told many times, like a favorite joke, I grinned back. "No, please tell me."

"When one lobster tries to crawl out of the box, all the other lobsters jump on his back and pull him back down."

Everyone in the room laughed as they sipped their tea.

I laughed, too. I had no idea how prescient that story would become.

CHAPTER TWENTY-TWO

WHAT'S A LEGAT?

★★★

When I tell people I was a Legal Attaché, also called a Legat, head of an FBI office overseas, the first question I am asked is "What's a Legat?"

I'm never surprised by this question. I learned soon after my arrival in New Delhi that even people within the FBI were sometimes not clear on what a Legat is allowed to do overseas and the restrictions that are placed upon what would be the normal course of an investigation in the United States.

Every day, I fielded emails, some from new agents who reached out with "Can you help me with this . . ." type questions. I was initially surprised that a new agent would not follow the chain of command and go through their supervisor to reach out to a Legat office. However, I soon learned that many supervisors and higher-level management were equally uninformed and would ask the same questions. I answered each and every query and did my best to explain what the Legat is allowed to do in a foreign country and why their expectations could, or could not, in some cases, be met.

The second question I am asked is "I thought the CIA was the international intelligence agency. What does the FBI do?"

The short answer is, yes, the CIA is predominantly focused on foreign intelligence. However, they do have a presence in the United States, although it is limited with no law enforcement capabilities.

Conversely, the FBI is, predominantly, a domestic agency, whose personnel all work in an overt capacity overseas. The FBI's seventy-plus Legal Attaché offices and sub-offices are staffed by only a few hundred agents and support personnel. By comparison, the number of CIA officers who live and work overseas is unknown.

Legat offices are located within US embassies and serve under the authority of the Department of State's Chief of Mission, also known as the Ambassador. Before I left for India, I was told to remember I had two bosses, the first being FBI Director Robert Mueller and the second being the Ambassador for each country I covered within my assigned territories.

Overseas, the work of the FBI and CIA overlap to some degree, however, it differs in that the FBI meets regularly with foreign law enforcement while the CIA's liaison is conducted predominantly with intelligence agencies.

Although I was stationed at the US Embassy New Delhi and was the FBI's representative in India, I was also responsible for operations in Nepal, Bangladesh, Bhutan, Sri Lanka, and the Maldives. The US Embassy New Delhi (which handles diplomatic relations with Bhutan) had a political appointee as the Ambassador, while Nepal, Bangladesh, and Sri Lanka (which covers the Maldives) had ambassadors who were all career State Department diplomats. Therefore, I not only had my FBI boss, Director Mueller, I had four ambassadors to whom I answered regarding any FBI matters within their mission. In Beijing, my responsibility was for China and Mongolia, with two ambassadors for whom I worked in those respective countries.

Contrary to the FBI's role in the United States, the FBI has no law enforcement authority in foreign countries. They also do not have arrest powers, and in most countries, are not allowed to carry a weapon.

Instead, the Legal Attaché programs create relationships with foreign law enforcement in order to be able to work with those officials to detect and investigate crimes against the United States. This includes, but is not limited to, terrorism, foreign intelligence, and other criminal activity that poses a threat to the United States' economy and national security.

Conversely, the FBI Legats act as liaison conduits when foreign law enforcement has a request for assistance should their investigations have a nexus to the United States. In those instances, the Legat will obtain their official requests and ensure they are forwarded to the appropriate FBI personnel. In FBI verbiage, this is called a "lead," which is the term used for requests, and evidence, made by the FBI to a foreign law enforcement agency, and vice versa, those requests made by the foreign law enforcement to the FBI.

Should a foreign law enforcement agency request assistance of the FBI on an incident that occurs in their country, such as a terrorist attack, the Legat office provides deployment of FBI personnel to assist with the investigation. The FBI will also deploy personnel to a foreign country should a terrorist attack occur that involves US citizens.

Should a foreign law enforcement agency request specialized training in specific areas of investigation, such as international terrorism, crime scene and physical evidence techniques, or the forensics of tracking illegal international financing, the Legat office is responsible for reaching out to FBI personnel with that particular expertise to deploy a team for training purposes.

Whenever the FBI works jointly with their foreign law enforcement counterpart, all efforts are coordinated with US Embassy representatives of the Department of State, to ensure the Legat's actions will not adversely impact foreign relations. In addition, the Legat also must maintain close relationships with other agencies represented at the US Embassy, so that information and intelligence can be exchanged, at times to coordinate efforts and other times to avoid overlap of investigative or intelligence jurisdiction.

The FBI Legat is a member of the US Embassy country team and serves as the lead federal law enforcement official for all crimes that fall within the FBI's jurisdiction. As such, the Legat advises and briefs the ambassador for each country the Legat office covers on law enforcement matters.

For instance, when traveling to other countries I covered out of New Delhi and Beijing, protocol dictated that I provide an in-brief with the Ambassador prior to meeting with my foreign counterparts. I would advise the Ambassador on my objectives for the visit should there be a conflict of which I needed to be made aware. After my liaison meetings with my counterparts, I would meet with the Ambassador once again, to provide an update regarding the coordination conducted between the FBI and the officials with whom I had met.

Although theoretically, FBI Legat offices are all given the same framework for working with foreign counterparts, as well as other US Embassy personnel, Legat offices differ depending on the country where the office is located, as well as the criminal, terrorist, or national security threats to the United States. For instance, Legat offices located in the Middle East might handle more terrorism-related leads, while other Legat offices might handle more international criminal fraud leads. I learned during my years as a Legal Attaché, although I might have my day planned, those plans could change in the span of minutes, depending on the situation in the host country, or an event that might have occurred in the United States. A willingness to be flexible and accept drastic change is a necessary attribute to be an FBI Legal Attaché.

Legat offices also differ in that some offices cover multiple countries, while other offices cover only one country. Therefore, those Legat offices that cover multiple countries might spend a great deal of time traveling to meet with their foreign law enforcement counterparts, ambassadors, or other US agency personnel represented at those embassies.

Over the course of their time serving overseas, a Legat might be asked to participate in a variety of activities that include training; presenting at international conferences; providing written reports on issues specific to FBI headquarters, as well as other government agencies; conducting interviews within country on behalf of the FBI (always with the approval of foreign counterparts); and participating in working groups with foreign counterparts or other agencies within the US embassies. Legats also liaison with counterparts representing other countries within the host country, including but not limited to the United Kingdom, Canada, Australia, and New Zealand. These relationships are also vital for sharing information and coordinating efforts, although their specific focus might differ to some degree.

Prior to leaving for an overseas post, all Legat office personnel receive specialized training at FBI Headquarters and the FBI Academy at Quantico. Much of the training is conducted by the FBI's International Operations Division (IOD), which is responsible for managing oversight to all Legat offices and operations around the world. Most of the training consists of multiple presentations and briefings, however, the two weeks of predeployment training spent at the FBI Academy at Quantico turned out to be the most fun. These two weeks were different because spouses were invited to attend training alongside FBI personnel. Out of the dozen or so people in the class, Keith, always up for an adventure, was the only spouse who opted to participate—surprising, since this seemed a once in a lifetime opportunity for a spouse to be a part of the inner workings of the FBI.

Some of the training was focused on classroom lectures, with which most FBI employees were familiar. The days inside tended to drag along. By the end of an all-day session of listening to one speaker after another, everyone was ready to go home. Keith, on the other hand, became the poster boy for raising his hand and asking questions, just when everyone else was ready to move along. One afternoon after class was dismissed, one of the male agents deploying as a Legat pulled me aside and said, "You need to tell your husband to shut the fuck up. He asks too many questions and wastes too much time." I laughed. I had been enjoying Keith's enthusiasm. I had rarely talked about my work and never talked about anything of a classified nature. This was Keith's first insight into my world.

During the second week, we spent time on the Tactical Emergency Vehicle Operations Center (TEVOC) course, where we learned how to drive a vehicle safely while avoiding potential terrorists or kidnappers, maneuvering away from trailing surveillance, maneuvering a vehicle out of an accident or away from another threatening vehicle. Even the instructors started to get a kick out of watching Keith act like a little boy at a bumper car pavilion. Never in his life had Keith received carte blanche to ram other vehicles on purpose, drive as fast as he wanted, perform tactical maneuvers against other cars, and wrangle out of tight situations. On one of our last training runs, an instructor sat in the back seat of our car with a movie camera, which would be critiqued later in the classroom. When the class reconvened to watch our film, all we saw was the camera as it rocked and rolled, floor to ceiling shots with the instructor hanging on to the door handle to keep from being slammed around. And in the background, we heard Keith laughing uproariously and yipping like a cowboy every time he crashed into another car. His exuberance was infectious.

Those two weeks watching Keith's unapologetic joy at being a part of my world made me realize that much of what I did in the FBI had become ordinary and commonplace to me. It was my job, and I hadn't thought about how it might be viewed by a civilian. Keith's career as a chemical engineer and network security engineer was an open book for me. Watching him take part in my career made me recognize Keith's strength, to be my husband and partner without ever knowing what I did on a day-to-day basis. I wondered if I would be as unwavering in my support if the tables were turned.

INDIA

CHAPTER TWENTY-THREE

NAMASTE

★★★

To other countries, I may go as a tourist,
but to India, I come as a pilgrim.
—Martin Luther King Jr.

India assaulted my senses as I stepped off the plane and onto the tarmac of Indira Gandhi International Airport. I breathed in the dust, which settles in the high heat just before the monsoon season. The scents of sandalwood incense, bodily sweat, curry and cardamom and chai, and the sweet stench of decay hung in the heavy humid air. The smells were both familiar and foreign.

It was about 3:00 A.M., normal arrival time for many flights from the United States. I had arrived for my permanent assignment—accompanied by thirteen suitcases and one husband—to be Legat New Delhi, which is located in the US Embassy, one of the largest US diplomatic missions in the world, with almost twenty federal government agencies representing the United States throughout the Indian continent.

I had dreamed of India since reading *The Far Pavilions* by M. M. Kaye as a teenager and vowed I would see it someday. That dream first came true when I was sent to India two years previously, on a forty-five-day temporary duty assignment (TDY). I had learned on my previous trip that westerners either loved India or hated India; there was no middle ground. I had fallen in love.

There was much to dislike about India. If you stand in one place, you see poverty and dirt and chaos that will bring you to your knees. You will ask yourself how you and the rest of the world can allow so much of humanity to live such an abject existence. The display of homelessness, the filth, the riotous disorder, and the caste system, alive and well despite official commentary to the contrary, is inescapable. The heat and humidity during a monsoon season could and would destroy anything in its path. Shoes rotted, clothing fell apart, mold grew on every surface.

But I had also learned during my TDY that India is a tapestry, like one of the finely woven pashminas from Kashmir. Viewed as a whole, the intricacy of the hair-fine threads was invisible. But if you take the time to look closely, you can see the colors and the complicated weave, how they complement and contrast, each thread held up by the other, no beginning and no end. For me, India had become that tapestry. I wanted to explore the complexities of India's history, culture, food, language, and architecture. I could live there forever and never fully understand or grasp the depths of a civilization that stretches thousands of years into the past, with its multitude of customs, rituals, and conflicts.

America felt two-dimensional by comparison. I was accused of romanticizing India, but I loved and I hated it in equal measure. It was India's contradictions that I came to love the most.

My first day as Legat New Delhi was a blur. Although I had arrived in the middle of the night on a Saturday, I was still jet-lagged on Monday morning. The initial adrenaline rush of arrival was starting to wear thin. The former Legat had departed post not long after his arrival, having learned that India was not to his liking. I had to rely on the current Assistant Legal Attaché (ALAT) to brief me on where I should focus my efforts in the coming months. Although a nice guy, the ALAT hated India. Upon my arrival at the Legat Office, his first words were "I'm glad you're here. Now I can get the fuck out of this place." He had spent his time in India unaccompanied. His wife, who had initially moved to Delhi with him, had pulled up stakes and left him to his own devices shortly after her arrival. India hadn't been to her liking either.

The ALAT made one concession before his departure; he'd planned a trip to Sri Lanka to introduce me to my foreign counterparts the next day. After that, I was on my own to travel to all the other countries I would be covering to introduce myself.

The FBI was working with the Sri Lankan government on an international terrorism investigation, which was to be one of my top priorities for the foreseeable future. In Colombo, Sri Lanka's capital, the ALAT would introduce me to everyone at the US Embassy, after which we would have separate meetings with the Sri Lankan police and intelligence service. After this whirlwind trip, he would leave his New Delhi post permanently.

Before he flung himself out the door, I also learned from the ALAT that I had an upcoming inspection, several terrorism investigations to coordinate in multiple countries, and a visit to coordinate for John Pistole, Deputy Director of the FBI, second in command only to Director Robert Mueller. If this wasn't enough to intimidate, just as important and far more impactive, I had the distinct impression that Rachel, the LOS—Legat Operations Specialist and office administrator—had taken an inexplicable dislike to me from day one. She had been polite but cold and had offered no advice to ease my transition. To add insult to injury, I would not have an ALAT replacement for over six months. It was up to me to cover all FBI operations in India, Nepal, Bangladesh, Bhutan, Sri Lanka, and the Maldives.

When Keith and I first arrived, we stayed at the Hyatt Regency, a five-star hotel, until our housing was ready. The first apartment we had been assigned was a long distance from the embassy, on the ground floor, surrounded by dirt, with no lawn, no gate between my apartment and the street, and a herd of cows making camp near a sliding glass door.

When US personnel are stationed at embassies around the world, they are provided with housing by the US government. The State Department handles the assignment of houses, which is determined by the employee's position in the embassy, their government salary level, and the number of children in the household. Although I would be head of an agency with a higher GS grade level than most, my childfree household lowered the standards of my housing. This system was theoretical, however, and sycophancy often favored those who were willing to buy thicker knee pads and pile on the Chapstick.

When I got back to the office and described the apartment to Rachel, she shrugged as if she didn't care—which she did not—and said, "You should take what you get." I was too busy to try to figure out what was eating her, but after a few days, I was getting an inkling she wasn't happy about having a female boss. She laughed openly with the men in the embassy, so I knew her taciturn behavior towards me wasn't her personality. I don't know why

I bothered to complain to her, but I desperately needed someone who could give me advice.

I headed off to the ████████ to talk to the office manager, Alicia, who I had gotten to know during my previous TDY. She and I had spent a lot of time together and had become friends. Luckily for me, she had not transferred out, and I looked forward to a good vent session with her. Alicia was outspoken and reigned over the ███ office with an iron fist. She had been stationed in Delhi for a few years, so she knew everyone at the embassy, as well as the inner workings of how things really got done. I came to rely on her heavily in the subsequent weeks.

Alicia set to work right away to help me find better housing accommodation. She knew, ████████████████, that I would spend a great deal of time at the embassy, oftentimes round-the-clock. Living in close proximity to the embassy was essential. She introduced me to the ██████████████████ ██████████████████, who had a great sense of humor and was willing to cooperate████████████████, despite public opinion that the FBI ████████ refuse to work together. Once Alicia laid out my predicament, he immediately told me one of his staff was soon to depart post and the house she had lived in had not been assigned yet. As she was a single female with no children, her housing assignment would fall within the appropriate guidelines for my residence. ████████████ Alicia put me in touch with a member of the housing board to discuss my change of residence. He agreed to put my appeal before the board, and a few days later I had found a permanent home.

Our new house was only about a ten-minute drive from the embassy, unless I happened to get behind a camel cart, elephants being led through the streets, or a herd of cows that had decided to take a nap in the middle of an intersection, which could hold up traffic for hours. This happened to me on more than one occasion while living in Delhi. Since Hindus consider cows sacred, no one dares to shoo them away or physically move them to another location. Cows reign supreme in the pantheon of sacred animals in India. They roam where they wish, sleep where they want, and eat whatever they can find. On many mornings, after opening the gate to my driveway, I was met by a herd of cows meandering down the residential street, chewing their cud in a leisurely fashion.

With our new house, we also inherited the cook, Elaine, hired by the previous occupant. I found her western name to be odd, until she told me she had been raised Catholic. I was wary to hire Elaine, who was probably tasked with reporting my every move to the Indian intelligence services particularly in light of the fact the previous American occupant of the house had been a ▮▮▮ employee. But Elaine had a stellar reputation as an outstanding cook and housekeeper, so I decided to keep her on. After we hired a driver—who happened to be Elaine's brother—and a gardener, Elaine began to rule the household staff with absolute authority, which left me free to spend all my time at work. I had been told by just about everyone at the embassy that household staff will watch your every move, gossip about you behind your back, and run to other American embassy employees' household staff to share stories of private matters and indiscretions committed within sight or hearing. I resigned myself to the fact that privacy in my own home was going to be limited.

One of my first orders of business was to get ready for the office inspection. An inspection entails the review of every investigation, case file, and liaison effort within the embassy and with foreign counterparts. Multiple reports were to be detailed and prepared for a team of FBI agents who would travel to Delhi, pore over every file in the office, and determine whether the New Delhi Legat office had been doing an adequate job.

Since I had recently arrived, I should not have been responsible for what the previous Legat had or had not accomplished. Nevertheless, if the inspection team found the office wanting, it would land on my shoulders. I had no one in my office to consult, so I stayed long hours at work reading every single file, every single piece of paper, and every single investigation that the Legat office had been involved in for the past few years. In addition, I made a point to spend time with my counterparts in other agencies at the embassy to learn if and how they had interacted with the FBI office.

In the midst of my inspection preparation, I also planned the upcoming visit of Deputy Director Pistole, which required a great deal of liaison with the Central Bureau of Investigation (CBI), the FBI's equivalent in India, as well as the Intelligence Bureau (IB), the CIA equivalent, to set up meetings for Mr. Pistole. In addition to arranging and organizing Mr. Pistole's meetings, I coordinated with his security team to ensure his safety during his visit.

Just a couple of weeks prior to Mr. Pistole's arrival, I received a telephone call late one evening from my Unit Chief, Carl. He had a message from Walt, the Deputy Assistant Director (DAD) of IOD, second in command of

Legats around the world. Walt had ordered Carl to inform me, if anything went wrong with Mr. Pistole's upcoming visit, I would be removed from my position as Legat and brought back to the US immediately, a demotion known to Legats as a curtailment. Walt was notoriously cold-blooded about removing Legat personnel for the smallest infraction and had racked up several curtailments during his short tenure. Anytime another Legat or ALAT was curtailed, word accelerated through the grapevine faster than a flame races down a lit fuse.

Since my arrival in Delhi about four months earlier, I had had only one day off due to a high fever and explosive diarrhea from a bout of food poisoning that had landed me on the toilet with a garbage can in my lap. Plus, I hadn't enjoyed one single full night's sleep. Agents and attorneys from the FBI and DOJ rarely saw fit to determine what time it was whenever they needed to talk. Although my own mom figured out exactly when to call me so that she didn't wake me, my attempts to explain to my colleagues that time ticks along numerous zones around the world fell on deaf ears. Their workday was my workday, even if it was in the middle of the night for me. One DOJ attorney made a habit of calling me almost every morning between 2:00 and 3:00 A.M. Delhi time. I reminded him, on a couple of occasions, that his late afternoon phone calls from Washington, DC, were the middle of the night for me. He either didn't care or he didn't listen.

After Carl's apologetic voice passed along Walt's threat of removal, I found myself saying to Carl, "Why don't you just remove me now? I'll start packing my fucking bags." I knew Walt's threats meant he had already given the curtailment some thought. I had come to the conclusion he was the kind of person who believed using fear-based incentive was an actual leadership quality. Plus, I think he enjoyed using his powerful position to torment others. Regardless, I was now in his sights.

Carl quietly said, "Are you OK, Kathy?"

"No, goddamn it, I'm not OK. I've been busting my ass and all I get are threats? You know goddamn well nothing makes that man happy."

"It's all going to be OK. Don't worry about it." He hesitated and then said, "Just make sure nothing goes wrong."

Carl knew as well as I that Walt was a fucking asshole. My future depended on nothing more than the way the wind blew when he made his decision to curtail me or not.

Shortly after Carl hung up, I received another phone call from one of the other unit chiefs in IOD, a female.

"Kathy, are you OK? Carl said you're really upset."

"No, I am not OK. I've been working my ass off, ALL BY MY FUCKING SELF, COVERING SIX GODDAMN COUNTRIES AND ALL I GET IS A FUCKING THREAT! No, I'm NOT fucking OK!"

"I know how you must feel but try to calm down. We'll do our best here to make sure everything works out."

I appreciated her phone call. I'm sure Carl had run to her and said, "Maybe another woman can talk her off the ledge." But the two of them had no control over Walt, and they knew it.

After I hung up the phone for the second time, I laid my head down on my bed, buried my face in a pillow, and cried for the first time since arriving in Delhi. All the things that could go wrong with Mr. Pistole's visit kept running through my head. If something went wrong, I would never be given another chance to work overseas, overshadowing anything else I might want to do for the rest of my Bureau career.

Just prior to the threatening phone call from Carl, I had been informed that the inspection team scheduled to travel to Delhi shortly after Mr. Pistole's official visit had canceled their trip. The chief inspector, a female, was concerned about getting sick because she had heard India was filthy and polluted. A friend of mine, who was to be part of the inspection entourage, called me to let me know. He knew how much work had gone into the inspection report; how it had taken me months of preparation while having no predecessor to consult, no ALAT to assist, with the upcoming visit by Mr. Pistole overshadowing everything else. The chief inspector, ostensibly responsible for verifying an office is running smoothly, had canceled her trip because of the possibility that she might get sick. I couldn't muster the energy to be angry.

A couple of weeks later, Deputy Director Pistole arrived back in Washington, DC, from New Delhi, after a successful visit of productive meetings with CBI, IB, and the Minister of Foreign Affairs—no glitches, accidents, or screwups. I was at home late one evening when I received a phone call from Walt himself.

"Kathy, I just got a call from Mr. Pistole. He sang your praises and said you did a great job with his visit to Delhi. I just wanted to give you a call and ask if you need anything in your office. Do you need a new Bureau car? Do you need any equipment? Is there anything I can do to make your job easier?"

You goddamn, mother-fucking asshole! I hate your fucking guts!

I had to take a deep breath and hold it for a few seconds before I responded, "I could use an ALAT. When do you think you could get someone out here to help me? I've been by myself for almost six months, covering six countries."

"I'll get on that right away. Congratulations. Good job." A couple of months later, I had an ALAT.

Despite my rocky start, India began to feel like home. I recall coming back to Delhi from a conference in the US. The embassy car had picked me up at the airport and dropped me off at my house. Walking up the driveway, I could hear the family of lime green parrots singing in the garden; the scent of the frangipani blossoms floated on the humid air. I felt like I belonged to this place. I realized, regardless how my tenure had begun, that I loved my job. I loved being in India, and I loved being a part of something larger than myself. I was only beginning to understand how this time in my career would change my life.

CHAPTER TWENTY-FOUR

KITTY PARTIES

★★★

There are some factions within the FBI who call the Legat program the "wine and cheese" circuit. This is to say, popular opinion believes that Legal Attachés have nothing better to do than attend diplomatic social parties where they stand around and drink martinis while consuming dainty little canapés offered up from a silver tray held by a tuxedo-clad server. I never attended one of these parties while I was overseas. The few social parties—which still involved work—I attended were at the end of a long and busy day, at which time I arrived in a rumpled business suit. I rarely chose to partake in alcohol and appetizers because I was usually too busy shaking hands and handing out business cards, and wanted to prevent myself from saying something I should not while under the influence of alcohol. This was easy while I was stationed in Delhi. Most of the countries I covered were strict adherents to Islam, Buddhism, or Hinduism, all of which frown upon alcohol. China and Mongolia would prove to be another story.

Each US Embassy has a Community Liaison Office (CLO), which is partly responsible for helping trailing spouses get acclimated to their new surroundings. They regularly set up tours and gatherings, make introductions, and, in general, make it easier for a spouse to have a social life.

It didn't take me long to discover that embassy life for trailing spouses—the informal name given to spouses who chose to not work while overseas—was actually more of a wine and cheese circuit than it was for those employed full time at the embassy.

It didn't take Keith long to be invited to activities in which most of the other spouses participated. His first invitation was to a "tea party," hosted by the US Ambassador's wife. At the time, the only female head of agency, other than myself, was the attaché for the Department of Agriculture, Hannah. When the invitation went out to all spouses, Hannah's husband called Keith and said, "Are you going to the tea? If you're going, I'll go. But if you're not going, I'm not going by myself." Keith, an outgoing and gregarious New Yorker, wasn't about to pass up the opportunity to see what embassy life was all about.

After Keith attended the tea, he became a favorite amongst the embassy spouses who soon learned Keith was not only willing to go shopping with them but was an excellent source of insight when it came to the male opinion. As a result, he was soon invited to attend tea parties with spouses at other foreign embassies. Tea parties in India are often called "kitty parties," a way for women of middle to upper class stature to socialize. This concept was explained to me by my cook and housekeeper, Elaine, who went on to tell me the term "kitty party" had been adopted by women from foreign embassies, the US Embassy included.

I had already met with one of the attachés from the German embassy and Keith had coincidentally met his wife at one of the kitty parties. We were invited to dinner at their house, which we accepted as it would be a good way for me to liaison on a social basis. During dinner, the attaché's wife informed me—out of earshot of her husband—that she needed a "companion" to keep her company during the long hours her husband would be working. I don't know if she was a mother who took upon herself the care and organization of running the household. All I was aware of at that moment was that I had witnessed her being overly familiar with Keith during dinner. I asked, "Do you think that person is going to be my husband?" I kept my voice calm, but I forced my face into a hardness that let her know, in no uncertain terms, Keith would not be taking on the role of her "companion."

Keith had applied for a job at the US Embassy with the State Department. It was time he started to put that predeployment training to work.

CHAPTER TWENTY-FIVE

FOLLOW THE LEADER

★★★

A dozen of my counterparts from other embassies—███████████████ ████████████████████████████—were sitting with me in a dingy room; one dirt-encrusted window lent meager sunlight to the bare bulbs swinging from fly-specked, cloth-covered electrical wiring overhead. Most of the people waiting expectantly around the scarred conference table were strangers to me.

The room I happened to be sitting in was located at the headquarters of the CBI. Shortly after I had arrived in Delhi, the Director-General of CBI, Mr. Vijay, had invited me to this meeting.

In the few weeks I had been in country, I had met only one or two of the other attendees at liaison gatherings. Developing relationships with them was important to my position, as I would need their cooperation on critical and time-sensitive issues; information would be provided and expected in return, quid pro quo.

I don't remember the specific reason Mr. Vijay had arranged the meeting, but I recall it involved increased sharing and cooperation with the Indian government on issues involving terrorism. India, a country rife with factions of dissenting opinions and religious beliefs, had become increasingly concerned about security in the post-9/11 world. This concern would prove to be prescient, considering the Mumbai attacks that were to occur in 2008, less than two years hence.

Mr. Vijay was a substantial man, his height and girth exceeding the average Indian male. He had a large square head, thick silver hair accented by a silver-black brush covering his upper lip. He normally carried the stature of his position with brash arrogance. This day, he was uncharacteristically humble, appealing to the group by acknowledging that India's law enforcement apparatus was inferior to just about every law enforcement agency represented. Since 9/11, the sharing of intelligence amongst countries had become a matter of crucial importance. Mr. Vijay knew the countries represented around the table took those issues seriously and needed their cooperation to protect the citizens of his own country. Allowing the group a private debate, he left the room.

I had guessed from the informal exchange of greetings, and warm familiarity amongst the group, that I was the newest member of this circle. I was still in a whirlwind—studying reams of information and intelligence, working sixteen-hour days and seven-day work weeks, taking middle of the night telephone calls from the Department of Justice and FBI field offices. My mind and body swayed between exhilaration and exhaustion.

Expecting a barrage of chatter at the Director's exit, I waited quietly for one of the more experienced veterans of Indian diplomacy to begin the discussion. My weariness wasn't the only thing holding me back from voicing my opinion. Immediately after arriving at the US Embassy, I had made a point to meet with every State Department section head and all other US agency attachés represented at the mission. I knew I had to work longer and harder to prove myself, a woman in a role previously held only by men, soon to be the only female Legal Attaché in the entirety of the FBI.

At each introductory meeting at the embassy, I encountered negative feedback regarding my office. My predecessor had apparently been an arrogant, self-serving prima donna who treated everyone with disdain and refused to cooperate on issues that were relevant not only to the FBI, but to the broader US mission in India. I had been told he hadn't liked India and complained constantly about the poverty and filth and chaos. After a few short months, he had somehow managed to get transferred to a location in Europe that met with his higher standards. My job was to piece together the shattered relationships he had left in his wake. Not yet knowing how many of the people sitting around the table had had the unfortunate experience of meeting with my predecessor, I was determined to tread lightly.

The room was quiet, everyone looking around the table with an air of expectation. Finally, one of the other attachés turned his head in my direction and said, "What are *you* going to do?" I stared blankly, resisting the urge to look over my shoulder to see if he was addressing someone else. "Me?" I asked, hearing the insecure squeak of panic in my own voice, embarrassed, and hoping he hadn't noticed. *I just got here! What the hell do I know?*

"Yes," he affirmed, with a terse nod, eyebrows slashed together, deepening the wrinkle between his eyes. "What is *America* going to do? Because whatever America does, we will all follow."

After his declaration, sluggishly trying to comprehend what he was saying, I looked slowly around the table. Nods of agreement toppled like dominoes, one after the other; ███████████████████████████ ████████, and on and on and on.

Clarity, an electrified current of understanding, rippled lightly across my skin. They were not asking me, Kathy Stearman, FBI Legal Attaché. They were asking me, Kathy Stearman, the United States of America. For the first time since taking on my position as Legat, I felt the responsibility of representing the FBI, and my country, settle tentatively and uncomfortably on my shoulders. I desperately wanted to get it right.

As I contemplate now, with not a little fear and trepidation, our post–Donald Trump government, I ask myself if the above scenario is being repeated in State Department, CIA, and FBI offices around the world. The United States is not without its own convoluted and misguided history; however, I know from personal experience how much of the world has looked to us for leadership and protection. And I ask the question, "Are we, representatives of the United States, still invited to those dingy rooms with scarred tabletops?"

CHAPTER TWENTY-SIX

AS THE WORM TURNS

★★★

"Rachel, are you OK this morning?" I looked up at her as she deposited a stack of envelopes from FBI headquarters in my inbox. I hesitated to ask Rachel a personal question. She kept her distance from me, and our conversations were, at best, politely strained.

Since I had arrived in New Delhi, Rachel had made it clear she was unhappy to have me as her new boss. At my initial attempts to strike up friendly conversations that involved topics other than work, she firmly rebuffed me.

On any given morning, Rachel was bubbly and cheerful with the mail courier, who delivered our diplomatic post every day. She always took the time to chat with other embassy employees who stopped by to bring me intelligence reports or cables that needed my signature. But this morning, there was no conversation coming from her office, which was right next to mine. The mail courier came and went with a quiet "Thank you." No chatter with staff from ██████████ Diplomatic Security about their weekend activities. I had become accustomed to Rachel's cool demeanor towards me, but she was always animated with other embassy personnel. Clearly, something was up.

Standing in the open doorway of my office, Rachel looked down at the floor and when she looked up, tears were streaming down her face. I was shocked. Rachel's face had never revealed anything but calm detachment in my presence. "Rachel, what's wrong? Is Ray OK? Did something happen to one of the girls? Whatever it is, I'll help you. We can fix it together."

Now she was sobbing, gulping huge breaths while tears and snot rolled off her chin.

I got up from my desk, and without thinking, reached to give her a hug, something I would never have dared before. She laid her head on my shoulder and whispered into my suit jacket, "I've got worms."

"What? You've got *what*?" I was not sure I had heard her correctly.

"I've got WORMS!" The last word came out in a wail.

I couldn't help myself. Disgust became reflex as I pushed myself away from her, recoiling from her touch.

I *hate* worms. I have hated worms my whole life. Of all the creepy, crawly, slithering, squirmy creatures on earth, I hate worms the most. Throw a snake at me any day. I don't like them, but they're not like worms. Worms are stealthy. They can crawl into tiny spaces and minuscule orifices, curling into a tight, slimy spiral only to be discovered at a later date.

I am not sure where my fear comes from, but I'm pretty sure it started when I was about four years old. I was with my mom and two older sisters digging up loamy, black soil from under the wood pile to fertilize Mom's flower beds. Scooping earthworms and white grubs from the moist ground, my sisters proceeded to smear them on me, my little halter top baring my back from neck to waist. I've never forgotten the cold viscous feeling of those worms as my sisters dropped them by the handful onto my bare skin.

Since coming to India, I had been regaled with stories about intestinal worms, brain worms, worms, worms, worms. One horror story I had recently heard was of a family who had continual worms and dysentery. Every embassy residence is stocked with a water tank on the roof and potable water is brought to the residence via trucks owned and operated by the embassy. As it turns out, the water tank of this unfortunate family had been invaded by a monkey who had fallen in, the lid slamming shut with no escape route. The monkey was discovered decomposed in the same water the family had been drinking.

"Rachel, how do you *know* you have worms?" *Maybe she's wrong. Maybe she just thinks she has worms.*

"Because I saw it in the toilet this morning."

"What do you mean you saw it in the toilet this morning?"

Rachel had stopped sobbing and now started to look annoyed. "When I looked at my poop this morning, I saw the worm."

"You look at your *poop* every day? Who looks at their poop?" I asked, not sure if I was missing something about this whole wormy scenario.

"I look at my poop, don't you?" She was clearly annoyed by now, and her snuffling had turned to a curled upper lip and eyebrows drawn together in an annoyed frown, a look to which I had become all too accustomed, because she had trained it on me on a daily basis for weeks.

"Well, I don't normally look at my poop, but I'm going to *start* looking. What did you do with the worm? Did you flush it?"

"I called one of the nurses from the Health Unit and she came over to get it. They want to track all the worm cases in the embassy. It was nine inches long."

I felt the hair jump to attention on the back of my neck and the skin crawl down both arms. *A nine-inch worm!* "Do you think you have more?" I asked, as I sidled further away from her.

"The nurse said I probably only had one because I haven't lost any weight recently. She said I might have pinworms, though, and asked if my butthole itches."

Before I could even ask what pinworms are, I felt a distinct tickle somewhere in the vicinity of my own butthole.

"What are you gonna do about them?" I was almost afraid to ask. I could already envision sneaking into the office after hours to scour everything Rachel had ever touched with a good dose of Clorox.

"I have to take special medicine to get rid of any worm eggs in my body. Ray and the girls have to take it too, in case they have them. Then we have to wash all our sheets, towels, and underwear in hot water and bleach."

I was already two seconds away from calling Elaine to tell her to strip every bed, find every towel, and collect the contents of every underwear drawer in my house. Once I told her what was up, she would have every surface worm free. My house already smelled faintly of bleach, from the daily floor mopping and the washing of our food in a mild Clorox solution, which was a necessity to get rid of—what else—worm eggs and the subsequent gestation of my own intestinal worm.

"OK, Rachel, here's what I'm going to do. You take your medicine from the Health Unit. I'm going to call my brother-in-law, who's a doctor. I'm going to have him send me some medicine that we can all take on a regular basis, so this won't happen again, OK?"

Rachel, normally impeccably groomed with flawless makeup, stared at me with her mascara-streaked face, lipstick bitten off where she had tried to hold back her sobs. With a hangdog expression, she nodded and turned to flop down on the "sick" couch in the main entrance area. I heard her whisper to herself, "Ray is never going to want to have sex with me again." The sobbing started all over again.

Jeez, that would be the least of my worries.

A few days later I looked up from my desk to see Rachel leaning against the door frame, head down, hands clasped in front of her. I waited for her to say something, never sure if a jab was headed my way.

"I owe you an apology," she said softly.

"Really? Why do you owe me an apology?" I thought I knew what she was going to say, but I wanted to hear her say it.

"When you got here, I didn't want to work for you. I don't like working for women. I find it easier to work with men. But you're OK and I've treated you badly." Rachel glanced up and then looked down quickly, completely out of character with her usual haughty demeanor.

"I know, Rachel. I knew it from the start. But I knew if I gave you enough time, you would realize I'm laid-back and actually fun to be around."

"How did you know?" she said, still looking down at her hands.

"Rachel, I've been in this job for a long time. You're not the first female to dislike other women. But, can we be friends, now, and have a good time working together?"

Rachel looked up with a smile, nodded, and said, "Thanks, Kat."

I smiled to myself as she walked out of the room. She had never called me Kat before. And all it took, apparently, was a case of worms.

CHAPTER TWENTY-SEVEN

MONKEY BUSINESS

★ ★ ★

I stared across the scarred, wooden desk past Mr. Kumar, my assigned contact at the CBI. Mr. Kumar's head was hunched down into his neck, his wiry little body slumped against the back of his creaking chair. A monkey sitting in the open window just over Mr. Kumar's right shoulder stared back at me with sad, yellow-brown eyes. "Yes," the monkey's eyes seem to say, "I did it. I'm guilty." The monkey slowly turned his head away from me, his pink-pointed Yoda ears twitching as he stared down into the courtyard. He raised one leg and planted it on the windowsill, one arm crossed over his knee as his furry paw dangled down, swaying back and forth in the same, languorous rhythmic motion as his tail, which hung down into the room. His little chest rose and fell in a sigh as his pink, hairless, old-man's face turned to look at me, once again in apology, before turning back to his perusal of the clamor down below, which no doubt involved the daily activities of members of the CBI. I could picture the scene; an officer urinating against a far wall, several officers squatting in the shade, having the ubiquitous cup of chai, or another officer stretching his arms up to hang laundry from the numerous lines that crisscrossed the inner courtyards of CBI headquarters.

Of course, I was assuming this monkey was a he. Everyone else in the building, with the exception of a few women who served tea, was male so why should this monkey be any different?

I knew the monkey in Mr. Kumar's office wasn't a langur, often seen riding on the backs of bicycles and motorbikes, which zigzagged through the congested cacophony of Delhi's city streets and alleyways. Langurs were larger with tails that curled over three feet. Langurs were also very territorial; the US Embassy had hired a langur trainer to bring his langur to the embassy compound and pee along the walled perimeter in order to discourage other monkeys from climbing over. No, the monkey staring at me was a rhesus macaque, a species of monkey seen all over India and the other countries I covered.

I first became acquainted with monkeys shortly after my arrival in Delhi. A memo, known as the "Monkey Memo," was distributed to everyone in the US Embassy, with a warning to beware of packs of monkeys roaming the streets of Delhi in search of lone humans to terrorize. The memo went on to describe how a female member of our embassy had been walking to work by herself when surrounded by a troop of monkeys, which stepped closer and closer to her, baring their canines in warning. An Indian woman who happened to be driving past recognized what was happening, pulled her car alongside the soon-to-be victim of a monkey mugging, threw open the passenger door, and yelled for her to get in. Embassy staff was advised to not venture out alone in the city and steer clear of gangs of monkeys headed their way.

The memo became a point of comedy at every water cooler in the embassy and the Monkey Memo was talked about and laughed over for days. I laughed along with everyone else until I received a phone call to my office from my cook, Elaine. I had given Elaine my office number in case she ever needed me in an emergency. Otherwise, she waited until I got home to ask any questions. She ran the household capably, from cooking to cleaning to laundry, so I rarely heard from her during the day.

Elaine's panicked voice yelled out of the telephone receiver, "Madam, the monkeys are here! I am trapped!"

"What? Elaine, what are you talking about?"

"There are many monkeys outside the door, and they won't let me out of the house!"

What the hell am I supposed to do about a troop of monkeys? I thought.

"Elaine, stay in the house and don't try to open the door again. I'll send Keith home to shoo them away."

"Yes, madam, thank you!"

It was often hard for me to leave the office, so I called Keith, who was working at the embassy with the State Department's Overseas Building

Operations staff and asked if he could drive home and chase away the monkeys that were holding Elaine hostage. It took a few minutes for me to explain the situation to Keith, but he finally understood and headed off to the rescue, ready to chase away a band of marauding monkeys with a broom or rake from the laundry shed.

After that incident, I took the threat of monkeys more seriously, although I found them fascinating and loved to sit and watch their antics, preening themselves and play-slapping as they chased each other. One day, Keith and I were sitting in a restaurant on the second floor of Khan Market, a series of shops near our neighborhood, when I looked out the window and watched as a monkey sitting on a low wall shit in his paw and threw it down on a spice seller who had been squatting on the sidewalk below, measuring out colorful spices on an old-fashioned scale.

"Keith," I said, "remind me to never buy spices from that guy down there, OK?" as I watched the spice seller glare up at the monkey.

I had also gotten accustomed to seeing monkeys in and around the Indian government buildings I visited on a regular basis. One day, I was sitting in the office of one of my counterparts at India's Intelligence Bureau, and watched, fascinated, as a monkey crawled across the rafters of the ceiling above me. I completely lost track of what was being said as I watched the monkey's progress, disappearing into a dark space in the far corner of the room. Oddly enough, the rest of the room, which was fully furnished and well-appointed, was completely at odds with the ceiling, which was apparently under construction. Several visits later, I realized this was indeed the case and missed my normal viewing of monkey antics during my visits.

I spent a great deal of my time visiting my Indian counterparts at CBI. CBI Delhi headquarters was located in a decrepit old building, no doubt constructed by the British during the rule of the Raj. It was, at one time, a classic example of British colonial architecture, gray stone walls now crumbling under the weight of decades of monsoon damp and mold. The brick- and stone-lined courtyards leading from one building to the next were a minefield of muddy holes and crumbling rock, which were particularly hazardous as I picked my way across in high heels.

The entrance where I was always delivered by my embassy driver was a rusted and locked wrought-iron gate. If a guard was on duty, he would unlock the gate and pull it aside on screeching hinges. Usually, I could see the guard in the distance, squatting against the side of the building, chai cup in one hand, beedi—the hand-rolled cigarette of India—in the other. On those days, I would have to climb through a turnstile situated at one side of the gate. The turnstile was much like the ones you see in the New York subway, but this one was much older, ornate and made of the same wrought iron as the main gate. It was partially rusted shut and would only turn halfway around. As I squeezed through, the stile arms, dusted in reddish-brown iron oxide, would grab my suit from shoulders to ankles, leaving perfectly defined reddish-orange tiger stripes along the fabric.

By the time I wrestled with the turnstile, I would be hot and sweaty in my summer weight wool suit. My Indian counterparts wore light cotton shirts and slacks in the summertime, but there didn't seem to be an equivalent for a western woman. Plus, I didn't think it prudent to wear only a light cotton blouse that would have ended up dripping with sweat and clinging to every inch of drenched skin. I was already an anomaly, I thought it best to sweat inside my suit and preserve my modesty.

The path to Mr. Kumar's office went through a series of courtyards. Everyone would stare in my wake, but no one tried to stop me. They had become accustomed to the tall, strange western woman who had a penchant for wearing men's clothing. The courtyards smelled of stale urine, telltale marks of wet dribble against the courtyard walls. Men's underwear hung from clotheslines strung from window to window above. Mr. Kumar always offered me tea and almond cookies and after my first trip to the toilet, I realized why most of the men opted for the open-air urinal of the courtyard. Thereafter, I politely sipped at my tea and refused a second cup in hopes of avoiding the noxious-smelling closet of a toilet down the hall. I had no idea where the few women in the building used the toilet, but as I watched the young women who poured my tea, staring shyly behind long lashes, I couldn't imagine how their saris remained pristine as hems dragged along the floor.

I had arrived in Mr. Kumar's office that morning to query him about a request I had made several months before. Each time I had called him to ask when he might provide a response, he was quick to say, "Very soon, Miss Kathy, I will have an answer very soon."

Today I had decided to make an appointment to confront Mr. Kumar in person. "Mr. Kumar, I gave you this request over three months ago. Do I need to further clarify the request? Can you please tell me why it's taking so long?"

Mr. Kumar looked at me mournfully, looked down, and in a low voice said, "The monkey took your paperwork, Miss Kathy."

"What?" *He couldn't have said what I think he said. Is he giving me the old, "Teacher, the dog peed on my homework" routine?*

"Miss Kathy, the monkey stole your paper."

That was when I saw the monkey sitting just beyond Mr. Kumar's bowed and dejected shoulders, which were not much bigger than the monkey's. Staring at the monkey on the windowsill and trying not to laugh, I said, "You know, Mr. Kumar, I actually believe you." And then I couldn't help myself. I started laughing out loud. Mr. Kumar's glare only made me laugh more.

Mr. Kumar and I had a love-hate relationship. On the surface, he was all smiles and teeth and invitations to share a cup of tea. I was pretty sure he secretly and purposely looked for ways to be uncooperative and vindictive in order to sabotage any progress I was trying to make in developing a working relationship with CBI. He had once invited me to a meeting with his management, at least three or four levels above his position. During the meeting, I was chastised for something that I can no longer recall and realized Mr. Kumar had lured me into this meeting so he could watch me getting dressed down by his superior. I remember politely clarifying my position with his management, then asking Mr. Kumar if I could see him in his office before I returned to the embassy. This was the last straw.

Once we got back to his office, Mr. Kumar stood in front of his desk as he preened his moustache, grinning like the Cheshire Cat. I smiled back at him, my teeth bared, as I steadily walked toward him. He slowly backed up against his desk and when I was close enough that he was looking up at me—considerably taller by several inches and outweighing him by twenty pounds—I pointed my finger in his face and said, "Don't you ever do that to me again, are we clear?"

"Yes, Miss Kathy, yes. I won't do that to you again," he said, but his eyes were resentful. After that incident, he was always respectful and professional, although I'm pretty sure he hadn't forgotten.

Now that Mr. Kumar had to admit that a monkey was responsible for the theft of FBI paperwork, there was no sign of the Cheshire Cat. I felt sorry for him, and, for a few seconds, a bit disappointed we would no longer be playing our little cat and mouse game.

CHAPTER TWENTY-EIGHT

GROSS NATIONAL HAPPINESS

★ ★ ★

"Miss Kathy, you Americans are all the same. You don't wait to get to know someone before you do business with them. That is not how we conduct relationships in Bhutan."

Mr. Wangchuk, a foreign minister stationed in New Delhi, whom I had invited to lunch for our first meeting, delivered his criticism with a smile.

I felt chastised in the face of his delivery, which was calm and measured. Mr. Wangchuk was from the country of Bhutan, a tiny Buddhist kingdom nestled in the Himalayas. I often pondered if this isolated country, which had allowed visitors only since the 1970s, could continue to pursue their "gross national happiness" or if they would get crushed in what was sure to become a struggle for power, as Bhutan is located between India and China, two powerhouses wrestling for primacy on the world's stage.

Mr. Wangchuk waited for me to respond, a beatific smile on his smooth, round face. "Can we get to know each other first?" he continued.

I had been assigned to cover Bhutan out of the New Delhi Legat office. The US does not have its own embassy there, so all consular issues are handled out of the US Embassy in Delhi. Although I had no investigative leads to cover with Mr. Wangchuk, a foreign minister, part of my liaison efforts was to make contact with the Bhutanese government to invite one of their officers from the Royal Bhutan Police to attend the FBI National Academy Associates [FBINAA] as an international student.

The FBINAA is a competitive leadership course, which attendees consider an honor to attend. Those who graduate from the program, held at the FBI Academy at Quantico, are considered the "best of the best" in their law enforcement communities. In each class there are officers from numerous US states, with several slots designated for international law enforcement.

One of the missions of the FBINAA is to promote cooperation. The FBI invites law enforcement officers who are the most likely to take on higher level positions in their organizations. When they are at the higher pinnacles of their agencies, having graduated from the FBINAA, they will better understand the FBI and the FBI's investigative process.

Although the FBI supports domestic investigations, the liaison developed and maintained with foreign law enforcement officials, especially in instances where international borders are blurred and overlapped, can assist the FBI and our foreign counterparts in apprehending terrorists or criminals, helping to bring an investigation to fruition more quickly. Cooperation between my office and my foreign counterparts was vital.

Part of my job as Legat was to seek out those law enforcement officers, counterparts in the countries I covered, as qualified applicants to attend the FBINAA. I made it a point to maintain contact with the officers who had already graduated from the program. Each time I traveled to Sri Lanka, the Maldives, Nepal, or Bangladesh, I invited the graduates out to dinner so we could get to know each other. This way, we could build up a level of trust.

I was already acquainted with some of the graduates; I had even been introduced to their children and their wives. To this day, I still have FBINAA graduate contacts in some of the countries I covered, although I now consider them friends.

To date, Bhutan had never agreed to send an officer to the FBINAA, and I had made it my mission to co-opt Mr. Wangchuk to remedy this situation.

"I'm sorry, Mr. Wangchuk, you're right. I'm just very excited to have the very first Bhutanese police officer attend the FBINAA."

"But, Miss Kathy, we don't have crime in Bhutan. Why would we need special training?" This I could not believe. Bhutan was a country so strict it outlawed cigarettes. Surely someone in their Buddhist, happiness-loving way of life had broken the law by taking an illegal puff every now and then.

What could I say in the face of his conviction that Bhutan was devoid of crime? Maybe he was right. I hadn't yet traveled to Bhutan, because I wanted to wait until I had an official invitation to meet with potential candidates for an FBINAA slot. I was already beginning to believe I had blown my chances by being an ugly American and charging out of the gate before observing the niceties required by a society that prided itself on friendliness first.

"Mr. Wangchuk, I hope this will not be our last meeting. Please allow me to invite you to lunch again very soon so that I can tell you more about the FBI."

With a smile that could rival any Buddha statue, he closed his eyes briefly and nodded once.

During subsequent lunch meetings with Mr. Wangchuk, I got to know him better, asking a myriad of questions. I was curious about Bhutan, its people, culture, food, history, and language. It was a place I hoped to visit both professionally and personally. Mr. Wangchuk was always readily available to meet with me and, in return, asked numerous questions about the FBI.

Although I met with Mr. Wangchuk several times over the course of my time as Legat New Delhi, I never received an official invitation to visit Bhutan. And, during my tenure, he never agreed to send an officer from Bhutan to the FBI Academy. But Mr. Wangchuk taught me the art of slowing down and recognizing that this amazing job I had was not all about paperwork and investigations. It was also about the friendship and respect that comes from taking the time to understand and respect another culture so different from my own.

Several years later, I would at last receive a call from the Delhi Legat office, telling me Bhutan had finally agreed to send a candidate.

CHAPTER TWENTY-NINE

HANNIBAL LECTER

★★★

I breathed in the stale smell of curry, incense, unwashed bodies, and beedis as I walked down the jetway at Kolkata airport. From this first whiff, Kolkata seemed not much different from Delhi, except for the underlying smell of vegetation decay. Kolkata is significantly south of Delhi and closer to the coast, abutting the Hooghly River, a sinuous arm of the Ganges, which eventually empties into the Bay of Bengal. The air was a thick soup of moisture and mold.

As I stepped to the top of the staircase, I had a sweeping view of the entrance hall below. I looked around for my contact with the Kolkata Police Department, expecting to see a lone figure in a wilting once-starched khaki uniform. Instead, my eyes met with an assemblage of khaki-clad men, all holding rifles, ostensibly poised to storm the beaches of some desert nation.

Frowning, I moved down the steps, feeling inquisitive eyes follow my every move. As I reached the bottom, a tall, slim officer stepped forward, his bearing straight and professional, hand outstretched. Mr. Gupta and I had spoken on the telephone several times although we had never met face-to-face. Smiling and pleasant, he appeared to be young for his position as a Deputy Inspector General.

This odyssey had begun several months prior to my arrival in Kolkata. Shortly after arriving in Delhi, I had become embroiled in an investigation looking into an individual who had been involved in both a kidnapping and a terrorist attack against an American Cultural Center in Kolkata, India. The FBI had assisted India's CBI, by tracing phone records to the subject of the investigation, Mr. Azam. After weeks of seeking approvals, from both the State Department and FBI General Counsel, to appear in a foreign court as a US diplomat, I was finally given official permission to travel to Kolkata and testify to the validity of the FBI-provided evidence.

I reached for Mr. Gupta's hand, introduced myself, and asked politely if there was something going on, since the airport seemed to be filled with gun-toting police officers. Mr. Gupta, visibly attempting to restrain his head bobble to a minimum, and looking uncomfortable in the process, said to me in his lilting, singsong accent, "Madam, there has been a problem."

In India for a few months, my main problems so far had consisted of avoiding the scathing criticism of the Ambassador during country team—a regular meeting of the heads of agencies represented in the embassy to brief the Ambassador on issues of importance—and managing my digestive system on a daily basis. So, any problem involving a troop of armed police officers didn't readily pierce my psyche in light of these two daily embarrassments. Still, I thought it best to pay attention, so I asked politely, "And what problem might that be, Mr. Gupta?"

"Madam Kathy, there was an article in the newspaper this morning alerting everyone to the fact that you will be testifying in court today against Mr. Azam. As Mr. Azam has many terrorist colleagues, we have become concerned for your safety and well-being. We are therefore providing an armed escort during your stay in Kolkata."

Well, shit! Is it too late to back out? I told Keith just this morning there was nothing to worry about, routine testimony, no problem.

I must have stared at Mr. Gupta a few seconds too long as he began to talk rapidly, saying I would be perfectly safe, there was nothing to worry about, the testimony had been postponed to make sure the prison was safe, I would go to a nice hotel first to wait . . . *Whoa! Wait a minute; what's this about going to a prison?*

"I'm sorry, Mr. Gupta, could you please back up just a minute? Why is the testimony delayed?"

"Madam, we feel it is unsafe to remove the prisoner to another location, therefore, we will hold the trial inside the prison. We are now making the prison safe for you to enter."

Up until this point, pooping my pants had been at the top of my list of things I would like most to avoid. However, the idea of being blown up in an

Indian prison was slowly starting to creep to the top. *OK, I'm an FBI agent . . . a female FBI agent at that, and I'm not about to let these guys—and they were all guys—scare me.*

"Okay, Mr. Gupta, let's stop standing around making targets of ourselves and get this show on the road." I think Mr. Gupta was a little confused by my vernacular, but he got the message as I headed for the exit. High stepping ahead of me, he quickly opened the door and led me to a line of cars waiting just outside the entrance ramp. Several vehicles in front and several vehicles behind, our motorcade wound its way out of the airport and onto the roadway to Kolkata.

Shortly after getting on the road, I looked at the vehicle just in front of my car and saw a pickup truck filled with soldiers sitting on wooden benches attached haphazardly to the sides of the truck bed. They each had a rifle laid across their laps with the muzzles pointing straight at me. Or rather, the car I was riding in. One bored officer was busily stuffing his left index finger two knuckles deep up his nose, digging away at some crusty pebble. It did not inspire much confidence.

As I watched the soldier excavate his sinus cavity, I hoped he would NOT venture upon a surprising find that would cause his trigger finger to jerk involuntarily, launching a few rounds into the car in which I was "safely" ensconced. These guys did not look like they hit the shooting range on a daily basis. The best I could hope for was to avoid the first couple of rounds and hit the floorboard as the next few headed my way.

Nose Picker, having decided to forego his pan of gold, had gone back to his hunched boredom, so I relaxed a little and started to look out at my surroundings. The airport being a bit on the north side of the city, where roads were pockmarked with broken asphalt, our entourage wriggled along at the pace of an undulating caterpillar, swerving back and forth to avoid potholes and herds of cows. Years ago, I had watched the Patrick Swayze movie *City of Joy*, which depicted the slums of Kolkata. Looking out the windows of the car, the scenes from the movie came alive before my eyes, mile upon mile upon mile of corrugated tin shacks, little more than roofs with three sides. Women in bright saris squatted in front, stirring rusty pots over cow dung fires, while ragged and dirty children ran barefoot through the maze of alleyways. My speedy passage through this tableau gave me the feeling I was racing alongside a celluloid movie reel, everything beyond the dirty glass unreal, existing only in stories and imagination.

Topping a low hill, I saw in the distance a low-lying verdant field, dimples of water twinkling in a sun just breaking through the morning haze. Shimmering in the light and looking like a modern-day version of the Emerald City stood an anachronism of glittering white crystal and shining steel rising majestically above the rust browns and gray dust of the surrounding poverty.

"Mr. Gupta, *what* is that building over there?"

In a voice filled with pride, "Oh, Madam Kathy, that is our IBM!"

"IBM?" *Seriously?*

"Yes, madam, India has many technical experts."

Slums forgotten, brightly clad saris moving out my vision, all I could see was the building in front of me, literally sparkling like a diamond. Recalling how many times the electricity popped off at my house in Delhi, as well as at the embassy, I wondered how in the world IBM was getting enough electricity to power such a building. And who were they hiring to fill such a vast space? I hadn't realized India's tech boom had grown so rapidly as to be able to provide the number of engineers needed to populate such a high-tech office building.

My disbelieving eyes still glued to IBM, I heard Mr. Gupta say, "Madam Kathy, we will be at the hotel very soon. There you may rest for a few hours and have some tea. I will return for you this afternoon to take you to prison." *An ominous statement if ever I heard one . . .*

Mr. Gupta had certainly reserved a spectacular hotel for me, albeit at US government expense. He obviously assumed I could afford it with my government credit card. The Taj Bengal was part of the Taj Hotel Group, one of the most successful luxury hotel chains in the world. I was thankful for the diplomatic discount, otherwise I would be explaining to FBI Headquarters why I couldn't have waited four hours on the front steps of an Indian prison and be satisfied with drinking tea from a chai wallah, one of the ubiquitous street tea vendors.

After checking into my room, I hung up my suit jacket, kicked my shoes off and lay down on the bed. I had gotten up before dawn to catch my flight. Dealing with the chaos of Indira Gandhi Airport was always exhausting. Closing my eyes, I tried not to think of getting blown up or whatever else might await me in prison. Remembering the newspaper article mentioned by Mr. Gupta, I decided to order a pot of tea and a *Times of India* newspaper.

Service is outstanding in India, and my tea and paper were delivered quickly by an impeccably uniformed young man, smiling and friendly, unabashedly staring at me, something with which I had become accustomed. I was a tall white woman wearing what appeared to be men's clothing—not something you see every day on the streets of a country that still boasts the colorful and traditional elegance of the sari.

Sitting down to read the article, I flashed back to my first encounter with the *Times of India*. My primary liaison in the Indian government was with the CBI. Part of my job was to give them leads, which were requests for information regarding US investigations with a nexus in India. Although my requests to CBI were always unclassified, they were nonetheless confidential, at least in theory. CBI defined confidentiality differently and seemed to enjoy leaking my requests to the *Times of India*.

One morning during a country team, I found myself being yelled at, by the Ambassador, who was, in addition to Director Mueller at the FBI, my boss at the embassy. An article had appeared on the front page of the *Times*, my name and quotes attached. Attempting to explain I had simply made a routine request of my counterparts, the Ambassador continued to berate me for allowing CBI to leak FBI information to a newspaper. I looked sheepishly around the room, where heads of other agencies busily took notes or picked at their fingernails. I realized I had no allies, at least for that showdown. *Cowards! Ball-less sacks of shitdust!* Throughout the scolding, I nodded my head, in certain agreement that I was nothing but a lowly worm on the fishing pole of American diplomacy. After some minutes, the Ambassador's morning gas having passed through his lower intestine, his diatribe ended, and he locked his stern eyes in my direction, white eyebrows drawn together in a shaggy point. I nodded one last time—yes, I was indeed chum—as he moved on to his next victim.

Thus began my three-times weekly morning meeting with the Ambassador. Shortly thereafter, I was eating breakfast at home, before heading to the embassy, when my Indian cell phone rang. It was the embassy's regional security officer (RSO), Henry. Henry and his cadre of agreeable young men—and they were all men—were part of the State Department's Diplomatic Security Service, responsible for embassy security. Henry's office was next to mine and we had hit it off right away. Hearing Henry's voice so early in the morning gave me the same feeling I was becoming familiar with—onset rocket-projectile diarrhea.

"Kathy, heads up, there's an article about you in the *Times of India* this morning. You might want to read it and be prepared to get yelled at in country team meeting." *Why does that grumpy old fuck always yell at me?*

I sighed. "Thanks, Henry, I appreciate the phone call."

Hastily reading the newspaper that morning, and every morning there-after, I wasn't able to avoid being yelled at by the Ambassador, but I no longer felt compelled to agree with his opinion that I belonged at the bottom of an Indian sewer.

Lying on the hotel room bed, I opened the newspaper to headlines that marched across the page: "FBI Man to Depose in Today's Terrorism Trial." Well, I had that going for me. They were expecting a guy to show up. Maybe the terrorists would throw a bomb at some unsuspecting western male reporter instead. What's with the confusion over my gender anyway? *Can no one get my gender straight in this country? I know I'm an anomaly, but can't they tell I'm a woman?* I was starting to feel not a little insecure about my own femininity.

I could only imagine what I would face in tomorrow morning's country team: *Yes, Mr. Ambassador, I did appear on the front page of the* Times of India. *But to be fair, they called me a man so I couldn't possibly have been responsible for the leak. Why would I call myself a man? Can't you let me off your freakin' fishhook for one minute?* I probably wouldn't say that, but I would be thinking it, while nodding along in agreement that I just needed to be wiped off the bottom of someone's shoe.

Tired and even more anxious, I met Mr. Gupta and my wayward entou-rage of trucks and cars and we headed to the prison. I'm not sure what I was expecting. I knew I wouldn't be seeing a prison like we have in the US with electrified fences topped by concertina wire, narrow windows looking out onto a wide-open space, monitored 24/7 by guard towers on every corner. But I certainly wasn't expecting this.

From a distance, the prison looked like the small palace of a minor maharaja, all red brick and crenelated towers. But nothing prepared me for the medieval, crumbling chaos that awaited as we got closer and entered an inner courtyard. As the driver came around to open the door for me, dozens of cameras flashed as reporters jockeyed to take my photo. I stepped out and away from the car as quickly as I could, my head down, shoulders hunched against the punch of an explosion or the crack of a rifle shot. Reason will tell you that nothing is going to stop either of those events should they happen, but your body prepares to defend itself, nonetheless.

I was quickly ushered into a room, empty of everything except a tentlike structure, set against one oozing, damp, and crumbling stone wall. The other three sides were blocked with curtains dangling from the ceiling on makeshift rods. Each curtain was divided, and I walked through the nearest side to find a small wooden table dotted with circles of tea residue, edged with beedi burns, nicks, and slashes in the wood. Mr. Gupta motioned me toward a rickety chair sitting alongside the table.

"Madam Kathy, you may wait here until we are ready for your testimony," he said and instructed one of his lesser officers to bring some water. The young officer placed in front of me a carafe of water with a less-than-clean glass and then skittered away, wide eyes cast down, looking out at me sideways as if I were a basilisk and could petrify him into infinity with one gaze. I smiled and thanked him, knowing that one sip of that water would earn me a trip to the prison toilet, a place I was loath to visit. I already regretted my earlier pot of tea and the onset of a full bladder should this drama drag on, as most things did in India.

My chair kept wobbling back and forth on the uneven stone floor, and when I looked up, two or three heads poked through each side of the curtain. They lined up, seemingly disembodied, one on top of the other, gawking, smiling, and waving. I felt like a two-headed calf at the county fair, or worse, a monkey in a zoo looking at people on the other side of the bars who were trying to get the monkey to shit in its hand for pure entertainment value.

Not wanting to disappoint, I smiled and practiced my pageant queen in a Macy's Day Parade wave. Noting this didn't seem to satisfy, I gave them my Queen Elizabeth limp-wristed wave. This generated a few claps. As I was trying to conjure up another form of entertainment, Mr. Gupta rescued me.

The makeshift courtroom was another long, cold, and damp stone-lined space, with a raised platform set at one end of the room. On the platform was an oversized, once beautifully carved antique desk helmed by an elderly Indian gentleman, his shoulders thrown back in stately command, obviously the magistrate. Perched at the edge of a precarious chair at one end of the desk was a young male clerk, fingers already poised in frozen anticipation over a vintage typewriter, which probably hadn't been new since the days of the Raj.

In front of the magistrate stood a smaller square platform, enclosed by a waist-high railing, the witness box where I would be standing to provide testimony. Just to the side of the witness box was a row of chairs occupied by about a dozen tiny, wizened men, all wearing identical black satin robes, shiny and green with age, topped by once-white wigs.

My eyes swept over the English-styled courtroom and landed on something probably rarely seen in a modern courtroom. Set up in the middle of the room, just behind the witness box, stood a cage, walls of rusted, but still sturdy, iron bars. The ceiling of the cage was enclosed, to my relief, and two armed officers stood at either side of the door, closed with a padlock the size of my head. Inside the cage, a man gripped the bars on either side of his head, his face pressed through the opening as far as the space would allow. He was glowering at me with menace, eyes half-closed, mouth turned down in a sneer. I stared back, giving no ground, and with shoulders straight, stepped up into the witness box.

I turned to the magistrate and practically jumped out of my skin as he yelled . . . yes, *yelled*, "Madam, please state your name!"

"My name is Kathy Stearman." Clerk and typewriter came to life simultaneously, clamoring barrage of ancient keys echoing from ceiling to floor.

"Madam, are you married?" Decibels rebounded off the stone walls.

"Yes, I am married." A short burst of keys bulleted out of the typewriter.

The magistrate, waiting until the fade of the last stroke, then bellowed, "What is your maiden name?"

"My maiden name is Kathy Stearman."

Heads nodded in unison, followed by another short burst.

The magistrate boomed, "What is your father's name?"

Playing along, I stated, "My father's name is James Stearman."

I waited for the racket to repeat itself but heard instead a collective intake of breath. Moth eaten heads to my right huddled together, chattering magpies, hands flailing in discussion. One head broke free and scurried to the front of the magistrate's desk, whispering across the expanse. Decision made, he scurried back to the flock. I know what they were thinking. How could I possibly be married yet still carry my father's name? Expecting another barrage of questions, they simply stared in confused silence and then finally, as if some invisible wire was attached to each, they nodded as one.

The clerk quickly recorded this vital piece of information for all posterity and the ensuing silence once again allowed the magistrate to roar, "What is your religion?"

"I have no religion." The group of magpies huddled together so quickly I was surprised they didn't give each other concussions. Whispers ensued, hands flailed again, and instead of consulting with the magistrate, one wizened little soul stepped forward, smiling as if to a child and said, "Madam, you *don't* understand. What is your religion?"

Enunciating slowly, trying to politely appease his condescension, I said, "Yes, I *do* understand; I have no religion."

Shock crossed his features and he scurried back to the flock. Some consensus made, the brave one stepped forward once again and said, "Madam, please, you must understand. Some people are Hindu, some are Buddhist, and some are Catholic. What is *your* religion?"

"Yes, I *do* understand that people have different religions. But I have *no* religion."

My statement seemed to have stumped them all . . . it was so quiet; a pin drop could have generated a cacophonous clamor. Mouths agape, they all stared in frozen wonder at a phenomenon they had obviously never before encountered. As entertaining as this drama was proving to be, I anticipated my full bladder of tea to kick in any minute, and I was ready to move things along.

"May I make a suggestion? Perhaps you could write 'none' in the space for religion."

Gray-white curls began to bobble in unison and the magistrate, obviously anxious to get to his tenth chai of the day or his umpteenth beedi, bellowed, "None!"

Crisis averted, the testimony proceeded with questions about the evidence the FBI provided, how the FBI obtained it, and so forth. After reviewing and signing my official statement, I was soon released from my little box.

I was immediately surrounded by the murder of crows, each more than six inches shorter than I, looking up at my combined height plus three-inch heels, topping six feet. Smiling and friendly, they didn't say anything until the brave one, obviously their leader, said, "Madam Kathy, your English is very good." I smiled wryly and replied, "Well, thank you. It is my first language after all." There were agreeable smiles and nods all around.

What I think they meant to say was my English was very clear. I had already learned that most westerners, when dealing with locals in India, didn't bother to slow down their speech or clearly enunciate their words. Having already dealt with people from several countries with numerous accents, I had gotten into the habit of speaking slowly and clearly, not using any American slang. I was happy to know my linguistic strategy was working.

As I passed the prisoner's cage, out of the corner of my eye I saw an arm snake out, fingers curled in my direction. I paused to look over. The prisoner smiled at me, his rotten teeth and spaces between resembling one of the crumbling towers on the prison roof. "Madam. Madam. Come here. Come here," he said as his hand moved back and forth in a beckoning motion. This man, responsible for the death of several individuals, had been sentenced to death himself and was now awaiting confirmation from the court. I wasn't about to go anywhere near him.

"I don't think so, Hannibal," I said, and kept walking.

The next day, my photo in the *Times of India* did indeed prove I was a woman with a caption that read, "First FBI Official to Testify in an Indian Court."

The Ambassador didn't even look in my direction during country team. I was a little disappointed.

CHINA

CHAPTER THIRTY

NI HAO

★ ★ ★

All war is deception.
—Sun Tzu

I couldn't see beyond the tarmac below my plane window. Any sense of time was obscured by the ubiquitous smog that covered Beijing almost every day, the landscape sucked dry of all color, only shades of gray remained. As the wheels of the plane touched down lightly, I sensed that my stint in Beijing was going to be completely different from my sojourn in India. I felt my chest tighten as I looked over at Keith beside me, as if breathing the toxic air outside the window had already filled my lungs.

"You don't seem happy." It was a statement, not a question.

"I'm OK," I answered. "I just miss the sunshine already."

When my time in India was drawing to a close, I had been thrilled to be offered the position of Legat Beijing, where I would cover China and Mongolia. I had spent several weeks in China during my time at FBI Headquarters and knew what it would be like to live there permanently. Keith had traveled over at the end of one of my temporary assignments in Beijing, so he was also aware of what life would be like in this gray and dreary city, where quaint hutongs and traditional alleyways were being destroyed daily; replaced by skyscrapers and construction cranes that stretched toward the horizon, which was obscured on most days by a thick, coal-smoke, and photochemical smog. The miasma of pollution and spices from the food carts dotting street corners lay heavily in the shadows cast by China's rise to modernity.

When I told Keith about the offer, he said, "You've been training to be Legat Beijing for almost your whole career. Why would you consider saying no? I think we should go."

Prior to my transfer to Beijing, I was scheduled to take a three-month-long refresher course in Mandarin Chinese in Washington, DC. Being in Washington would also allow me to receive briefings on China from the FBI and other US government agencies within the intelligence community.

My briefings were interesting, although I was already aware of most intelligence I received. The best advice I acquired was from a young woman from another government agency, who had spent the previous few years in Beijing. She didn't bother to talk about Chinese intelligence. She looked at me over her desk and said, "I know your background. I'm not going to tell you anything you don't already know. So, here's my best advice for you. Buy zit cream, lots of it."

I smiled at her, not responding. I had never had acne or pimples in my entire life. But then I thought, maybe zit cream could be used for some clandestine purpose that I might need to understand. She saw my confused look, so she followed with, "You already know the air pollution in Beijing is horrible. Living there for a long time, you're going to get zits like you haven't seen since you were a teenager. Trust me. The best zit cream is Neutrogena Rapid Clear. Take several tubes with you; you can't buy it over there."

I took her advice and several months later, I sent her a silent word of thanks. To my horror, my face broke out so badly it could have been used for a game of connect-the-dots. Not only did I use the tubes of Neutrogena I had taken with me, I bought several more tubes every time I traveled back to the US. It turned out to be the best predeployment intelligence I received.

A couple of weeks prior to my arrival in Beijing, I received an email from the LOS in Beijing, Tara. Tara had a great reputation and I looked forward to working with her. The FBI has some amazing personnel who serve in embassies as Legat Operations Specialists, some of whom have served in multiple Legat offices. With their vast experience, they were often responsible for teaching a Legat many aspects of his or her job, myself included. After our rocky start, I had been lucky in Delhi to have worked with Rachel. She was worth her weight in gold. Her work and work ethic were impeccable and any Legat office she served in would be lucky to have her. In the end, she and I developed an open, friendly relationship, and I learned a great deal from her.

Tara informed me she had been diagnosed with breast cancer and would have to travel back to the US for several months of treatment. Although I wasn't obligated to agree, she asked if I would be willing to hold her position open until she was well enough to return. I knew it must have taken a great deal of courage to ask. We had never met, and she had no idea what my answer might be. What she didn't know was that I was also a breast cancer survivor, having gone through numerous surgeries, chemotherapy, and radiation, the same treatment she was facing. I remembered clearly the support I received from all my colleagues in the San Francisco office. Even though it was going to be difficult for me to operate without an LOS, there was no way I wasn't going to honor her request.

Keith and I were met at the Beijing airport by the ALAT, Ed, who I already knew from working together on previous investigations. He was due to depart Beijing permanently in about five months. On the drive to our assigned apartment, he told me IOD was going to send a temporary LOS for a month or so to help while I got settled into the office. The current Legat, David, would overlap my arrival by two weeks, then he would depart post permanently to return to the US. David was also a former colleague of mine, so I thought I would have time to pick his brain before he left.

On my first day in the office, I did the normal check-in procedure by getting my official badge, signing paperwork, getting passwords, and all the other administrative minutiae required for working in a highly secure, classified space. When I finally walked into David's office—soon to be mine—I asked him if he had time to brief me on issues and investigations on which I would need to concentrate after his departure. He looked up from a Chinese dictionary he was using to translate a document and said, "I'm busy. I don't have time."

"OK, no problem, I'll come back later." Thinking I could at least catch up on current investigations, I started to read case files. Later that afternoon, I poked my head around the door and said, "Do you have some time for me now?"

"No, I'm still busy" came the curt reply. I went back to reading files.

After this scenario was repeated the next day and the next, I stopped asking. I realized David was not going to provide any insight as to what I should concentrate on in the coming months. When I had left Delhi, not only had I accompanied my successor to meetings with our foreign counterparts, but I had written a comprehensive, multipage report on every country covered by Legat New Delhi, listing every single counterpart I had dealt with, their names and bios, a list of cases I had worked on and a list of cases that would require his immediate attention for the next two or three months. I had essentially left him a road map. I hadn't wanted to leave him with a shit storm like the one I received when I arrived in Delhi. I hadn't expected the same treatment from David, but I had expected professional courtesy, which was, unfortunately, not forthcoming.

I was lucky that the temporary LOS who had been sent to Beijing was experienced and knew her job well. Since we were both new to the Beijing Legat, we had to learn the functioning of the office together. This was just as well as the ALAT, Ed, was about as forthcoming as the Legat. One day I stuck my head in Ed's office and asked him to obtain some information for me. His response was "I already have a wife at home, I don't need one telling me what to do here," as he went back to napping or handling a personal issue, which I had already learned he was prone to do.

At that point I called IOD and asked how quickly they could get my ALAT replacement to Beijing. Ed's successor, Ryan, had already been chosen, and I wanted him to arrive as soon as possible. Ryan had school-age children and he couldn't arrive in Beijing until their school year had ended at his current assignment. I resigned myself to the fact that I would have to grit it out for the next few months until Ed's departure. Fortunately, IOD continued to supply me with stellar temporary LOS's so the office administration could function while I did my job as Legat.

❖

China had become one of the most important priorities for the US intelligence community. The relationship between the US and China had grown significantly economically and politically, while numerous American companies had moved their manufacturing operations and subsidiaries to the People's Republic of China (PRC). The number of investigations the FBI covered involving China had increased dramatically to include international parental kidnapping, cybercrime, terrorism, and espionage.

Numerous congressional delegations traveled to Beijing to meet with embassy officials, myself included. I briefed members of the House Intelligence

Committee, the Senate Intelligence Committee, delegations from other areas of the US government who wanted to show their constituencies they were doing their jobs where China was concerned, and representatives from private sector companies who wanted to do business in China.

US Embassy Beijing, the second largest US embassy in the world, was also the mission where ambitious State Department employees jockeyed for assignment, to solidify their reputation on their way to more advanced positions. In other words, US Embassy Beijing was the place to be.

It didn't take me long to realize who to distance myself from and to learn who would be an ally. The day I moved into the Legat's office, after my predecessor's welcome departure, one of the guys from the IT department came in to move my State Department computer. As he was on his hands and knees pulling cables and wires, he sat back on his heels and said, "So, where does your boss want this moved to?"

"Well, since I'm the boss, why don't you put it over there," I said, pointing to the top of a credenza. Without missing a beat, he said, "Uh-oh, I guess this means you're not going to be baking me any cheesecakes, huh?" I burst out laughing, not just because he had a quick wit and a dry delivery, but I had already gotten accustomed to a few State Department employees in Beijing who were either haughty or didn't like the FBI.

On the other hand, my second boss, Jon Huntsman Jr., US Ambassador to China, turned out to be an ally of the FBI, unlike the ambassador in India.

One of my favorite predeployment trainings prior to working overseas took place at the State Department's Foreign Service Institute (FSI). Although I had been overseas on temporary duty assignments prior to my permanent assignment, and was familiar with the inner workings of an embassy, the FSI program provided more in-depth information regarding how to conduct oneself as an American diplomat. Not only did FSI define the inner workings of an embassy, but they also taught the finer points of interacting socially with the Ambassador. One should always address the Ambassador as Mr. or Madam Ambassador; one is to rise when the Ambassador enters a room; and one is never to go through a doorway in front of the Ambassador.

This last rule of protocol made for some awkward situations. For example, while I was stationed in Beijing, there were times when I prepared to enter a doorway at the same time as Ambassador Huntsman. I always opened the door for him and said, "After you, Mr. Ambassador."

"Now Kathy, I'm a gentleman, and you're going to go through that door first, or we can stand here all day." And then he would smile and wait patiently.

The first couple of times this happened, we went back and forth with "No, Mr. Ambassador, after you," and "No, Kathy, after you."

I finally learned he wasn't going to break his "gentleman code," but every time I passed through a door before him, I was sure someone from the Regional Security Office (RSO) responsible for embassy security would arrest me on behalf of the protocol police.

I sorely missed Ambassador Huntsman's banter when he departed post and the new Ambassador arrived. One day, I found myself arriving at a doorway at the same time as the new Ambassador. I opened the door, stood aside, and said, "After you, Mr. Ambassador." He did not look at me. He did not say thank you. He did not acknowledge I was there. For all I knew, he might have thought I was posted there all day, every day, for the express pleasure of preventing him from getting carpal tunnel syndrome from having to open a door on his own.

❖

Although Legat Beijing was extremely busy, in addition to China, I covered one other country, Mongolia. The amount of time I had to travel to liaison with my foreign counterparts was greatly reduced as I wasn't allowed to reach out to my Chinese counterparts in other parts of the PRC, such as Shanghai or Guangdong. Nor was I allowed to travel freely in-country unless it was for personal reasons, during which time I'm sure I was still monitored. Travel to Mongolia was limited as well, due to extreme weather changes, especially during winter as high winds and heavy snows precluded travel except in warmer months. Thus, I did not go there as often as I would have liked.

In spite of its massive size and population, Beijing was an easy city in which to maneuver. Plus, I had been assigned an apartment just across the street from the embassy. My commute was a whopping five-minute walk to the embassy compound. As an American with top-secret security clearance, Keith had gotten a job at the embassy with the State Department, working in the IT department. As we settled easily into our new life, we knew there would be completely different challenges living in China.

CHAPTER THIRTY-ONE

BIG BROTHER

★ ★ ★

You had to live—did live, from habit that
became instinct—in the assumption that every
sound you made was overheard, and, except in
darkness, every movement scrutinized.
—George Orwell, *1984*

Because US Embassy Beijing is such a high-threat post, living and working there could sometimes feel like we were all living under a glass dome, which the massive embassy atrium resembled. The stress of being under scrutiny by the Chinese intelligence services was sometimes a catalyst for relationships to develop—sometimes where they shouldn't—and other times would bring about the demise of other relationships.

I knew Keith and I would be monitored. Our every move would be watched, and our apartment was more than likely bugged. It didn't take long to see signs that someone had been in our apartment while we were at work. There was nothing I could do, nor did I ever try to find any cameras or listening devices.

We had heard stories of personal computers being broken into, photos erased, personal finances erased or corrupted, or at the very least, all their files read and copied for any information that might be used against them by the intelligence services. Since Keith worked in the IT section, he received a special dispensation to take our personal laptop into the embassy with him every day, kept in a locker and out of reach of people who had unfettered access at our apartment to freely troll the computer.

When Keith and I went to the wet market to buy groceries, he carried that laptop in a backpack. When we went out to a restaurant, the laptop came along. When we went to a movie, the laptop was our trusty sidekick. We never left it alone in our apartment. I was loath to lose all the photos we had taken over the past few years; nor was I anxious for the Chinese to read our personal emails or peruse our finances. Years later when we arrived back stateside, one of Keith's first comments was "I'm so happy I don't have to carry that god-damn computer around anymore."

One day, Keith found a fresh poop in the toilet and a big smear of green boogers on the bathroom wall. Someone had obviously taken the time to sit down, enjoy a leisurely shit, inspect the contents of their nostrils, and leave evidence of their disdain for us to enjoy and clean up. Of all the things we had learned to deal with in Beijing, this one threw Keith into a frenzy. He began yelling at the chandelier, "You all can go fuck yourselves! Fuck you! Don't ever shit in my fucking toilet ever again!"

I'm not sure why he yelled at the chandelier. There was no evidence that was the location of one of the listening devices. It probably just seemed convenient as it hung from the ceiling in the middle of the living room. I knew to never provoke the intelligence services in any way, but in time, when I got pissed off at finding something deliberately moved or displaced, I found myself also yelling at the chandelier. It seemed as good a place as any to vent my spleen.

On another day, Keith went to our apartment for lunch. Apparently, the Chinese surveillance team responsible for the lunch shift was taking a nap, because Keith was just opening our apartment door to step out when a man wearing black clothing was preparing to put a key in the lock to enter. Keith didn't say anything to him. He didn't have time. The man in black bolted for the stairwell as fast as he could run, the door slamming behind him.

Keith and I were also aware we couldn't have in-depth conversations in our apartment. I obviously never talked about work and Keith never spoke of his work either. Because Keith had a top-secret clearance, he was allowed into my office. When we needed to have a personal conversation, or an argument for that matter, we always headed for the security of my office space.

Surveillance did not stop at my apartment, nor did it stop while I was out on the street. One day, Ryan and I were driving back from a meeting at the Ministry of Public Security (MPS) headquarters. On that day, we happened to be in one of our FBI vehicles, an older model bulletproof Suburban. We never discussed our meetings in the vehicle, nor did we ever talk about anything but innocuous topics, waiting until we were back in the security of our classified space. All at once a woman's accented voice boomed from somewhere inside the dashboard, "The voice recognition software is now shutting off."

We turned to each other, eyes wide, and said in unison, "What the fuck?" Then we started laughing and couldn't stop. Ryan was laughing so hard he started choking. I laughed and laughed and laughed, my eyes tearing up. I don't know why that moment struck us as being so funny. Maybe the stress of walking a verbal tightrope every time we stepped outside our office had gotten to the both of us. Maybe it's the surprise of *not* being surprised that the vehicle had obviously been listening to every word we were saying. Maybe it was the gratification of getting to do what we were doing, having the experiences we were having, living in a country that, while frustrating at the best of times, was also fascinating and exhilarating. We had the rare privilege of representing the FBI in a job to which few people will ever be exposed or learn about, aside from the most innocuous of details.

CHAPTER THIRTY-TWO

THE POWER OF THE BLOW JOB

★★★

"Oh, for fuck's sake! He has to be sent home!" Sharon slammed her hand down hard on the top of the conference table, looking around in scorn. I looked down at the tabletop, smirking, as I witnessed the expressions on the faces of the men around the table. And they were all men. Their expressions clearly said, *Shit, here's another woman ready to put another guys' dick on the chopping block.* And they would have been right.

US Embassy Beijing is one of the highest-threat posts in the world, meaning the Chinese intelligence services are extremely aggressive in their tactics to compromise the integrity of the embassy and any American citizen working within its confines. When I first arrived in Beijing, I was fully cognizant of the threat posed to me, my staff, their families, and Keith.

Everywhere I went in my first few weeks, I saw the same Chinese male following me, sitting at a table near mine at Starbucks, trailing along behind me at the flower market, observing me at local restaurants. He stood out because he wore nicely tailored black slacks and jacket and a neatly pressed white shirt. He never stared at me, nor did he try to approach me. He became my shadow everywhere I went outside the embassy. After a few weeks, I no longer saw him and, frankly, stopped looking for him. I'm sure he had gotten bored with watching me drink coffee, buy vegetables, and slurp the best dumplings I have ever tasted at the local dumpling house.

I had already been asked numerous times by my counterparts at the Ministry of Public Security, "Why are you here in Beijing? Are you a spy?"

Every time my answer was the same: "No, I'm here to act as the FBI's representative to provide liaison between our two countries in order to enhance better understanding of each other's law enforcement practices and facilitate exchanges of information regarding matters of mutual interest, blah, blah, blah." My rote answer changed to some small degree every time I was called upon to repeat it, but the message was always the same. I am who I say I am, not something more.

Although their physical surveillance *could* be amateurish—perhaps the intelligence services wanted me to know I was being followed, and they sure were not subtle about checking our apartment—the Chinese intelligence apparatus was quite sophisticated when it came to how they organized an approach to American personnel. To monitor the direction of the threat, and to determine exact information the Chinese were interested in obtaining, ██

███

███

██████████████████ As a member of this team, I witnessed Sharon's frustration regarding yet another cleared American man who had become involved with a Chinese woman, who also worked at the embassy.

Classified embassy jobs are staffed with Americans hired by their respective US agencies. But a good percentage of jobs, within the unclassified offices of the embassy, are staffed by foreign nationals—citizens of the country in which the US embassy is located.

Americans routinely interacted with foreign nationals on a daily basis—through the travel office, where everyone went to make travel reservations, both professional and personal; through the motor pool of vehicles used by authorized personnel; as well as in the community liaison office, which held events to familiarize family with their new country of abode. Friendly relationships could and did develop. I myself had developed friendships with many members of the foreign national staff in India. However, I never lost sight of the fact that my every move and comment could be reported. China was an entirely different story. Chinese intelligence services would consider it an intelligence coup were they successful in compromising someone within the US embassy. Therefore, I kept myself under tight lock and key when it came to who I talked to, when and where I had conversations, and who I socialized with.

One of the favorite mechanisms utilized by the Chinese intelligence services was the use of "honeypots," young, beautiful women who were directed to target a specific American male, develop a sexual relationship with him, and then compromise him so he would be willing to give up the keys to the kingdom, i.e., any classified information to which he might be privy.

As I sat and waited to see what the response would be to Sharon's outburst, I was glad that it wasn't me doing the haranguing this time. I was tired of defending the position that any man who had developed a sexual relationship with a Chinese national needed to be sent home in order to protect the integrity of the embassy. Most times, the man in question was sent packing. Sometimes the men circled the wagons to protect one of their own. This was one of those times.

The current "fallen" employee had been caught, after hours, having sex on his desk with a young Chinese female who worked in another section of the embassy. Never mind that he had been caught in flagrante delicto with said young woman, sprawled across his desk. Never mind he had a high-profile position in the embassy. The State Department was making noises that he needed to stay in Beijing because of his specific expertise.

I sat quietly, for once, and listened to the arguments go round and round as to why he should stay or go. This whole argument wasn't new to me, especially as it related to the protection of the American embassy in Beijing.

When I was stationed at FBI Headquarters in Washington, DC, I had been the program manager for the build-out of the new US Embassy in Beijing. The US government was determined that the new embassy would be built with the utmost security in mind. No one wanted to repeat the multiple security debacles surrounding the construction of the US Embassy in Moscow.

The embassy in Beijing would be the State Department's second largest overseas construction project, the largest being Iraq. Every single piece of construction equipment to go into the classified building was shipped to Beijing under armed guard, and all subsequent construction of the same building would be conducted by security cleared American personnel. As such, the intelligence community put together a team to provide briefings and training for those personnel from both the architectural and construction firms designing and building the embassy, informing them of the high-level threat they would be under once they arrived in China.

Part of my job had been to set up a program through which the construction and architectural personnel could report any approaches by Chinese intelligence services. This included approaches by the honeypots. It was a given that most men—the construction crew was overwhelmingly male—were going to have sex when spending months on end away from home. And when they have women throwing themselves at them for monetary or political gain, it does not really matter, the dick wants what the dick wants. Telling them to say no is like telling a dog to not lick its own balls.

The purpose of the program was to ██████████████████████████ ██ ████████████████████████████████. Each man who developed a sexual relationship with a foreign national had to report it and follow that report up with a face-to-face interview with ████████████████████████████████.

I spent several weeks in Beijing helping to set up this program. After a few days of listening to men talk about their sexual exploits, some in graphic detail, I realized they seemed to get titillated by sharing details of their sexual prowess. The experience solidified my belief that all men have a price. Marriage, kids, solid relationships, it does not matter. One man even said to me apologetically, "It was the best blow job of my life." Frankly, I didn't give two shits if he got blow jobs around the clock. What mattered to me was that he would be willing to share classified information, should the flow of blow jobs cease, until he fessed up some tasty tidbit to pass along to the Chinese intelligence services.

I still held out hope that there were a few men on the site who would not fall to the wily ways of the women planted to solicit information. One was a construction site supervisor. He was quiet, soft-spoken, polite, professional, and well-groomed for someone who worked on the dirty, dusty, and chaotic quagmire of machines and concrete. He was also married with children. I looked forward to seeing him every day when he would pass me by with a polite, "Good morning, ma'am." Then, one day, I looked up from my desk to see him sitting across from me, ready to make a report.

"No. Not you, too." I said it calmly, but obviously could not keep the disappointment off my face. He held his hard hat between his knees and looked down. "I'm sorry. She's just so beautiful. I think I'm in love." *Jesus H. Fucking Christ!*

After I got back to Washington, DC, from one of my temporary duty assignments to Beijing, I found myself criticizing every man who crossed my path. The men I worked with, the men I saw on the street, the men in the car next to me at a red light. If he had a penis, he became the brunt of my internal, and sometimes external, scorn. I started to look at men, watch them, and wonder what their breaking point might be, their purchase price. A woman twenty years younger, someone new, someone different, a blow job? There were only a handful of men I felt couldn't be compromised. But then I'm sure they too had a purchase price. I had experienced plenty of men who behaved badly in the FBI. But being faced with it on an ongoing, daily basis for weeks on end had driven me into new territory.

One day Keith asked me, "Do you hate men?" He didn't ask it in an accusatory way. Nor was he annoyed when he asked it. Rather, he seemed sad, as if that might include him.

Keith's question had stunned me. I didn't realize I had been venting my frustration toward the male gender. I had to stop and think about how to answer him. Part of me wanted to say, "Fuck yes, I hate men!" The reality was that I had begun to realize, with overwhelming clarity, that a considerable percentage of men around the world look at women as a commodity. Did they not respect women at all, their wives, their daughters, their mothers? Was the act of a blow job the ultimate subordination of a woman? Was that why it was so satisfactory? Was the secret desire of the male gender to have a woman at his beck and call, common language and conversation an unnecessary and unwanted waste of time?

"No, Keith, I don't hate men. I'm just tired of being disappointed." And that was it. I was disappointed. My job had shown me a perspective of men that other women don't get. I was tired of watching men I liked, worked with, even respected, dissolve my own expectations of how they should conduct their lives. And that was the key to my disappointment; my own expectations were set too high.

Maybe I should just say it, ladies. Maybe I should say one of the most antifeminist things I could possibly utter, and it goes something like this—if we could just learn to channel the power of the blow job, maybe we could rule the world. That glass ceiling we've been trying to crack would already be shattered into a million crystalline shards if we realized men can be ruled and manipulated and led by the power of a simple act of oral physical contact with an erect penis.

I used to laughingly say that when I left the Bureau, I would write a book called "The Power of the Blow Job." This chapter will have to suffice.

CHAPTER THIRTY-THREE

KONGTUI KAILAN

★★★

"Sheng Kailan can really drink!"

Mr. Zhang swayed as he raised his baijiu glass above his head, splashing liquid over his thumb and forefinger as he attempted to maintain a grip on the tiny stem.

Sheng Kailan is the Chinese name given to me by one of the foreign nationals who worked at the US Embassy in Beijing, Mr. Wu. Upon my arrival at the embassy, I had been told to go to Mr. Wu as he was the person to order business cards—English name, title, and contact information on one side, with corresponding Chinese characters on the other side. I suspected Mr. Wu enjoyed this position at the embassy as he could report all newcomers and their Chinese names to a contact in the Chinese government. I wasn't too worried, I had been to China several times prior to my permanent assignment, so the Chinese government already knew exactly who I was.

When I gave Mr. Wu the Chinese name I was given at the Defense Language Institute (DLI) many years before, Shi Kaidi, he scrunched his eyebrows together and looked at me in confusion.

"This name has no meaning. Chinese names must have meaning."

I told Mr. Wu the name given to me by my teachers who had taught me Chinese was a transliteration of my real name. Because it sounds like my English name, other students in the class were able to remember it more easily.

My explanation did not move him to acceptance. He shook his head and said, "I will give you a new name, a name that has good meaning." Hence, I became Sheng Kailan, which roughly translates to an energetic or flourishing orchid about to open. According to Mr. Wu, the name meant I was a woman on the verge of great things. *OK, I'll take it.* Maybe this new name was an auspicious beginning to my tenure as Legat Beijing.

Mr. Zhang raced around the table with his glass in one hand and a bottle of baijiu, a clear distilled liquor which is about 50 percent alcohol, in the other. Baijiu is the most popular liquor in China and this particular bottle was distilled in the village of Maotai in Guizhou. The occasion was Chinese New Year, and all my Chinese counterparts were in high spirits. Baijiu is served in tiny glasses that are about the size of two thimbles. When toasted with a glass of baijiu, one is supposed to knock it back in one shot. I had already learned during my time in Beijing that baijiu can taste a bit like jet fuel smells. However, since I had been lucky enough to attend quite a few formal dinners where only the best was served, I hadn't had to consume too much rot-gut white lightning. This particular baijiu was really smooth and, therefore, dangerous.

The Chinese New Year event was also attended by my counterparts from other embassies in Beijing, including Great Britain, Australia, New Zealand, Germany, and France. Not much food had been consumed, although dish after dish kept arriving on the table. I'm not sure why, but this particular table was long and rectangular, more in the western style of dining, versus the Chinese style—a huge round table with a lazy Susan in the middle. The toasts began shortly after everyone had arrived and it was considered rude to not participate. You were expected to drink after each toast, and at some point, make your own toast to the hosts and the fellow attendees . . . one by one.

By the time Mr. Zhang was singing my praises as a "good drinker," my Chinese counterparts were all swaying, red-faced and smiling, racing from one side of the table to the other to stand behind the person they were toasting. Eventually we were all on our feet, glasses in the air, toasting "Xinnian Kauile"—Happy New Year—to each other.

I looked around the table. I seemed to be the only person not fazed by all the alcohol, other than my Assistant Legal Attaché, who was Mormon and did not drink. The Chinese are a bit suspicious of anyone who doesn't drink so they had chosen to ignore Ryan during the festivities. He remained seated, sampling the plates of food, ignored by the rest of the crowd.

Calculating in my head, I figured I had consumed about forty glasses of baijiu but for some reason, I remained clear-headed. I was always studious about participating in toasts at dinner functions while not drinking too much. I knew I had to be careful about saying something I should not, inadvertently providing a tidbit of classified information to a foreign government willing to use nefarious means to obtain valuable information. During this celebration, I had consumed more alcohol than any other time in Beijing. Yet, the baijiu had done its best on the rest of the group but left me steady as a tree.

I smiled at Mr. Zhang and said, "Mr. Zhang, do you know what they say where I come from? When someone can really drink and not get drunk, we say they have a 'hollow leg.'" It took some explaining before they understood what a hollow leg meant, but once they did, laugher ensued and I instantly became Kongtui Kailan, which roughly translates to "Hollow-Leg Kathy."

Shortly after my anointing, the party started to break up and Ryan and I headed to the embassy vehicle waiting to take us home. As we were about to drive away, Mr. Zhang came racing out to the car with two red and gold boxes in his hands.

"Kailan, Kailan, wait!"

Ryan rolled down the window and Mr. Zhang passed the two boxes over to me.

"You are the best drinker we've ever met. This is our gift to you." I looked at the label and realized he had given me two bottles of the highest quality baijiu I had ever been served.

I arrived back at my apartment and stepped inside, still feeling normal, still feeling like I had full control over my limbs, my voice, and my reason. Keith, sitting on the couch waiting for me, immediately said, "What have you been up to? You smell like a distillery."

I walked to our bedroom and sat down on the edge of the bed. I could hear Keith's voice asking, "Have you had anything to eat?" The bones in my body seemed to melt at once. All I remember next is falling backwards on the mattress. Light clicked off in my brain as I passed out, oblivious to the world.

The next morning when I got up, the suit and overcoat I had worn home were draped over a chair. I could smell them a mile away. I decided a "hollow leg" just might be the best asset to have when trying to prevent yourself from letting your guard down and giving away secrets.

CHAPTER THIRTY-FOUR

WOLVES, VODKA, AND TIME

★★★

"Maybe during one of your next visits, Miss Kathy, we could take you wolf hunting."

I looked down at the foot-long haunch I had been gnawing on. *Did I just eat a wolf?* My brain reeled through photos of wolves I had seen and thought, *Nah!* Wolf legs are long and skinny, designed for speed. Whatever I was clutching in my greasy fingers was far too meaty.

After I had been seated for lunch, a Fred Flintstone–sized platter had landed in front of me. There were only two things on the plate, one of which smelled like a small pile of pickled cabbage and carrots. The second appeared to be the leg of some animal I couldn't identify. A tall, slim bottle of unopened vodka was placed to my right, along with a tiny glass. I looked around the table and noticed each place setting had its own bottle of vodka. Clearly, I was in new territory.

"Miss Kathy, you are welcome to use a knife and fork, but we eat with our fingers here." Temujin demonstrated by picking up his own haunch with both hands and biting into the steaming flesh. He looked up at me, chin shining with grease, and gave me a closed-mouth smile while chewing rapidly.

"Hey, I'm from the land of fried chicken, which we consider to be finger-licking good. When in Rome . . ." I gripped my own haunch with both hands and bit into some of the tenderest meat I had ever eaten.

Now sated by a full belly of meat, the wolf comment came as a surprise. I gave a sideways glance at my own personal bottle of vodka. *OK, only a third gone. I can't be that drunk . . . yet.*

"Wolf hunting?" I asked, knowing by the greasy grins on their faces they were more than happy to elaborate.

"Yes, Miss Kathy, we have an infestation of wolves here and we hunt them down with bow and arrow. They kill our sheep and goats and horses. It is quite a fun sport. Maybe you would like to go with us."

For some reason, I have always had a soft spot for wolves. Everything I've read about them indicates they are highly intelligent and communicate within the pack to ensure their survival. I could sympathize with the farmers and ranchers who lost cattle and stock to this wily predator, but something inside me understood that wolves are slowly losing their place in the world and the survival instinct runs deep in their bones.

"Well, sure, that would be interesting. But do I have to kill a wolf myself? Can't I just watch?"

Hmm . . . wolf hunting. Not something I had considered that morning as I had stared out the airplane window on my flight from Beijing, looking out over the seemingly infinite, undulating waves of grasslands that had given Mongolia its horse-riding nomadic culture. This was my first official visit as the FBI Legat. In addition to my duties in China, I was responsible for all liaison and investigations in Mongolia. I was here to meet my counterparts from the Mongolian National Police Agency, their FBI equivalent, and General Intelligence Agency, Mongolian's equivalent to the CIA.

In my previous postings, I had found that first meetings usually occurred over a lively and prolonged meal introducing the newcomer to the food and tradition of the country. Mongolia proved to be no different. After being picked up at the airport, I had been driven out of Ulaanbaatar in a four-wheel drive vehicle on roads that were paved but had seen better days. Mongolia has few highways, most of which lead to and from Ulaanbaatar, the capital of the country. Although Ulaanbaatar was not an attractive city, it had several beautiful temples and monuments. Much of it was built with gray blocks, square and squat, without thought to architectural aesthetics. In many areas, it looked exactly like the Soviet era concrete jungle it was. Occasional billboards within the city could be seen advertising cell phones and other paraphernalia used by city dwellers, all in Cyrillic. During my later visits, I realized my first impression of Ulaanbaatar had been dulled by its surroundings.

Mongolia's redeeming qualities were in the beauty of its landscape, pristine and unblemished. No roads, billboards, or strip malls marred the landscape as far as the eye could see, which stretched in unbroken waves until it reached the mountains in the far western part of the country. I longed to get on a horse and ride off into the silent grasslands of the least densely populated country in the world.

This visit was my third attempt to introduce myself to the Mongolians. My first two flights had been canceled due to high winds sweeping across the steppes. Apparently, wind shears in this part of the world can knock a plane completely off course, causing crashes and skids across the runway when landing in the outskirts of the city.

The Mongolians were also a surprise to me. My first and only introduction to Mongolia had been through the legends and stories I had read about Genghis Khan. Genghis and his horde of nomads had been portrayed as blood-thirsty heathens, sweeping down into China, raping and pillaging everything in their path, only to make a sharp right and head west, to the horror of the European continent. Genghis himself was portrayed as powerful and formidable—wispy beard and moustache on round features.

The men sitting at the table with me, however, were completely different from what I had expected. Instead of the short, oftentimes wiry to frail stature and Chinese features I had become accustomed to in Beijing, these men—and they were all men—were *big*. Tall and broad and strong. Although black hair was ubiquitous, their features were slightly more Caucasian than Asian, lending them a passing resemblance to Native Americans.

This observation played out during one of our first conversations while sitting around the long rectangular dining table in a low-roofed building that resembled a log cabin renovated to appear more urban. A large fireplace dominated one wall. Curiosity had gotten the better of my counterparts; as soon as we were seated, I had been peppered with questions.

"Miss Kathy, where are you from?"

"Miss Kathy, why did you join the FBI?"

"Miss Kathy, do you find Mongolia to be beautiful?"

"Miss Kathy, who are your ancestors?"

Ancestors? That was a new one for me. People in the United States often ask where your family is from, especially if you're Caucasian, which assumes that ancestry will most likely be European in origin. But I had never had it phrased in quite the same way the Mongolians approached it. Ancestors. The word made me feel as if I should be circling a campfire out on the steppes, a yurt pitched behind me, short and sturdy Mongolian horses grazing nearby.

"Well, I've been told I am part Cherokee on my father's side, but I have no proof other than family conjecture, although my father looks Native American."

"Miss Kathy, you are our sister!" Smiles and nods in my direction, whispered murmurings amongst the group. The Mongolian language sounds like a combination of hisses and gurgles, as if they had gathered a pocket of saliva on either side of their tongue and were trying to talk through it. As I listened to their exchanges, I felt a smile cross my face, partly from the vodka I had been consuming and partly because I recognized the thrill that always runs through my body when I happen upon something unexpected, something different, something I had only dreamed of encountering. Here were a people who lived in one of the most remote regions, at the top of the world, surrounded by a way of life that knew its earliest days almost 3,000 years ago. I was thrilled to be included in their circle.

"What do you mean, I am your sister?" I asked. They all started chattering at once, each talking over the other in their hiss-and-gurgle-accented English.

"Miss Kathy, Mongolians believe we are the ancestors of the Native Americans. When land was connected over the Bering Strait, it was the Mongolians who crossed into North America and settled your country. We are also brothers and sisters to the Koreans. Mongolians traveled into Korea many centuries ago and gave the Koreans their culture. So now you are sister to Mongolians *and* Koreans."

All this was relayed by Temujin, the senior representative and apparent spokesman for the group. His smiled broadly at me, black eyes disappearing in epicanthic folds beneath his dark, caterpillar eyebrows. His whole face took on a blissful Buddha-like expression.

Toasts of vodka ensued as they welcomed me into their "family," followed by even more toasts when I informed them I was from Kentucky, the land of swift and graceful horses. Being a nomadic people, they revered horses. I had just solidified my place around their campfire forever.

Easing into work territory after all the food and conversation, thinking their consumption of vodka might smooth the way, I asked, "How would you like to work with the FBI in the future? Are there any investigations in which we can assist? Is there any training you would like to receive from us?"

With the exception of China, most other countries I had covered were eager to work with the FBI, to take advantage of resources offered, and to learn as much as possible about new investigative techniques. Why would Mongolia be any different?

The group fell silent and glanced around at each other. *Well, shit, now I've gone and ruined it.* I had been chastised by my counterparts in Bhutan that Americans don't bother to get to know each other before doing business. I understood this was a cultural concept throughout Asia. But my time was limited, and I didn't know when I would or could make the trip back to Ulaanbaatar from Beijing in the near future. I needed to know what they wanted or expected of me during my tenure as Legat.

Temujin spoke up. "Miss Kathy, several years ago one of our high-level officials was assassinated and we were never able to find his killer. Do you think you could help with that?"

"Well, I can certainly try. What did you have in mind?" I asked, confident that the FBI would surely be able to shed some light on their dilemma.

"Could you turn back the time on one of your satellites and find out who killed him?"

Not sure I had heard correctly, for the second time that day I glanced at my bottle of vodka, now absolutely positive I had imbibed far more than I realized. *Nope, only two-thirds gone.* By normal alcohol consumption, I should have been under the table slumbering away, the reek of alcoholic fumes wafting around my head. But Mongolian vodka, pronounced *Chinggis* Khan vodka, not *Genghis* Khan vodka—I had been corrected—was both smooth and slightly sweet. Rather than feeling like I had been guzzling jet fuel, I felt as if a warm furry animal had settled somewhere in the vicinity of my midsection and was purring away in contentment. Plus, I had the advantage of a hollow leg.

Straining to conceal the *What the fuck?* I was thinking on the inside, I diplomatically said, "No, no, I don't think our satellites can turn back time." *Wow, I've met foreign law enforcement who thinks the FBI is pretty badass and can do just about anything, but this takes the cake. I wonder what else they think we can do?*

I was pretty sure they meant to ask if we could obtain digital information from a satellite feed. But, trying to make light of the situation, I laughed. "You know, it would be pretty amazing if we could turn back time. The mystery of who killed John F. Kennedy could finally be solved."

My comment was met with blank stares, probably more from *not* believing the FBI couldn't turn back time than not really knowing or caring who John F. Kennedy was.

Realizing I had just lost my audience, at least for this visit, I nevertheless felt a combination of warmth and relaxation completely out of character for me in these situations. I glanced at my vodka bottle. Shit, almost empty! I had completely forgotten that I was flying back to Beijing in the late afternoon. I looked at my watch and realized with horror that I was about to miss my flight.

Relaying this information to Temujin, they all hopped up as one and headed for the door. Temujin could tell I was not only in a hurry, but less than steady on my feet. I had gotten cocky. Knowing Chinese baijiu could have little effect on me, I assumed Mongolian vodka would be the same. Although the Mongolians had consumed just as much, if not more, vodka than I had, they appeared alert and battle ready. Perhaps their nomadic metabolism coupled with living in an extreme environment had provided them with an immunity to the mind and body altering influences of alcohol.

Temujin said, "Don't worry, Miss Kathy. We'll call ahead to the airport and have them hold the plane for you."

In a country of less than three million people, half of whom lived within the capital city of Ulaanbaatar, the fact that the national police could hold an international flight to await my drunken arrival most definitely penetrated my vodka-induced brain fog.

True to their word, Temujin and his Mongolian horde had saved the day. Boarding last on my flight, I made my wobbly walk of shame down the aisle. All eyes were turned in my direction, not with hostility, as would happen in the United States if one self-centered passenger caused that delay and inconvenience. Rather, I was looked at with a curiosity I had come to recognize. Asian eyes laser focused on a tall, slightly tipsy white woman wearing what appeared to be a man's suit.

As I slid into my seat and buckled up, my last thought before drifting into a tipsy slumber was *What would I do first if I could turn back time?*

PART FIVE

BEYOND THE HORIZON

CHAPTER THIRTY-FIVE

WHO ARE YOU?

★★★

*Occasionally I'll be sitting somewhere, and I'll be
listening to someone perhaps not saying the kindest
things about me. And I'll look down and I'll sort of
pinch my skin to make sure it has the requisite thickness
I know Eleanor Roosevelt expects me to have.*
—Hillary Clinton

One day, when I was stationed in New Delhi, I found myself sidling around the duck pond—the pool in the middle of the embassy atrium—during a spectacular monsoon downpour. The US Embassy in Delhi was designed by Edward Stone, the same architect who designed the Kennedy Center in Washington, DC. The center atrium was originally open to the sky until ducks decided to fly into the pond to splash around, followed by a messy shit along the edge of the white marble pool, which was drastically slippery when wet. People had slipped on the duck shit, only to fall into the pool, which became brown and green sludge after a long season of monsoon rains. By the time I arrived, the opening had been covered with netting. However, during rainy season, it was prudent to step close to the walls—an adventure in itself—as the walls were usually covered with the skittering of dozens of bright green geckos.

As I was stepping along to avoid both the sheets of rain and the wet marble around the duck pond, one of the administrative staff from the Regional Security Office (RSO) popped out her door and saw me mincing along. As she followed along behind, she said, "You know, we were all talking about you at lunch the other day. We decided you walk like a cop."

I didn't know who the "we" specified in her sentence was, but I was pretty sure it was the little gossip cabal I had seen her with in the embassy restaurant.

Not really giving a shit that they talked about me, but curious what "walking like a cop" meant, I asked, "What do you mean?"

"Well, you walk around like you own the place."

I wasn't sure how she and her little gang of gossips could have come to that conclusion. The monsoon season had started exactly one week after my arrival in Delhi and I, like everyone else, either tiptoed around the duck pond to avoid a dunking, or ran through the puddles of rain when going from one building to the next in order to avoid a drenching, which was an exercise in futility on most days. I looked over my shoulder at her and shrugged without comment.

The way I'm perceived physically has resonated in how both men and women view me. Numerous people in my life have commented on the way I walk or rather the attitude I have when I walk. People who know me say they can recognize me by the sound of my footsteps. As early as high school, I was told I walked the hallways with my head held high, like I was "stuck up" and "better than everyone else." I wasn't. I was just shy, and my composure was my protection. Apparently, I started building a shield at a very young age.

Part of the shield I had built around myself, after joining the FBI, involved the way I dressed. Early in my career, I wore business suits with slacks and sometimes business suits with skirts. My skirt-wearing habit had come to a speedy halt after my time in the New York office. Riding the subway in panty-hose and high heels was hazardous on a good day. What changed my wardrobe from skirts to all pants was the fact that every single day, someone's briefcase would tear a long rip in my pantyhose. Tired of buying new pantyhose on a daily basis, I had switched to all business suits with pants.

Over the years, I had established a uniform for myself, which consisted of a dark suit and a white or light color tailored cotton shirt. My "freak flag," to borrow from David Crosby, was my jewelry, which became my personal statement, the one item I wore that revealed an aspect of my personality, while adding a feminine touch to my ensemble. This was a subconscious choice until one day in the San Francisco office, one of the other women I worked with asked, "Just how many white shirts do you have?"

"Maybe twenty. It makes it easy for me to get dressed every day. I don't have to think about it."

"Yeah, but you show your personality with your jewelry. I always look forward to seeing what jewelry you wear every day."

After graduating from the FBI Academy, I had always tried to wear clothing that covered my cleavage, didn't bare my arms too much, or wasn't too tight on my body. I did not want to stand out and I didn't want anyone to truly know me. My exterior has always been completely different from who I am on the inside. I wanted to be taken seriously. As the years passed, without even noticing, my wardrobe became more severe and businesslike.

A few weeks into my tenure in Delhi, my cook and maid, Elaine, stopped me one morning as I was leaving for work. She stood in the doorway, wringing her hands in front of her, looking down at her feet. She bobbled her head and in her singsong voice said, "Madam, we are all very concerned."

"Who is *we* and what are you concerned about, Elaine?" Was this one of those tidbits of gossip people had warned me about, which could spread throughout the embassy grapevine like wildfire? I tried to be professional with Elaine and our gardener and driver, but Keith and I were uncomfortable with the idea of having household staff. Yet they were invaluable to us because I worked long hours and traveled for days at a time to the other countries I covered while Keith worked at the embassy with the State Department.

Keith and I did not know how to navigate the open-air markets where fly-swarmed animal carcasses hung from the rafters, and vegetables and fruit were displayed in boxes above dirt floors, but Elaine did. Our food had to be cleaned with a solution of Clorox water and rinsed with distilled water from the tank on the roof of our house before being cooked, a process with which we were completely unfamiliar. Because we felt guilty for having help, Keith and I had probably overcompensated with Elaine, allowing her freedom to ask a lot of personal questions and make household decisions that she hadn't cleared through us.

"Madam, me and Manish and Gaurav are concerned that you might be a hijra." Now she looked in my eyes with something akin to both pleasure and malevolence. I had already picked up on the fact that Elaine liked me a lot less than she liked Keith. Keith was home more than I was, and having a big personality, he had befriended her and her family, all of whom lived in the apartment attached to the back of our house. She couldn't understand why I was the "boss" and I felt her resentment toward me in the looks she gave me, the disdain she displayed when I made a request of her, and the deference with which she acted toward Keith.

"What's a hijra, Elaine?" I was in a hurry to get to work, but now I was curious. I loved learning about India, to better work with my Indian counterparts. This might be a valuable lesson.

"A hijra is a man who wants to be woman and dresses like a woman. Maybe you are a woman who wants to be a man."

"What? Why would you think that, Elaine?" I was starting to get annoyed. I was late for work and standing outside in my business suit during monsoon season, temperatures close to 100 degrees with 100 percent humidity.

"Madam, you wear men's clothing every day. You are not feminine. You don't look like a woman." Now, I was *really* pissed.

I've been called names in my career—bitch, ball-buster, and man-hater, just to name a few. Hearing men call me hateful names always resulted in some verbal response on my part. I hadn't always been that way. I was actually a quiet, shy little girl, coming out of my shell only as I reached my twenties and gained confidence in myself and found my voice. Working in the FBI not only helped me find that voice, it forced me to become something more; someone aggressive, outspoken, and not afraid to push back against someone pushing me.

I had learned to curse, and my cursing was a point of contention for some people, particularly men and women who are not familiar with the FBI, where cursing is not uncommon. But cursing had helped me keep men at arm's-length and was a way for me (and other agents, male and female) to let off steam in a high-stress environment. Being a rapid-fire, cursing, ball-buster has been part of my protective shield. Most men aren't attracted to a strong woman with a strong voice, much less one who isn't afraid to land a few well-thought-out insults in their direction. According to Katherine Dunn in her book *On Cussing*, "When we use bad words, they may not communicate much actual content, but they can carry emotional TNT." Cursing made me less attractive to men; therefore, curbing whatever desire they might have to make advances towards me.

Yet I was still a woman and Elaine's words had sent a shiver along my skin. I felt my eyes twinge in hurt. Outside my "uniform," I loved to laugh and joke and kid around. I loved colorful clothing and jewelry and makeup. I loved being feminine, but I also loved the fact that I was tall and physically strong. Sometimes I felt like two different people warring for the same body, the same mind.

"Elaine, this is the way professional women dress in America. There's nothing wrong with what I'm wearing. I'm still a woman underneath, I promise." At that, I walked to my car before she could see how hurt I felt.

❖

While living in China, Keith and I worked in separate buildings at the US embassy in Beijing. My office was in the "classified" building, therefore inaccessible to those who did not carry a high-level security clearance. As a result, the majority of embassy staff rarely saw me. During the times I mingled with the general embassy populace, I was usually headed to a meeting. I had very little time for everyday chitchat in the central atrium, the large and airy gathering place for exchanging pleasantries or gossip. People knew I was the FBI Legal Attaché, and since that lent mystery and fear, most people were reluctant to talk to me anyway. The few times I spent outside my building and in the main building of the embassy were when I met Keith for lunch in the cafeteria.

One day, Keith and I were sitting together having lunch when a few young guys from another embassy section sat down on the other side of the table. Conversation on my part never consisted of anything but pleasantries. I was usually in a hurry to get back to work and I was always cognizant of security. Any conversations within the main building were not as secure as the building in which I worked.

Keith was well-known around the embassy. He was friendly and chatty and, because he worked on the computer systems, knew everyone. On this particular day, one of the guys looked over at Keith and asked, "Why do the two of you always sit together at lunch?" Keith, a puzzled look on his face, answered, "Because we're married." The young man sitting across from me jerked his head back as if stung by a bee. Eyes sliding over my face without meeting my eyes, he turned back to Keith and said, "You're married to *her?*" Keith, not picking up on the implied insult said, "Yeah, why?" A shrug of the shoulders was his only answer. I, however, couldn't resist giving the asshole my best "fuck you" smile, followed by a squinting stink eye. I knew what he was thinking—the discrepancy between how he, like most embassy people, perceived me, compared to the puppy-dog friendliness of Keith, made our union incomprehensible to him.

Another evening, I received a middle-of-the-night phone call from FBI Headquarters. I needed to go into my office at the embassy and read some classified traffic that was time sensitive. It was wintertime and freezing, so I threw on my sweatpants, a sweatshirt, my Uggs, a puffy down jacket, scarf, hat, and gloves and headed across the street to the embassy. My midnight treks to my office weren't unusual. My job was round-the-clock, and if something was happening on the other side of the world that I needed to know about, I had to be briefed in real time. I had gotten accustomed to few nights when I was able to sleep a whole night through without interruption.

By the time I had gotten to the Marine gate, which guarded the classified building in which I worked, I had flashed my embassy identification, buzzed myself through a dozen doors, and greeted other US Marines as well as the Chinese armed police who acted as the security force around the embassy perimeter and main gates. I had shed my hat and scarf along the way and was punching in my security code to enter my building when the Marine on duty yelled at me through the bulletproof glass. "Ma'am, who are you? You aren't allowed in this building!"

I turned to him and held up my badge, thinking it would be enough to settle him down before he came out the door at me with a weapon. "I don't recognize you. Who are you?" he said again, this time with more urgency.

What the fuck? This Marine, not much more than a kid, had spoken to me numerous times and watched me buzz myself into the building at least a dozen times a day, every day.

"I'm the FBI Legat." Exasperated, I walked closer to the glass and held my badge to give him a closer look.

"Oh. Sorry. I didn't recognize you without your . . ."—his hand waved from his face down to his stomach and back up again—". . . clothes."

I continued to buzz myself in, thinking how different I must look to him. I had pulled my hair back in a ponytail, I had no makeup on, and I was wearing shapeless clothing that made me look like a lump. This poor kid was probably traumatized, thinking that some strange woman had tried to break in to the classified building in the middle of the night. I'm not sure what might have traumatized him more, my makeup-less face or the fact that he might have to do his job and shoot me in order to safeguard some of the most highly classified information in the US intelligence community. And then I started laughing. I could only imagine the conversation that would take place the next day during the guard duty shift change. *Man, you should see what that FBI Legat looks like without her makeup.* Apparently, I can walk like I own the world, but I don't always look like it.

CHAPTER THIRTY-SIX

SIG SAUER 229

★★★

Before I left the United States, I knew very little of the security protocol that would ensue should a US Embassy compound be breached by terrorists, protesters, a foreign faction set on wreaking havoc on embassy property, or an angry mob with the intent to slaughter US citizens.

My first experience came shortly after I arrived in New Delhi when we had our first lockdown drill. A lockdown drill is when most embassy staff is directed to a "safe haven," a room or rooms in the bowels of the embassy compound where embassy personnel are to stay until the all-clear is sounded or, in the case of an actual invasion, until help arrives to evacuate US personnel.

Keith worked in another building on the embassy compound. During our drills, he was to go straightaway to one of the safe havens, while I would be provided with a weapon and remain inside the main embassy building as part of the security team, along with the Marines, Regional Security Office (RSO) personnel, and other law enforcement, such as the DEA.

Mobs are not uncommon in India. I became accustomed to reading about protests that could turn into raging violence and mayhem in a matter of minutes. The embassy decided we should conduct tabletop exercises to prepare for a potential breach of the compound. As head of agency, and head of the FBI in New Delhi, I was a key member of this exercise. Keith and I talked at great length about the possibility of a breach and what we would do if such an event should take place; he was reluctant to be separated from me. I needed him to understand that I had to do my job, regardless of what that job entailed. I could do my job better knowing he was safe, even if I was not.

One evening, I was working late in my office. My LOS had already gone home for the night. The office was quiet, as was the rest of the embassy. All at once I heard over the embassy intercom, "The embassy has been breached. The embassy has been breached!" Jolted out of what I was doing, I ran to the door and looked out to see gun-toting Marines running back and forth from office to office, all of which were located around the perimeter of the duck pond. My hands itched for a gun I didn't have, as Legats are not allowed to carry guns overseas, with the exception of a handful of embassies located in highly dangerous countries.

As one of the Marines rushed past me, I grabbed his arm and said, "What the fuck? Is the embassy surrounded? What do you want me to do?" Seemingly unconcerned that the embassy was about to be breached by some angry mob, he paused in front of me and calmly said, "Good evening, ma'am. Didn't you get the memo? We're conducting an exercise tonight. Nothing to worry about." Adrenaline rushed down my arms and legs, the initial surge of energy overridden by relief.

On subsequent nights when I worked late, I became accustomed to hearing Marines rushing by my office door, calling out commands to each other. Every now and then, one would pop his head in and let me know the embassy was "all clear."

A few years later, while stationed in Beijing, the same type of drills were conducted on a regular basis, just as in Delhi. Once again, Keith had gotten a job at the embassy and was working in the IT department. Everyone in the IT department was a cleared American as Chinese nationals were not allowed anywhere near the administrative aspects of the embassy computer systems. Still, Keith was directed to go to a "safe haven" in a different building than the one where I worked.

I had already become accustomed to leaving the embassy at night, hearing the pounding footsteps and the back-and-forth dialogue of Marines conducting their security exercises, which occurred on a more frequent basis than in Delhi. I was not surprised. The building I worked in was highly classified. Only Americans with a specific security clearance were allowed through the doors, which were guarded by a Marine post. Keith, who had obtained his security clearance in Delhi, was allowed in my building not only by virtue of his clearance, but also because he was part of the team that took care of the State Department computer systems. I told Keith that if he was anywhere near my building when the breach alarm sounded, he was to come to my office if at all possible. My building would be defended to the death, whereas the main embassy building where Keith worked would not be as secure. I had already learned this fact one day when a Marine showed up at my office door. "Ma'am, would you come pick out your weapon?"

"My weapon?" The context of what he said didn't register with me, although I had been told that those of us who would be members of the security team would be allowed to choose a weapon of their preference.

"I need you to choose your weapon if the embassy is overrun. And I need to show you where they're stored." This actually made me feel a lot better than the protocol in Delhi. There I was simply told I would be given a weapon, always unspecified. In Beijing, I was given a choice. My choices were a Sig Sauer 9mm P229 and any shotgun or rifle that might be available, preferably a Remington 870. These were my two favorite weapons, and I knew how to use them well. The likelihood of an infiltration of the US embassy was low. But if it happened, I would and could step up and protect those within its confines.

Although a gun doesn't play into an FBI's daily activities as much as one sees on TV, it is still a part of an agent's everyday life; gun paraphernalia, along with badge and credentials, are required to be carried and secured at all times. By the time I worked overseas, I had gotten over the anxiety that had plagued me at Quantico and felt confident in my ability to shoot my weapon.

But when that Marine placed the Sig Sauer in my hands, I realized I had learned to do my job with no thought of carrying a weapon. I had learned to carry words, developing relationships and liaison in the countries in which I had served overseas. I had learned that representing the FBI wasn't just about having a weapon, it was about sharing the FBI's mission, cooperating with foreign colleagues and working together.

CHAPTER THIRTY-SEVEN

INVISIBLE

★★★

The FBI's International Operations Division (IOD) is the little-known group of personnel responsible for the FBI's overseas operations, which includes the Legats. An Assistant Director (AD) is assigned to head the IOD and he or she—to my knowledge, there has never been a she—makes sure Legats are doing their jobs and, in theory, supports them in getting their jobs done. During my last two years as Legat in Beijing, Dick was my Assistant Director.

Dick came to the IOD under a cloud of rumors. Apparently, he had been caught having an affair with a female agent, who was also a subordinate. Dick was not a handsome man. He was tall and rail thin, bald, with beady eyes under a Cro-Magnon brow shelf. In his official FBI photo that was inevitably passed around after his appointment, he was smiling like he thought he was really cute. That's what happens when you abuse your position of power. Or perhaps when you stumble upon a female ambitious enough to sleep with you in order to move her own career forward. You start to think you are Brad Pitt.

In the FBI, as with almost all corporations and agencies, if you are the boss, you are not supposed to sleep with one of your subordinates. Usually, this kind of behavior would be grounds for dismissal. But Dick benefited from an activity that I had already coined a term for: the FUMU method of moving up in the FBI.

Shortly after Dick arrived in his new position in IOD, I was told by FBIHQ that he was going to travel to each region of the world and meet with all the Legats stationed in that particular region. Legats are divided into six different regions of the world: Europe, Middle East, Asia, Africa, the Americas, and Eurasia. As Legat Beijing, I was part of the Asia region. I was to join my other Asian region colleagues, twelve of us altogether, in Kuala Lumpur for a meet and greet with Dick.

At the time, out of approximately seventy Legal Attachés, I was the only female, obvious in a small crowd.

A conference room had been reserved in our hotel for the Legats to have coffee and drinks and a roundtable chat with Dick. Before entering the room, I stood outside the door and mentally put on my Stargate shield. This was emotional armor I learned about from some of my female agent friends when we were talking about being, more often than not, the only female in the room. We discussed how each of us prepared for that moment when the female steps in and all conversation stops, heads turning in her direction. The stares start at her head and end at her toes. Rarely do the stares end with a smile; some end with a smirk, depending on how fuckable she's deemed. Other men seem downright hostile. One of my friends quipped that she put on her Stargate shield so that nothing could touch her—not the stares, not the smirks, not the demeaning words that sometimes followed. I had taken her Stargate shield as my own armor.

When I entered the room, I found three or four of my colleagues already in attendance. Usually, the early ones are the ones who have strapped on the kneepads and buttered up the Chapstick, readying themselves to have their lips permanently sewn to the ass of the boss of the moment in hopes of getting a cherry-picked onward assignment. I got along pretty well with all my Legat colleagues, some better than others. There were one or two who didn't show their treacherous natures until later.

I immediately picked out Dick as he was talking loudly, drink in hand. He was in conversation with someone, so I walked over to the refreshment table, got myself a bottle of water, and waited for the "moment." The moment told me a lot. It's what happens when I, as the lone female, walk into the room. Would my new boss introduce himself as he should, as a good leader, or should I shoulder my way through the circle of ass-kissers and introduce myself to him? I watched and waited for about fifteen minutes, chatting with my coworkers. I caught Dick glancing in my direction a couple of times, only to look away quickly. Who did he think I was, the concierge, the waitress, random hotel staff? Or did he think ignoring all females after his recent conquest and subsequent slap-down would keep him out of the doghouse? I didn't know and I didn't care. The time had come to show him what a jackass he was being. I walked up to him during a pause in the surrounding lip-slurping, put my hand out, and said, "Welcome to IOD, Dick. I'm Kathy Stearman."

He looked at me blankly and said nothing. I stared at him, eyebrow raised that both stated and questioned, *Are you an idiot?* I waited and then reminded him, "I'm your Legat in Beijing . . . ?"

"Oh . . . oh, yeah. Well, um, nice to meet you." Then he turned on his heel and walked away. He didn't speak to me again that evening. Apparently, he deemed me invisible.

A few months later, I was back in Washington, DC, at FBIHQ for our annual Legat Conference, two long weeks of training that allowed me to catch up with friends and colleagues in the area, but also took me away from work in Beijing. Flying into Washington from the exact other side of the world left me jet-lagged and less than willing to tolerate the bullshit of watching almost seventy men jockey for facetime with the powers that be to campaign for their next promotion.

During these annual conferences, it was tradition that the Legats would have a group photo taken with Director Mueller. A couple of mornings after arriving, we were told to meet at the appointed location for the obligatory photo. The photographer, a female, always put me in the front row. I wasn't sure why until one year she whispered to me, "You represent all us females so I'm going to make sure you're out front, right beside the Director." Then she gave me a wink and a smile and continued to order the men into their places. By the smile on her face, I think she enjoyed telling the guys what to do and where to go.

I was standing in my front-row spot, with an empty place to my left waiting for the Director to arrive, when Dick ran through the door and slid into the space that placed him between me and the Director's spot. He wiggled his shoulders and ass, turned to me with his possum-faced grin, and said in a flirtatious voice, "Now don't pinch me on the butt, OK?"

My "I don't give a shit, I'm jet-lagged, tired, and overly done with your male chauvinist bullshit" attitude kicked in. I looked at him with my best stink eye and said, "Really? You actually just said that to me?" He took another look at me and I could see his jaw clamp shut. A "Fuck, I'm fucked" look crossed his face as he realized I was not just some random female, but one of his Legats. I stared directly into his eyes, not bothering to hide my contempt. He stared back, wide-eyed, as if caught in the gaze of a basilisk. Would that I could have rendered him immobile with one look. Director Mueller's arrival finally tore his gaze away from me as he couldn't resist turning his sycophantic, smarmy smile at the Director. Apparently, the opportunity to kiss the ass of Director Mueller was stronger than the fear of a basilisk. As soon as the photo was taken, Dick trotted away behind the Director as fast as he could go.

Dick would display his cowardly backside to me one more time in my not-too-distant future.

CHAPTER THIRTY-EIGHT

KARMIC JUSTICE

★ ★ ★

The price one pays for pursuing a profession or
calling is an intimate knowledge of its ugly side.
James Baldwin

"Kathy, this is Susannah. Would you please hold for the Director?" Susannah was Robert Mueller's personal assistant. I didn't even know her last name. She was like Madonna or Bono. She needed no other name. I called her "god." As I heard the click on the other end of my FBI cell phone, I lowered it away from my mouth and said quietly to Keith, "Well, this is it. Start packing your bags."

I had learned early in my career that the personal assistant, almost always a woman, to the Special Agent in Charge (SAC), the head of an FBI field division, was the gatekeeper. Though I was always polite to everyone, I made it my mission to be damn polite to whoever wielded the power to grant entrance. As the Director's gatekeeper, Susannah had become immune to charm and flattery. I'm sure she had seen her share of groveling, ass-kissing men, doing their best to wheedle their way into the inner sanctum. In the parlance of my dad, she was St. Peter, allowing entrance to only the deserving few.

As I waited for Director Mueller to fire me over the phone, I felt nothing. I was exhausted; mentally, physically, and emotionally. I had reached a level of acceptance that left me numb. Hearing Susannah's polite but abrupt greeting didn't leave me with the usual quake in my stomach. This was a phone call I had been expecting all week, which had begun in Beijing with the official visit of Attorney General (AG) Eric Holder.

As I was the highest-level representative for the Department of Justice at the US Embassy in Beijing, the Attorney General's office tasked me to arrange an official visit for AG Holder. Normally, the embassy would have had DOJ's Regional Legal Advisor handle the visit; however, the former advisor had departed post and her successor would not arrive until the day before AG Holder. The entirety of the visit landed on my shoulders.

The arrival of a high-level US official to an overseas embassy requires an enormous amount of work months in advance, especially at a high-threat post like Beijing. When I was first tasked to organize the visit, I called my unit at FBIHQ in Washington, DC, the International Operations Division, to ask if someone of higher rank should organize the visit. All other work conducted by my office, especially time-sensitive investigations, would still need to be handled in addition to preparation for the AG's visit. I had handled visits by Director Mueller before, but the Attorney General—the head of the Justice Department and seventh in line to the President of the United States—was another level of importance in the hierarchy. I needed to arrange meetings for AG Holder's visit with the highest levels of the Chinese government.

Dave, the agent in IOD who was responsible for overseeing the administrative issues for Legats covering Asia, said I could handle the visit or not, it was up to me. I was a little shocked, but not surprised by Dave's response; I had received little support from him since my arrival in Beijing. Even though the US Embassy Beijing was one of the most critical posts in the world, for the FBI and many other government agencies, I had felt ignored by my own agency.

While Legat New Delhi, I had learned to navigate the intricacies of IOD's administration, so I coped well with the lack of support. I had a good deal of autonomy handling the affairs of my office. I knew Dave would take care of his "boys" and make sure they had everything they needed. I was fine as long as he stayed out of my hair. Dave was ambitious and had already finished one Legat assignment. He was biding his time back at FBIHQ until he could get another overseas posting.

Even though I was aware that IOD didn't concern themselves overly much with Beijing, I maintained good liaison with my Chinese counterparts. It was also important that I work well with the US Ambassador in Beijing and all government agencies represented there, the State Department ██████, in particular. I knew Director Mueller considered China to be of utmost importance to the investigative and intelligence mission of the FBI.

Receiving no further guidance from FBIHQ, I proceeded to spend two months working with my small staff of three—LOS, ALAT, and analyst/translator—while planning the visit. On any normal day, I would go into my office with a full day planned, only to be surprised with something that was time-sensitive, or a request from another agency, or a last-minute meeting with my Chinese counterparts. Our regular workload did not cease, nor was it pushed aside to make room for AG Holder's visit. I was determined everything should go smoothly, so I held daily briefings with my staff to review official meeting requests with high-level Chinese government officials, to ensure an official invitation was sent by the Chinese government to AG Holder, to author research papers and talking points for AG Holder to review, and determine which issues were important for both countries to discuss during the visit. This last topic involved a great deal of negotiation since the US had specific issues of concern, while the People's Republic of China would have a different set of concerns to address.

Emails between my office and the AG's DOJ staff became a daily occurrence, as topics for discussion were introduced and discarded. My research papers and talking points became a fluid process that began and ended every day and left me tossing and turning every night, trying to bullet-point in my head all the things that could go wrong and inventing contingency plans for unexpected events. As it turns out, I omitted one contingency that had never entered my mind.

During the race to the arrival day, I had kept Dave in IOD informed of everything I had been doing. There had been very little feedback, simply an "OK, thanks for letting us know" kind of response. About one week before AG Holder's arrival, the Attorney General's security detail sent an advance team to Beijing to assess the meeting locations, the hotel where the AG Holder would be staying, and meet with everyone from my team involved with the visit, as well as those handling security from the Chinese government. The Attorney General's security detail consisted of FBI agents assigned to the protection detail on a permanent, rotating basis, all of whom had received specialized training in personal protection. Having worked with protection details for Director Mueller, I anticipated no problems with AG Holder's security staff.

During the week leading up to the visit, my office worked long hours with the advance team. We were all under a lot of stress, but I never sensed there were problems. No issues popped up regarding the itinerary over which we had labored long and hard for months. Justin, the head of the advance team, told me I was one of the best Legats he had ever worked with. He was pleased with the level of assistance my office had given him and his team in order to ensure the security of AG Holder and his entourage.

On the day of AG Holder's arrival, I waited at the VIP section of the Beijing airport with several members of the advance team, along with members of China's MPS security detail. The MPS detail all spoke English so there was no need for the interpreter, Simon, to attend to AG Holder after he deplaned; the AG would immediately be taken in a bulletproof SUV to his hotel.

Simon, an employee of the Department of State and Ambassador Jon Huntsman's official interpreter, was a linguistic genius and spoke impeccable Mandarin Chinese. During his assignment to Beijing, he had interpreted for several US presidents and other high-level US officials who visited China. Simon was well-respected by both the American embassy staff as well as the Chinese. I had made sure to introduce Simon to the advance team so they would be familiar with his face and his physical appearance as he would be the person walking and sitting closest to AG Holder for the duration of the visit.

As soon as AG Holder's plane arrived, I stepped outside the VIP terminal to meet Bud, the head of AG Holder's accompanying security detail, followed by a short greeting with AG Holder. During Director Mueller's visits, I rode in the vehicle with him so that I could provide nonclassified information and points of interest along the route from the airport to the hotel in downtown Beijing. AG Holder's staff had already told me he did not want me riding in the vehicle with him. Instead, I rode in a passenger van with members of the security detail.

At the hotel, AG Holder was escorted to the floor assigned to him, his entourage, and his security detail. The entire floor was blocked off for the group, and a command post had been set up to monitor, 24/7, anyone coming and going on the floor. As I walked down the hallway, checking on operations and making sure everything was running smoothly, I noticed several members of the security detail, which had just arrived with AG Holder, looked at me as if they didn't know who I was. Entering the command post, I observed photos of the entourage hung on the wall, but no photos of the Legat Office staff nor any of the State Department employees who would be taking part in the visit. I commented to the detail member sitting at the desk that he needed to make sure everyone was aware of the Legat Office personnel so we could be easily identified. He didn't comment, giving me a look of pure boredom. I went in search of Justin to make sure he briefed the new arrivals on the identities of all participants and found him hurrying toward me. The head of the Chinese security had tried to get on the elevator with AG Holder when he entered the hotel and Justin was concerned. I told Justin I would take care of it and tracked down the Chinese security officer to explain that, although I was aware he was accustomed to handling security for members of his own country, it was US policy that a high-level official such as the Attorney General would be escorted by US security detail *only*. He apologized and said he understood.

The first day of AG Holder's visit began early the next morning. After several meetings with US Embassy personnel, I escorted AG Holder to my office so that he could make a secure phone call. While he was on the phone, I explained to Bud how the Legat Office entry and exit system worked. Bud would be escorting the Attorney General to the motorcade first, at which time I would follow, accompanied by the rest of the delegation. I told Bud that he must ███ ███ ███ ███ ███████████████████████████████ which caused a ten-minute delay in leaving the embassy for the first meeting.

For those who have never participated in or organized a high-level meeting in a foreign country, every single minute is accounted for. Streets and roads and highways are shut down, stop lights turned off, and miles of security personnel posted along the planned route. To shut down a main thoroughfare in a city like Beijing, with a population over 20 million people, disrupts the entire city's transportation process. Ensuring the shutdown time is limited is extremely important to the city's commerce and daily activities.

I finally arrived at the motorcade, just outside one of the main entrances to the US Embassy and climbed into a van with the interpreter, Simon; the head of the DEA, Brad; and the remainder of the delegation. The Attorney General rode ahead of us in an armored vehicle, along with Ambassador Huntsman and members of the security detail. The first meeting was with a member of the Supreme People's Procuratorate, China's highest-level agency that handles investigations and prosecutions. I made sure to accompany Simon to stand by the Attorney General, as Simon would be glued to him for the remainder of the meeting and all subsequent meetings with foreign officials. As we strolled toward the Attorney General, we walked past several members of the security detail, all of whom noted our passage through the group.

When the meeting ended, the delegation regrouped at the motorcade to head out to the Ministry of Public Security (MPS) headquarters. The MPS is China's police and security authority; several MPS officers had been my main contacts and liaison partners. I had worked hard to develop liaison and create goodwill between our two agencies. It had taken me weeks to arrange a meeting between the AG and the Minister of the MPS, who in the power structure of the PRC, holds a higher rank than other ministers. In China, he is responsible for the US equivalent of all police and security agencies, apart from the CIA, whose equivalent is the Ministry of State Security (MSS). This meeting was crucial.

Arriving at the MPS, I passed several members of the Attorney General's security detail as I walked behind AG Holder and Simon into the meeting room. The detail was designated to stand outside the room for the duration of the meeting, then escort AG Holder to a lunch banquet immediately following. The meeting with the MPS lasted about an hour, although Ambassador Huntsman departed early for a previously scheduled engagement, so he would not be attending the lunch banquet.

After the meeting, the Minister and AG Holder exited the room to walk to the banquet, which was a five-minute stroll from the building where the meeting had taken place. I was relieved the meeting had gone well and was feeling pretty confident that everything was running smoothly.

I, along with the rest of the delegation, followed a short distance behind AG Holder and headed to the bank of elevators at the end of the hall. When I got about ten feet from the elevators, I heard a scuffle and raised voices. I was standing by several members of the AG's detail as well as Brad. I heard a voice yell loudly, "But I need to do my job!" I looked over the heads of the delegation in front of me and watched as Simon slammed into the wall opposite the elevator door, which at that exact time began to close. I ran up to Simon, who was holding his hand to his shoulder, his suit jacket ripped and hanging off his back. He told me that Bud, the head of the security detail, would not let him on the elevator with the Attorney General, the Minister, Bud, and the Minister's Chinese interpreter. Shocked at the level of violence and misconduct I had witnessed, I told Simon to take the next elevator down and hurry to catch up with AG Holder. The knot that had started to loosen in my chest was suddenly smothered by my own hubris that all was going well.

After I reached the ground floor and was walking toward the banquet, Justin, from the advance team, caught up to me and told me AG Holder's security detail did not want Simon to be interpreter anymore. When I asked why, Justin simply said, "Bud thinks Simon is dangerous. Bud wants him replaced by someone else."

As I stared at Justin, I couldn't tell if my anger or my panic was winning the war of which had the tighter squeeze on my esophagus. I told Justin, in words too clipped to be misunderstood, that the banquet was about to begin, and it was impossible to replace Simon. Justin wasn't pleased and told me Bud would be unhappy.

The banquet was to be held in an exquisitely restored mansion located on the grounds of MPS headquarters. The exterior displayed the bright reds of lacquered paint and curled eaves of ceramic tiles. The interior was a treasure trove of Chinese art and hand-painted ceramics located on pedestals and walls of the main dining area. I had been fortunate to have already attended functions at this location, so I had been looking forward to another opportunity to explore this elegant display of Chinese architecture.

As I was about to enter the building, already running behind and feeling mortified to be the last person to show up at an official function, two MPS officials pulled me aside and told me the Minister was very upset about the incident outside the elevator and wanted an apology and explanation. I tried to explain that it was an internal miscommunication amongst the Attorney General's personal security detail and that it in no way had anything to do with how the MPS had conducted the morning's activities. Despite my attempt to soothe their justifiably ruffled feathers, they insisted on an apology. I asked what form the apology should take, written or verbal, and who the apology should come from. By this time, we had all entered the main dining room and I had been led to a far corner where I was now surrounded by another, even higher-level MPS official who demanded an explanation. I again apologized and said it was an internal matter and I was taking care of it. Our low-voiced conversation was now noticed by both the Minister and the Attorney General, so I asked if we could proceed with the banquet with the promise I would take care of the matter on my end. That seemed to appease for the moment and the banquet proceeded without further incident.

After the banquet, our itinerary planned for AG Holder to return to his hotel for a break before an afternoon meeting with a Communist Standing Committee member, a political position even more powerful and influential than the MPS Minister.

The Attorney General was escorted to his room and I went to the executive lounge where Simon was waiting with Brad from the DEA. I asked Simon to explain to me in detail what had happened at the elevator. Simon told me, upon exiting the meeting room, he was walking by the Attorney General's side when one of AG Holder's security detail had grabbed Simon and asked his identity. Simon explained he was the interpreter and continued toward the elevator. When Simon tried to enter the elevator, already occupied by the Attorney General, the Minister, the Minister's interpreter, and Bud, Simon was grabbed from behind and pulled into the hallway. At this point, Simon was visibly upset and his interpretation of being "pulled" into the hallway was milder than the episode I had witnessed, in which Simon had been slammed against the wall hard enough to rip his suit jacket off his back.

I told Simon I was looking into the matter and asked if he had hurt his shoulder. He said he would go to the embassy's medical unit later in the day after he finished his interpreting duties. "I don't know what I've done wrong," he kept repeating. He asked me to find out what mistake he had committed, so he wouldn't do it again.

Simon then asked if he could sit down with the head of the detail, Bud, and talk to him. He wanted to put the incident behind him and carry on with his job. Simon then told me he planned to notify the Deputy Chief of Mission (DCM), second only to an ambassador in the diplomatic protocol chain at the embassy. I asked Simon to let me speak to the DCM first so that I could explain the entire situation, to which he agreed.

As I was talking to Simon, Justin came into the lounge and when Simon saw him, Simon moved away from my table to sit with other members of the delegation. Justin then proceeded to tell me that Bud refused to allow Simon to be present at the next meeting. He said again that Simon was unsafe and did not take orders well. Justin explained the detail did not know who Simon was at the time of the incident.

At this point, my stress level was banging on the roof of my head like one of those games of strength at a county fair. The mallet, in my case, was hitting the gong every few seconds. I sneered at Justin and said, "Really? The advance team was introduced to Simon last week. Simon walked by my side into the front door of MPS headquarters in full view of the Attorney General's detail. He sat right next to AG Holder during the entire meeting and exited the meeting room at his side. If the powers of observation of your fucking security detail can't determine who Simon was during all that time, then they should get another fucking job!"

I told Justin that Bud needed to explain to Simon what he did wrong so Simon could do his job. Justin said the Attorney General no longer wanted Simon by his side. Startled, I asked Justin to bring a leading member of the AG Holder's entourage, who hurried over to me but repeated there was nothing else he could do. At that point, I asked Justin to bring me Robert, Deputy Assistant Attorney General, the highest-level member of the Attorney General's entourage. When Robert arrived in the lounge, I reminded him that the upcoming meeting, which had taken me weeks to arrange, was with a member of the Communist Standing Party (CSP). Robert was noncommittal, but reluctantly said he would ask the AG to reconsider his decision.

While I waited for Robert's return, someone in the security detail had advised AG Holder that an FBI temporary duty employee, Lan, had been deployed to my office the week before. Lan, a native Chinese speaker, was utilized by Director Mueller whenever he traveled to China. She was assigned to the IOD section at FBIHQ and had been sent to Beijing to help out in the absence of my office manager. Lan is an excellent interpreter, but I was concerned she wouldn't have enough time to prepare as she had not familiarized herself with the talking points of the upcoming meeting. Plus, I was concerned about how the sudden change in interpreters would be perceived by the Chinese. Simon was known to the Chinese. Pulling Simon from the interpreting position would indicate to the CSP that the US didn't consider the meeting to be of significance. Protocol in China is paramount, and much time is spent on who attends a meeting, who sits where, and who gets to be seen.

Still waiting for Robert, I walked over to Simon, who was already on the phone with the DCM in rapid-fire conversation, having reneged on his promise to let me provide an explanation for the day's events to the DCM first. I asked Simon to hand me the phone and I proceeded to tell the DCM what had happened. He was agitated and told me he was going to speak with Ambassador Huntsman, who was still at another engagement, about the whole incident upon his return.

As I finished my conversation with the DCM, a staffer who had accompanied the delegation walked up to my table. I was still sitting down, going over in my head what I was going to do next. The staffer, a tall, burly male in his mid-twenties, made a point to stand as close to me as possible. He looked down at me, sneered, and said, "You'll do what we tell you to do." He then stood there and continued to glare at me. When he finally turned and walked away, Ryan, my ALAT, who had overheard, walked up and said, "What the fuck?" At that point, I couldn't help it. I started to cry. Not loud, wracking sobs, but silent, gushing tears. Ryan sat down in front of me and said, "Kat, you've got to stop crying. You've got to get yourself under control." I couldn't stop, nor did I try. The months of 24/7 work, coupled with the lack of support from my own unit at headquarters, had taken its toll. I hadn't realized how much I had been holding in until this young staffer, whose position was far inferior to that of an FBI Legat, had treated me with blatant disrespect. I grabbed a tissue out of my suit pocket and whispered, "I'm trying. I really am. I just can't stop." Ryan sat quietly by my side until Robert returned with bad news.

Robert quietly stared at my wet, red eyes but made no comment. He then explained the Attorney General wouldn't change his mind. AG Holder had said he needed to listen to his detail and trust their judgment. I told Robert that the DCM and the Ambassador were being informed of the incident and that it might be resolved if Bud took five minutes to meet with Simon. Robert just shook his head and walked away.

After wiping my face in the ladies' room, I told Simon he was no longer needed as the interpreter and arranged a car to take him back to the embassy. I contacted Lan and told her she would be interpreting for the Attorney General for the afternoon's meeting and that a car was coming to the embassy to pick her up. Despite being nervous upon arrival, Lan was calm, professional, and flawless in her interpretation for the afternoon meeting.

Later that afternoon, I called IOD to give them a verbal report of my daily activities. This was something I had done as soon as the Attorney General arrived. I knew I would be under scrutiny by headquarters with such a high-level official under my responsibility. As I relayed the day's events to Dave, who had been indifferent about my involvement in the visit from the beginning, he asked a few questions and then became quiet. He said he needed to brief Dick, Assistant Director (AD) of IOD, who oversaw all Legat operations worldwide. Already aware of Dick's reputation, I knew that it was in my best interest to put into writing everything that had happened that day, so I authored a lengthy email and sent it to IOD, copying both Dick and Dave.

That evening, I had arranged for a few Chinese vendors to set up tables in the executive lounge of the hotel where the Attorney General was staying. It was common for visitors to want to purchase pearls, silk, ceramics, and other items to buy as souvenirs. Because of the level of security required for AG Holder, he could not travel to the Chinese markets, so I brought the markets to him. The embassy had a list of vendors who provided quality jewelry and artifacts that were traditional examples of Chinese artisans. Each vendor, although well-known to the embassy and utilized for other high-level visits, was still checked through security to ensure the Attorney General's safety.

AG Holder arrived in the lounge and found a seat on a long sofa. Sitting on either side of him were Bud and other members of his security detail. The Attorney General stretched his arms along the back of the sofa and held court, laughing and chatting with the detail. Other members of the detail were sitting in chairs surrounding the Attorney General, their backs to the lounge where members of the entourage were perusing and making souvenir purchases to take home. I stood in the corner away from the group, watching quietly. No one tried to talk to me, and I didn't try to engage in conversation with anyone. I felt detached from my surroundings, but still completely aware my job was to make sure everything ran smoothly.

The next day, after a morning meeting with the Ministry of Justice, China's equivalent to the US Department of Justice, I had arranged with my Chinese counterparts for the Attorney General and his delegation to visit the Great Wall, a UNESCO World Heritage site, and one of the tourist destinations that all visitors to Beijing want to see. I had thought the afternoon would be relaxing after all the meetings and official dinners. Like most days in Beijing, the morning had dawned to the steel-gray skies of polluted air. I had gotten accustomed to the lack of sunlight in Beijing, leeching all color from the city, which now consisted mostly of modern structures built of steel and glass. Older structures such as the Forbidden City—which in rare sunlight can shine a bright orange-red—most of the time appear a drab terra-cotta, the peaked ceramic roof tiles glistening with noxious chemicals spewed out of local manufacturing plants.

The ride to the Wall was quiet. I sat in the back seat of a long twelve-seat passenger van. I spoke to no one and no one spoke to me. Actually, I don't remember any conversation at all amongst the group.

Earlier that morning, prior to the meeting with the Minister of Justice, a member of the entourage told me the Attorney General intended to contact Ambassador Huntsman to discuss Simon's dismissal as interpreter. I recall it was Robert, the Deputy Assistant AG, who communicated this to me. I had returned to my office and drafted another email to IOD detailing several additional incidents of unprofessionalism involving the security detail. Bud, the head of the detail, had told my ALAT that we should all listen to Bud as Bud was the equivalent of the thirteenth disciple. Everything he said should be taken as gospel and the Attorney General would listen to whatever advice he had to give. In addition to my email, I tried to contact Dick, the Assistant Director of IOD, to discuss what was going on in the area under my purview. His personal assistant said he was in the office but would not take my call.

I had had little sleep the past five nights, tossing and turning while my mind vibrated over the events that could and had gone wrong. I was already worn out mentally and physically from the months of planning, during which I had gotten no input from IOD, nor any guidance from the Attorney General's office, other than "just get it done." Riding in the van to the Great Wall was the most relaxed I had been in months. I existed in a place where there were no more decisions to be made, nothing more to be done; the waiting for the inevitable had drained away all emotion.

As we arrived at the portion of the Great Wall that the Attorney General would be touring, I noticed the entire region was socked in with fog. What would have been an impressive view of massive gray stones undulating over green hills and snaking down into lush valleys was a wall of thick, white mist.

Making the short climb to the lookout point that had been selected for the scenery that would have unfolded in a 360-degree panorama, I could only see a few feet in front of me. Lack of sleep and lack of appetite dragged my footsteps and I found myself lagging behind the group. I could barely see the Attorney General ahead of me, guided by one of my Chinese counterparts.

Ryan slowed down to fall into step beside me. "Are you OK, Kat?"

"Just tired. I can't breathe. I'll be fine. Go ahead and make sure everything is going as planned."

He gave me a look of concern but knew from experience he shouldn't argue with me.

A few minutes later, I finally dogged my way to the top of the viewing area. Everyone else was already assembled to ooh and aah over . . . what? There was absolutely nothing to see. Looking over the low wall, the eye met nothing but white and gray swirls of mist and fog so thick, not even the crenelated watchtowers that had provided residence and protection for soldiers guarding the kingdom could be seen.

As AG Holder and his entourage lined up along the edge of the barrier, staring over into the nothingness, I heard the guide apologize that the view was nonexistent. He proceeded to tell a short history of the Great Wall, during which time the Attorney General made polite noises and comments. The disappointment amongst his entourage was palpable.

I stood to the back of the group, recalling all the times I had traversed the Great Wall with visitors, the thrill of seeing the ancient, man-made structure disappearing over the horizon. As I was directed to step up to Attorney General Holder to have the obligatory photo taken with him, I wanted to be anywhere but there.

The next day there were no scheduled meetings. It was AG Holder's last day, and I had arranged with my Chinese counterparts for him to visit the Forbidden City. The Ming Dynasty imperial palace at the heart of Beijing is one of the most visited landmarks in all of China. On any given day, tens of thousands of tourists spend hours in the vast complex. On the day of the Attorney General's visit, the Chinese government had shut it down, allowing entrance to no one other than those included in the Attorney General's delegation. I had already visited the Forbidden City, as it is the first thing every visitor wants to see, and had acted as tour guide several times. But I found no pleasure in being able to traverse the massive stone blocks, with which the main courtyard was constructed, and see the vastness of the Hall of Supreme Harmony, not marred by flashing cameras, no selfie sticks in my face, and no ubiquitous cries of amazement of the hordes of admirers that descend every day.

Just minutes prior to leaving for the Forbidden City, I had received a phone call from Dave's boss, my Unit Chief, Jeff. Jeff told me quickly, and in unsympathetic terms, that Attorney General Holder planned to contact Director Mueller to complain that I had not been concerned about his safety during his visit. The Attorney General was planning to tell Director Mueller I had sided with an interpreter over the wishes of the security detail and my actions had put him in grave danger. Jeff said I would be removed from my position as Legat. I tried to defend myself, but Jeff cut me off, saying there was nothing he could do. This was becoming a common refrain.

Not trusting that either Dave or Jeff had relayed the incident in accurate terms, I then tried to call Dick again to explain the situation. His administrative assistant told me once again that he was in the office but would not take my call.

After the tour of the Forbidden City, the motorcade took the AG and his entourage back to the airport for departure. Pulling up to the private Gulfstream jet, I stepped out of the van I was riding in and walked to the steps of the plane. Before they stepped on board, several of the Attorney General's delegation pulled me aside to say they and other delegation members didn't agree with what "he" was planning to do to me. They told me they would try to "go to the mat" for me to ensure I wasn't punished for something I hadn't done. I made no comment. Nor did I say thank you. I simply nodded as they stepped up to the stairs.

As I turned around, the Attorney General came up to me, held out his hand, and thanked me for arranging the visit. I had had no contact with him during the entire visit. Normally, I would have provided briefings prior to each meeting. It was I, after all, who had authored his research papers and talking points, and decided which issues needed to be raised with the Chinese government. Instead, Eric Holder had surrounded himself with his detail and I had not been afforded the opportunity to do the job for which I had planned for weeks. An official visit isn't just about logistics, it's about information, and intelligence, and policy. Instead, I had been relegated to the back of the van and now was to be removed from my position.

I shook his hand, nodded at his thank-you, but said nothing. As the Attorney General climbed the stairs of the Gulfstream, I had already turned my back and was walking toward the VIP terminal.

When I got back to the office, Ryan told me the remainder of the security detail, which would fly back to the US on a different flight, had wanted to speak to him in confidence. They did not agree with how the incident had been handled, but could not speak out against Bud. They asked Ryan to apologize to me on their behalf. I looked up at Ryan standing in front of my desk. "Really?" I asked sarcastically. "Why don't you pass this on for me? I would tell them to go fuck themselves if I thought they could find their teeny, tiny little dicks."

"Come on, Kat, they don't mean it that way."

"Yeah, well I do. So, you just trot off and tell them exactly what I said because I no longer give a shit what they think, those spineless bags of shit dust."

Later that afternoon, I spent about two hours meeting with the DCM and Ambassador Huntsman. The Ambassador had asked to meet with me so I could give him a full briefing on what had occurred during the visit and wanted to learn more about the conduct of the security detail. I told the Ambassador the Attorney General was planning to have me removed from my post as he blamed me for the incident. Ambassador Huntsman was visibly ruffled and said, "That is not going to happen." The Ambassador said he wanted to speak to Director Mueller by telephone. The DCM suggested he author a letter requesting a conversation, to which the ambassador agreed. That afternoon, I emailed it to Director Mueller's office.

Before leaving my office for the day, I attempted, once again, to reach out to Dick to give him an update on the situation in Beijing. Once again, I was told by his personal assistant that he was not taking my calls.

Later that evening, as Keith and I were laid out on the sofas in our apartment, me staring at the ceiling in a semi-coma of lethargy, I received the phone call from Susannah. I held my breath for the inevitable.

"Kathy, this is Robert Mueller. How are you doing this evening?"

"I'm fine, sir." I waited. I knew from previous experience that Director Mueller did not appreciate or welcome extraneous details. He would choose the questions he felt relevant. There was no need for me to expound on the situation.

"I understand you've had a bit of trouble over there in Beijing. I received the Ambassador's letter and I apologize that you've had to deal with this situation. I would like to speak to the Ambassador. Would you be able to arrange a telephone call?"

"Yes, sir, I can. Would you like to speak to him this evening?"

"Yes, please. And, once again, thank you for dealing with this situation in Beijing."

"You're welcome, Director." I ended the call and said to Keith, "Well, I guess we're not leaving after all." But I didn't feel vindicated. I still felt nothing.

I made good on my promise and arranged a phone call between Ambassador Huntsman and Director Mueller. I don't know what was said, but I was never asked to leave.

The morning after the Attorney General's departure I received two phone calls. The first was from the Legat in Tokyo. "Hey, thanks for dumping your problems on to me," he said jokingly.

"What are you talking about?" I asked.

"You haven't heard? Right after the Attorney General left Beijing, Bud started having chest pains. Since they were closer to Tokyo than Beijing, they made an emergency landing in Tokyo. I was stuck with them until they could find out if he had a heart attack."

"Is he dead?" I asked, hopefully.

"No," he laughed.

"Too bad," I said. "At least he was out of my airspace when it happened."

The second call was from Dick. "Kathy, this is Dick. I just wanted to see how you're doing," his voice boomed at me cheerfully. Dick, being the spineless fuck he was, had waited until someone from his stupid-monkey grapevine had told him I had the full backing of Director Mueller. He had waited to make sure he was standing on the right side of things when the final bucket of shit hit the proverbial fan. If I was in trouble, then he was in trouble. Now that the tide had turned in my favor, he wanted to be friends. All this was running through my mind as I listened to him yammer on without hearing a word he was saying.

Finally, I interrupted him and said, "You know, Dick. I've been trying to reach you all week. But last night I received a supportive phone call from Director Mueller. I also have the full support of my Ambassador. I no longer need your fucking help." I didn't wait for a reply nor did I want one. I hung up the phone.

That afternoon, I passed Ambassador Huntsman in the hallway. I told him what had happened to Bud. The Ambassador shook his head. "Well, that's karmic justice for you." I nodded and we both went about our business.

Later, I received a copy of the photo taken with the Attorney General at the Great Wall. I had a smile on my face, completely incongruous to what I remember feeling as I stood on that wall. I think I must have been a little pleased that the trek to the Great Wall had been a bust.

CHAPTER THIRTY-NINE

THE BEGINNING OF THE END

★ ★ ★

*I will no longer mutilate and destroy myself in
order to find a secret behind the ruins.*
—Herman Hesse, *Siddhartha*

Shortly after Attorney General Holder's visit to Beijing, I was notified that Director Mueller had ordered an internal investigation into the incident involving the AG's security detail. FBI internal investigations are conducted by Special Agents assigned to the Office of Professional Responsibility (OPR). Not many people wanted to end up in the OPR unit. Some of those who did should never have been assigned to do what they were mandated to do, which was to investigate one of their own.

When I received the email letting me know two OPR investigators would be traveling to Beijing to conduct interviews with my office staff as well as other members of the US Embassy, a twinge of fear raced down my spine. I had known only a couple of people who had been assigned to the OPR. They had the type of personalities that enjoyed the failure of others, relished finding wrongdoing, even thrived on exposing the humiliation of that perceived wrongdoing. I believe the word borrowed from the German language is "schadenfreude." The German definition indicates the person who feels schadenfreude finds pleasure in someone else's misfortune. The investigators

I had known who were assigned to OPR made no attempt to hide their feelings of schadenfreude.

When the two investigators arrived in Beijing, they were polite and professional but kept their distance from us. I would normally spend a good deal of time with a visitor from the US, particularly one from my own agency. I spent no time with these FBI investigators outside the official interview.

My office staff and I were ordered to not speak to each other about our respective interviews; nor were we to inquire with others in the embassy with whom the investigators would be meeting. I wasn't too worried about what they would find. I knew everyone interviewed and I knew what they would say. When you work in a high-threat post such as Beijing, you know the people who have your back. I knew the people being interviewed outside my office had my back. I could not say the same about those being interviewed from the AG's security detail, nor from the entourage who had traveled to Beijing with the AG.

With dozens of interviews to be conducted and compiled in Beijing and in Washington, DC, the investigation took a few months. I was never told the outcome officially, but I heard through the Legat grapevine that Bud had not been removed from his position because the AG felt Bud's position as head of his security detail was too critical.

I was not surprised, though I had garnered other tidbits of information that had come my way in the wake of the "visit," which we had started to call it in my office. "Incident" didn't seem to cover the fallout, but "visit" encompassed the entire debacle. The Legat world is small within the FBI. Everyone knew everyone else and word had gotten around as to what had happened in Beijing. I'm sure quite a few Legats were feeling their share of schadenfreude, while others were thinking, "Shit, what if that had happened to me?" Fortunately, I had a couple of good buddies among the ranks of Legats through whom I received some information that had not come to light until the Beijing visit.

According to my sources, the AG's detail had gotten themselves into hot water in other countries. A member of the team had punched a Tokyo police officer while in Japan on an AG visit. The Tokyo Police Department wanted to press charges, but nothing happened. A similar incident occurred when a member of the detail hit a woman during an official visit to Brazil. Again, nothing happened.

When I heard the "unofficial" results of the investigation, I was not shocked. I realized I could not fight the power that emanated from on high. Men would always protect other men, and women were simply cannon fodder, a tragic casualty of war. It was finally the visit by the Attorney General that made me realize the betrayal I felt from men within my own organization; their willingness to preserve their own self-interests and their own self-centered trajectory rather than the overall mission of the FBI. They were willing to allow my career to be ruined, all in the interest of sticking together as men ensuring that women would always be kept on the other side of the door, patiently waiting to be invited into an antechamber, an event that was never going to happen. It was the day I stopped loving the FBI. Had I ever really been a part of it?

CHAPTER FORTY

PERFORMANCE UNAPPRAISED

★★★

"If you plan to excel in the FBI, what you probably have not learned in your very short, few years in the FBI, is communication is key. Good luck. I have a feeling you're going to need it." My finger then hit the send button on the email to Leon, my final communication as Legat.

These were my last days in Beijing. Although I was happy to leave China and head back to San Francisco, I was resigned to the fact that my departure wasn't going to be a celebratory occasion filled with laughter and tears and shared stories. No, my last and final act was sending a scathing two-page rebuttal to FBI Headquarters in response for a lowered performance appraisal I had received from someone I had never spoken to telephonically or otherwise.

Four months prior to my departure date, Leon had been appointed Unit Chief, head of the Asian Unit. All Legal Attachés covering Asia had received a group email from Leon stating he would reach out individually to introduce himself, learn about each office, and discuss issues and concerns each Legat might have. This policy was a step up from the previous Unit Chief whose comment to me had been, "Kathy, you're one of three Legats I never hear from. Let's keep it that way." The previous Legat meant I did my job, I did not complain or whine, and I did not need to have my hand held. As a result, I rarely reached out to FBIHQ unless absolutely necessary. News on the FBI grapevine was that Leon had only a few years in the FBI; his main ambition was to be a Legat. Every time I heard a story like Leon's I cringed. It takes a great deal of knowledge of the FBI's criminal, terrorism, and counterintelligence programs to be able to do the Legat job with assurance. I had waited until I felt confident enough in my own experience within the FBI to start working toward a position as Legat. More ambitious agents didn't feel the need to develop their skillset before representing the entire FBI in a foreign country.

A few weeks had passed when I heard from other Asian Legats that Leon had followed up on his promise and reached out to each of them telephonically. My time in Beijing was drawing to a close and I wanted to brief him prior to my successor's arrival. I had sent him an email welcoming him to the unit, stating I was available at any time to discuss the Legat Beijing office. When I received no reply, I emailed him several more times to no avail.

The FBI provides every employee with annual feedback on work performance, called a performance appraisal. The Unit Chief of the Asian Unit conducted my appraisal, even though the Unit Chief was technically not my boss, nor was he positioned at a higher level than a Legal Attaché. This system is one of the flawed aspects of how IOD handles Legat personnel. I was due to receive my performance appraisal just prior to my departure.

The highest rating one can receive is an "Outstanding," followed by an "Excellent," and so on down the scale until you reach "Unacceptable." I had received an "Outstanding" on my appraisal for the past several years, and the Legat Beijing office as a whole had received an "Outstanding" on the annual inspection of the work my office had conducted since my arrival in Beijing. I was surprised when I received my appraisal to see my performance downgraded to "Excellent" from someone with whom I had never spoken or had direct communication.

To add insult to injury, Leon indicated he had reached out to the Chinese officer who had been assigned to represent the Ministry of Public Security at the Chinese Embassy in Washington, DC, to ask him what my appraisal should be. As it happens, the liaison officer in question had been my main contact when I first arrived in Beijing. Leon stated that part of my performance was based on the "lack of cooperation and leadership" I had shown my Chinese counterparts. I was appalled. I thought I had become calloused and impervious to anything else the FBI could throw at me. For one of my own colleagues to believe a representative of a foreign power that was not an intelligence ally over a fellow agent was unconscionable.

When the liaison officer had been my contact, he was often arrogant in his unwillingness to be cooperative and hid behind smug smiles and glib statements, letting me know he was being obviously evasive unless it suited his purposes. There had been many times I had gritted my teeth and smiled in return, in order to maintain the diplomacy necessary between our two offices. However, we had not once butted heads or exchanged words that amounted to disrespect. In fact, I had received praise by high-level MPS officials, in front of Director Mueller, for my willingness to respond to MPS requests in a timely and professional manner. For Leon to have gone out of the chain of command to reach out to a foreign liaison officer, much less one from a ███████████████ was beyond reprehensible, especially when Leon had not bothered to call me to defend my position regarding the negative feedback he had received from the MPS official.

My office had weathered another visit by Director Mueller, which was carried out without a hitch. After the Director's departure from China, I had about six months left in-country and I was determined to do my job well and pass along any tidbits of wisdom I felt would smooth the transition for my successor, who had already been appointed.

I was scheduled to leave just a few weeks after my Legat Operations Specialist, Tara. Tara had been a godsend to me in Beijing. She was not only the best LOS I had ever worked with, she had become a friend. One day when we were gearing up for Director Mueller's most recent visit, Tara had been standing at the door to my office while I went down the checklist of things that needed to be done. After the fifth or sixth question, she put her hand on her hip and said, "Whatever you ask me, I've already done it." I laughed out loud because it was true. She was brilliant at anticipating what needed to be done and informed me of tasks completed that weren't on my list. Tara was determined to make our last few months together a smooth transition, for which I was grateful.

After receiving Leon's appraisal, all of my efforts to speak to him directly were met with negative results. FBI protocol regarding performance appraisals is such that the employee receiving the appraisal must sign it and return it to the reviewer, indicating agreement with the findings. A refusal to sign requires a rebuttal of the findings. Being unable to reach Leon, I had resorted to sending a written rebuttal to FBI Headquarters, except I planned to send a copy to Dick. I was not about to leave Beijing without a fight. In my rebuttal, I listed the timeline I had attempted to reach out to Leon over the course of months with no results. I listed the awards and recognition my office had received and reiterated the accomplishments my staff and I had achieved during the previous three years of my tenure. At the end of my rebuttal, I couldn't resist wishing Leon luck. As Dick was the same Assistant Director who had ignored me during the Attorney General debacle, I didn't expect any recourse from him. But I did want he and Leon to know this was a fight from which I wasn't going to back down.

I had become eligible for retirement a couple of months prior to my return to the US, so I could literally walk out the door any day. When a Legat retires while overseas, that person is moved back to the post of origin, which in my case would have been Washington, DC. Although I had loved living in the nation's capital, Keith and I both missed California. We had kept our house in San Francisco, so I applied for and received a transfer as the Supervisory Special Agent of a national security squad in the San Francisco field office. By the time I left Beijing, the final death knell had sounded on my career.

Curiously, my performance appraisal was stricken from my personnel file. I had not been given the opportunity to appeal what had been written about me, nor was there any communication with Leon. Later, I heard Leon was promoted to a Legat position, from which he was subsequently removed for unprofessional, unscrupulous, and unbecoming behavior involving financial transactions with foreign women.

CHAPTER FORTY-ONE

WITH ALL DUE RESPECT

★★★

Former FBI Director Robert Mueller is a tall, slim, square-jawed man who strides hunched slightly forward, as if leading with his shoulders. When he walks, he walks without a glance behind him, sure of his place as the leader; confident we will all be following. He carries himself like the former Marine veteran of Vietnam that he is. He rarely smiles and when he does, it is a smile of politeness and economy, not pleasure. His eyes, piercing and intelligent, belie the smile on his face.

During his visits to the US Embassy when I worked as Legal Attaché, he never made chitchat, never wanted to stay long enough in the country he was visiting to see local points of interest. The foreign officials he met were always perplexed he wouldn't take time out of his schedule after traveling through numerous time zones. I found myself constantly explaining his abrupt appearances, reiterating he was a terribly busy man.

There was one aspect of Director Mueller's agenda from which he never veered; he always took the time to meet and have photos taken with the Marine guards posted at the embassy. It was one of the few times I saw him become animated.

His grave demeanor reminded me of my father, a World War II veteran of the battle of Okinawa. Daddy hardly ever smiled, and when he did, the distance never left his gaze. Perhaps this is a common trait among men who have witnessed unspeakable atrocities in war.

I first met Director Mueller prior to leaving the US to head up the FBI office in New Delhi, India. Due to a series of investigations that would require my attention upon arrival, I had the opportunity to participate in two meetings with the Director. During these meetings, I was quiet, absorbing as much as possible about representing the FBI internationally. But I was also observing Director Mueller's leadership style, ascertaining what he would require from me as his representative in several foreign countries, and how I would need to impart that information to him when called upon.

Just before I departed for India, my Unit Chief commented, "Do you know you've had more face time with Director Mueller in the past couple of weeks than most agents have in their entire career?" The question surprised me. I hadn't given any thought as to how much "face time" I had been afforded. My only thought had been, *I'd better not fuck this up, because answering to Robert Mueller is going to require all my skills and leadership as an FBI agent.*

During Director Mueller's last visit to Beijing while I was Legal Attaché, I was sitting with him and the staff of agents who had traveled with him. In a few hours, he would depart to return to the US. One of the agents, Jared, turned to me and said, "Hey Kathy, when is the wheels-up party?"

I looked over at Jared, who happened to be my Navy SEAL classmate at the FBI Academy, and widened my eyes at him, desperately trying to tell him with my nonverbal cues to shut up.

Director Mueller, who never missed a beat, immediately asked, "What's a wheels-up party?" Jared, having worked more closely with Director Mueller, obviously felt more at ease in his presence. He laughed and said, "Kathy, why don't you tell Director Mueller what a wheels-up party is?"

Director Mueller looked in my direction, eyebrows raised expectantly. *Well, shit, I can't NOT answer.* "Well, Director, as soon as your plane is out of Beijing airspace, the people from my office and your security detail will come over to my house to celebrate a successful and secure visit." I hesitated, "Plus, there's going to be a huge amount of alcohol consumed."

Director Mueller pursed his lips together and humphed in the back of his throat, as if he had learned something new. He then turned, and with characteristic focus, began to discuss an issue of more importance than my wheels-up party. I turned my best stink eye on Jared, clearly signaling, *You're an asshole!*

A few hours later, I was sitting with Director Mueller in the armored vehicle on the way to his return flight to the US. He turned to me and asked, "May I ask you a question?"

Crap! I hope this isn't about the wheels-up party!

I was more shocked than surprised. Director Mueller did not engage in small talk, nor had he ever asked me a personal question. *You're the Director of the FBI. I'm going to say no?*

Hoping I didn't sound as wary as I felt, I said, "Of course."

"You've been Legat in multiple countries dominated by men, some predominantly Muslim. Did you ever feel you couldn't do your job because you're a woman?"

Now I was truly stunned. Silently, I continued to stare at him. His gaze, as usual, never wavered.

Should I tell him the truth? If I do, will he think I'm complaining? I wanted to make sure I did nothing wrong, *said* nothing wrong. This man was my boss, the head of the entire FBI. He could remove me from my position with just a few words.

I opted for the truth.

"Director Mueller, in all the countries I've covered, I have been treated like a queen. I have been respected and given everything I've asked for, if it was in their power to give it to me. But I *will* tell you that I have been discriminated against and harassed and treated far worse by my own male agent colleagues than I *ever* was by anyone overseas." Then I hesitated, and added softly, "And with all due respect, sir, you need to know that."

He studied me silently, looked away, then turned his laser focus back toward me. "You're right, I suppose I did."

I had grown to admire and respect this man. Throughout his tenure as Director of the FBI, which had begun exactly one week after 9/11, he had shunned the spotlight, made public appearances only when necessary, and asked nothing more from his agents than he gave himself. At that moment, I had never respected him more.

CHAPTER FORTY-TWO

THE LEFT BEHIND

★★★

How does one cope with leaving behind friends and acquaintances you've made overseas, knowing you'll never see them again, knowing you'll never keep in touch via any mode of communication, knowing that by doing so you're possibly preventing them from coming to harm?

Leaving the Legat world was difficult for me. I knew I would keep in touch with certain people from other US government agencies. That is easy. Keeping in touch with someone who is a foreign national is more complicated. I knew if I ever decided to apply for another government position requiring a classified clearance, I would have to list those people from other countries with whom I have a personal friendship.

I was less worried about everyone I had gotten to know in the area I covered in India. I had made wonderful friends in all the countries I had covered, with the exception of Bhutan. The Bhutanese were not unfriendly; they were simply reluctant to open themselves to the outside world, including the FBI.

The day I left Delhi, the motor pool driver who took Keith and I to the airport, Manish, showed up at our house with a dozen red roses. He had tears in his eyes as he told me he was going to miss me. Manish and I had developed a friendship of sorts. Whenever I needed a motor pool car to take me to a meeting or to the airport, Manish routinely volunteered to be my driver. I had gotten to know him, the names of his wife and children, and other small details of his life. I always inquired about his family and made sure I chatted with him as he drove me through the busy streets of Delhi from one place to the next.

Seeing Manish standing by the van with his arms full of flowers and tears in his eyes made me realize just how much I was going to miss India. Up until that moment, I had been too busy traveling with my successor to meet with our contacts to think about what leaving would mean to me. Manish's simple gesture started tears that did not stop all the way to the airport.

I could see Manish's face in the rearview mirror as he drove. He kept looking back at me, his big brown eyes wet and shining. As he pulled up to the airport entrance and got out to open the door for me, he said, "Ma'am, I will miss you so much. You remind me of my mother who I also miss very much."

His comment was the spigot that slammed to off on my river of tears. I reminded someone of their *mother*? I was only in my midforties! I had witnessed the harshness of the Indian culture toward women, especially older women who had less value than a camel in some regions of the country. Had my time in India really turned me into a worn out, downtrodden version of myself?

Manish's round, wet face was so hangdog I immediately felt ashamed of my own vanity. Here was a man who had touched my heart and who I had obviously touched in return. I knew that his comparing me to his mother was a sincere sign of respect and fondness. I reached out to give him a hug, something I would never have done in the course of our time as driver and Legat. He tentatively hugged me back, a public gesture rarely seen between a male and female in their culture. He sniffled and stepped away to retrieve our suitcases. After he accompanied us to the check-in area, he turned and walked away. I watched him as he turned and waved from the door. I waved back, knowing I would never see him again, wondering how many people I had gotten to know over the past few years would become only memories.

Leaving India was also leaving Sri Lanka, a country I vowed to return to someday, a country where I could easily move to and live out the remainder of my days. Nepal, the roof of the world with its generous people, and over-whelmingly welcoming hospitality, was another country in which I had made wonderful friends with whom I knew I would keep in touch. The Maldives, surrounded by countless and unnamable shades of blue and turquoise that stretched to the horizon in all directions, had been a place of friendship and acquaintance. I knew I would never be able to forget the camaraderie developed with my colleagues there, even though I was always the only woman amongst an all-male, Muslim police department. I had been treated with nothing but professionalism, respect, and friendship.

Leaving China was different. I had developed tentative friendships with some of my colleagues in the Chinese Ministry of Public Security. They knew and I knew that we would never keep in touch. Their government wouldn't allow it, my government would frown upon friendships with Chinese nationals and require me to answer countless questions, pass numerous polygraphs, and, no doubt, question my patriotism and integrity on a regular basis. Those friendships were best left behind.

Throughout my daily life in Beijing, I had gotten to know the people at my hair salon, the waitresses at our favorite restaurants, the language teacher at the embassy, the tea ladies and the vegetable ladies at the wet market. These women, and they were almost all women, were part of my day-to-day routine. But my life in China had been anything but normal, as I was followed, surveilled, and monitored on a daily basis. Although the Chinese government no doubt knew who I talked to on a regular basis, I felt protective of those I would leave behind, never to hear or see again.

On my last visit to the hair salon, my hair colorist threw her arms around me. She was so tiny, her head barely reached my chest, but she clung to me like a leech as she sobbed her goodbyes. She didn't ask to stay in touch. I think she knew we wouldn't.

Later that week as we packed up and prepared to leave, Keith and I went to our favorite sushi restaurant for the last time. We had gotten to know every single waitress on staff. Some evenings when we were there, service at all the other tables would grind to a halt as they would all stand around our table to chat with us. I always spoke Mandarin with them and had gotten to know each of them by name and background. I knew their villages and their hopes and dreams. The manager would eventually come along and shoo the servers away to take care of other customers, but they always found an excuse to drift back to our table.

One young waitress, who was originally from a village outside Beijing, approached our table on our last night. She shyly handed me a tiny package wrapped in colorful paper and ribbon. "This is my gift to you." Touched, I opened the gift to find a business card holder, covered with tiny beads depicting the face of a black cat, white whiskers on a yellow background. She said, "I made it myself just for you. I hope you like it." Then she handed me a piece of paper with her email on it. "Can I have your email too?"

Even though I knew I would never contact her once I left, I lied and wrote my name and email on a napkin. She grinned from ear-to-ear. Shortly after arriving back in the US, I received an email from her. I never responded. I have often wondered how she felt, not ever receiving an answer. Did she think her email didn't reach me? Or did she believe I had lied to her, which I had, but not for reasons she would ever understand. I had not wanted to be a person who made promises I knew I would never keep. But on the off chance the Chinese were monitoring her communications, and mine for that matter, I wanted to protect her, her innocence, and her generosity in befriending a total stranger.

★★★

PART SIX

ALL THINGS MUST PASS

★★★

CHAPTER FORTY-THREE

IT'S NOT ABOUT THE GUN

★★★

To perceive is to suffer.
—Aristotle

Jason glared at me. Sitting at the kitchen counter in my parents' kitchen, I watched as his head jerked back and forth, flushed jowls flapping, an enraged bull seeing only red, readying itself to charge the matador. "What? Now that you're back you think we should all just give up our guns?"

"No, that's not what I meant."

I had just moved back from China to San Francisco and was visiting my parents for the holidays. The house was crowded with siblings and squabbling spouses and children, the latter screaming as they chased each other from room to room.

Already annoyed with the chaos, I said slowly to my brother-in-law, "What I meant was that when I lived overseas, I never worried about getting shot because people don't carry guns. Here everyone has a gun. So, I have to learn to carry myself differently now that I'm back."

"Well, *here* we have the right to carry guns. Over *there* they don't." Jason plowed ahead with his argument. "Over there" for him was anywhere but here.

"Maybe they don't need guns *over there*. There are a lot of countries I traveled to and never once did I feel afraid to go out at night alone. Here you can look at somebody wrong at the stoplight and you might get yourself shot."

"That's exactly why we need to have guns here!" Jason's cheeks were blooming red blossoms by now, beads of sweat popping across his forehead. He obviously didn't notice the irony of his circular logic.

As Jason and I stared at each other, I sensed a new tension as it became clear my welcome home wasn't going to be all that welcome. Knowing I was never going to change his mind and lacking the energy or the desire to try, I said, "I'm sure you're right."

Thomas Wolfe says you can't go home again. The place you remember from your past won't be the same. My past and those in it remained static. They had stayed rooted in the same soil, the same rolling hills, circumscribed within the same county line across which the scary and fearful unknown existed.

I had been the one to change. My career with the FBI had not been about carrying a gun, it had been about so much more. The FBI had allowed my world to unfurl, and in the process, unlocked my heart. I was where I had always been, standing on the outside, looking in.

CHAPTER FORTY-FOUR

THE RETURN

★★★

I leave no trace of wings in the air, but
I am glad I have had my flight.
—Rabindranath Tagore

Living and working overseas in India and China was the part of my career I loved best, even though it was like walking a tightrope over a pond of alligators without a safety net. Sometimes the alligators represented my own agency, sometimes the State Department, and sometimes my foreign counterparts. I learned to be diplomatic and I learned to push back against those who would push against me. When agents asked about my work as Legal Attaché, I always said, "It was the *worst* job I ever had. And it was the *best* job I ever had." Coming back to the United States after living overseas proved to be one of the hardest things I've ever done.

Stepping down to a position lower than the one I had just left had been a mistake. Once you leave a place and move into a different role with a heightened level of responsibility, you cannot unlearn those lessons. It didn't take me long to realize that the FBI hadn't changed, but I had.

I had little tolerance for the politics of the San Francisco field office. Having dealt with the machinations within FBI Headquarters, my patience had worn to a brittle gloss, ready to fracture at any minute. I had developed an edge, and it was sharp.

The day I arrived to check in, the ASAC, second in charge of the field office, wasn't present, nor had anyone been assigned to brief me on the squad I would be supervising. I made my way to the administrative office responsible for providing security badges. Because I knew everyone in that department from years before, I was able to complete the administrative paperwork required in order to become an official member of the division.

Several days would pass before the ASAC contacted me. Although the Special Agent in Charge, head of the field office, would in my experience have normally spent time welcoming a new supervisor, the female who was SAC San Francisco didn't deign to meet with me the entire time I was in San Francisco. The only time she ever spoke to me was once when I was sitting outside the ASAC's office waiting for a meeting. She came strolling in, saw me sitting there, and said, "What are *you* doing here? Don't you have work to do?" She continued to stroll past me, on the way to her office.

As I stared at her retreating back, I felt something rise up in me that I had come to recognize. I was no longer going to be treated with disdain, not by men and not by women. What she didn't realize is that she was small potatoes compared to what I had been up against for the past few years.

I didn't stop myself from responding, "I'm slumming." She didn't turn around.

Prior to my arrival in San Francisco, she and I had never crossed paths. But I was pretty sure she was annoyed with me for an incident that had happened a few weeks previously. A meeting had been called at the ███████ to meet with then CIA Director David Petraeus. Normally only the SAC and ASACs were invited to a meeting at this level, but the ████████ had told Director Petraeus that I had been Legat Beijing. He had requested I attend the meeting. When we arrived ████████, Director Petraeus politely shook hands with the SAC and ASACs. When I entered the room, he walked over to me and said, "I've heard so much about you. Won't you come sit next to me."

As I sat down on the sofa next to him, I looked over at the SAC, who was shooting daggers in my direction. At that moment, I realized I had made an enemy.

The last squad I was assigned in San Francisco was a highly classified and experimental counterintelligence squad. The agents assigned to me were hard working and experienced, having been in the Bureau an average of about ten years. I loved working with each of them, and the analyst assigned to the squad was one of the best in the entire FBI. But one of the things that had changed about the FBI in my absence was an inordinate amount of oversight by FBI Headquarters, partly due to the fact that headquarters had become management heavy.

Shortly after I left for India, agents were encouraged to move to FBIHQ, on a temporary basis, in exchange for a financial bonus. Previously, agents who wanted to compete for promotions had to vie for positions at FBIHQ and make the sacrifice to move permanently to Washington, DC, an expensive area to live. When the incentives were put in place, agents who were short on experience but long on ambition and desire to make extra money ended up at FBIHQ. As a result, when I came back to San Francisco, I inevitably ended up trying to obtain permissions and funding from agents who had no idea what they were doing.

In addition, the FBI had adopted more administrative controls and I had to waste time on assessments that had little relevance to my squad's mission. I ended up spending more time pushing buttons and reading nonsensical documents than mentoring my squad.

The little patience I had began to fray, and I gave short shrift to those FBIHQ personnel who could not understand the enormity of what the agents on my squad were trying to accomplish. The agents under my purview were out doing dangerous things on a daily basis, but FBIHQ managers seemed unable or were unwilling to provide what I requested. Terrorism had absorbed funding and personnel at an unprecedented level and other FBI initiatives fell by the wayside. Having come from a high-threat post in a high-threat country, I made my concerns known.

My disdain came to a head one day when I was attending a meeting along with several other supervisors and the ASAC. The analysts responsible for compiling terrorist groups in the region covered by the San Francisco office were providing an overview of groups they considered to be credible threats. One analyst made the comment that only those groups on the list would be investigated; no other groups would be deemed worthy of attention.

I looked at the ASAC to see if he planned to ask questions. He appeared to be compiling a grocery list in his head as I stared at him. I asked the analyst for clarification regarding the last statement. "So, let me get this straight. If a terrorist group *not* on your list is purported to pose a threat, we're not going to investigate them because they're not on your list, correct?"

"Well, we would have to consider those groups on the list to have priority where resources are concerned."

I looked over at the ASAC, who now appeared to be taking a nap. I decided he needed to wake up. I slammed my hand on the desk, looked at the analyst and said, "That is utterly ridiculous. Are we not going to keep an open mind about terrorist groups we know nothing about? If it's not on the list, let's just ignore it. Is that what you're saying?" When I looked over at the ASAC again, he just looked back at me, saying not a single word.

I pushed my chair away from the table and said, "That's it. I'm done," and walked out of the room.

Later, several people came up to me and said, "I heard you yelled at everybody in the meeting," or "Wow, I heard you blew a gasket and stormed out of the room." San Francisco is a large field office but it's still a rumor mill, just like every other FBI office to which I had been assigned. I just shook my head and said, "That's not how it happened, but whatever."

A couple of days later I received a phone call from the ASAC: "Kathy, are you OK?"

"Yeah, I'm fine, why?"

"Well, you seemed a little put out the other day in the meeting. I just wanted to check on you."

"You could have spoken up and said something about the ridiculousness of what was being discussed," I countered.

"Well, I try not to interfere too much."

You're the fucking ASAC, you're supposed to interfere!

A couple of weeks later, I was sitting at my desk when one of the male supervisors, Sam, knocked on my open door. He peeked in, head cocked forward as if testing the air for cordite, ready to bolt at the first whiff of a potential explosion. I gestured for him to come in and sit down. I didn't know Sam well, but he seemed quiet and reserved. I had often seen him sequestered with other supervisors, part of an early morning coffee clutch. We always exchanged polite greetings when we met in the hallway or attended the same meetings.

"Some of us guys go out after work for happy hour. I thought we should invite you because you're the only supervisor we haven't invited."

I looked at him, not stating the obvious, *I'm the only female supervisor amongst you.*

"The others are a little afraid of you, so I volunteered to come invite you."

"Why are they afraid of me?" I asked, perplexed. I was always polite to the other supervisors, but I kept to myself, preferring to talk with my squad during any spare time I had.

"You say what you think, and you walk around here like you have so much confidence. And you have so much experience. I think they feel a little intimidated."

I raised my eyebrows and stared at him for several seconds. I didn't know what to make of his admission. Are men really afraid of women who exhibit confidence? I didn't feel insulted or annoyed by his comments. I felt bewildered, and then resigned. No matter what I did or how I carried myself, I could never change others' perceptions of me.

I knew I felt a low-level simmering anger that had been bubbling just beneath the surface for several months. Most days I felt like a steaming pot of water, tiny little bubbles on the inner edges of the pan; one tap on the side would lead to a full boil. I was angry because I had chosen to ignore the whispers, the taunts, and the backstabbing in an organization that was male dominated and testosterone driven. I had shoved it all aside, thinking, "Well, that's just the way it is." I chose to ignore it and by ignoring it, I allowed it to flourish unchecked. I was angry because no matter what I did, no matter what I said, no matter what position I attained in the FBI, I felt a betrayal by my own colleagues, culminating in the debacle surrounding the visit by the Attorney General.

"Thanks, Sam, I appreciate the invitation. I live in San Francisco rather than East Bay and since I cross the Bay Bridge every day, I don't think it's a good idea for me to go out drinking and then drive home. But I hope you guys have a good time." I meant it. I didn't wish them any ill will.

Coming home to the United States, I knew I had changed. My willingness to accept the status quo had changed. I was unwilling to accept the way women were treated—including, in some instances, the way women treated women. Even in my own marriage, I had learned that there are limitations to what women can achieve in their careers while juggling a relationship with a partner who is also a professional, with career aspirations of their own.

Keith and I had difficult times in our marriage while we lived overseas. I was frequently away on travel and, when home, I spent long hours in the office, followed by middle-of-the-night phone calls that not only disrupted my sleep, but his. Some days I felt as if I had invited him to travel with me to a strange country, only to drop him off and ignore him for long days and weeks at a time. We had decided to come back to California, a place we both loved, to move back into the little house we had patiently and painstakingly renovated years before. In this move back to the familiar, we hoped to be able to find each other again.

Even knowing the sacrifices my career had exacted from my marriage, I still missed the responsibility of being Legat. I missed the stress. I missed the fact that every day brought something unexpected and challenging. The thrill of walking through the doors of an American embassy, regardless of which country that embassy happened to be located, never faded. I was proud to be an American, proud to be entrusted to represent the entire FBI.

San Francisco, by comparison, felt like a village; boring and dull, lacking the thing I craved, but which had been sinking tentacles into me physically, like a drug. I felt exhausted and was worried that Keith and I would end up with serious health issues. The air pollution in Beijing had taken its toll, and several people who had lived in our apartment complex had been diagnosed with lung cancer, not a single one a smoker. I was wary of the same fate. After reviewing my blood tests, my doctor in San Francisco said to me, "I don't know what you've been doing, but your blood work and your cortisol levels look like you've been chased through a jungle by a lion . . . for a very long time."

A little over a year after returning to San Francisco, I put in my request for retirement. I felt I had little left to give and the agents on my squad deserved more. On my last day, I placed my gun, badge, and credentials on my ASAC's desk, and signed the documents to release my FBI property. As I stared at my gun lying on the ASAC's desk, I realized my career had meant so much more to me than carrying a weapon. Most people think of guns when they think of the FBI. But the job is not about a gun, it's about something bigger than yourself, something you must live in order to fully understand.

A few minutes later, I was silently escorted out the door by a young girl, who looked about twelve, but was probably in her early twenties. As I heard the metallic snick of the security lock behind me, I felt a flutter of regret. I would never again enter a door as an FBI agent.

CHAPTER FORTY-FIVE

POWER

★ ★ ★

I thought leaving the FBI would be easy. I was wrong. The initial few months after retirement, I had promised to give myself time before deciding what to do next. It felt like a vacation. What I didn't bargain for after the euphoria wore off was the predictability of my days, how one followed the next and all blended into sameness.

"Normal" for over twenty-six years had been a mysterious, secret, enthralling world that others seek to know, but can only get a voyeuristic glimpse of in movies, TV shows, and books. I questioned whether I could go back to a normal life when I had never possessed that elusive ingredient necessary for "normal."

I had lived life where maintaining secrecy with classified information was paramount. I had learned to pretend to be naive, uninterested, so that people wouldn't ask me questions for which I would never give answers. Secretiveness of necessity had informed my day-to-day activities, as well as my relationships. Secrets shaped my view of the world and the people in it. I held myself to a higher standard because the FBI makes you more accountable to yourself, to the public, and to your country. Although I was, by nature, a quiet person, the secretiveness changes your personality. I had to learn how to assess who I had become while moving from the secretive lifestyle I had adopted in the process of becoming an FBI agent to the normal lifestyle of a civilian.

I began to put my resume on the market, seeking out the type of jobs a retired FBI Legat Attaché would look for in the private sector, such as "Global

Director of Investigations," and "Insider Threat Advisor," or "International Security Consultant." I had a couple of interviews that intrigued me, but most corporations were interested in my experience in China and required frequent travel there, a country to which I was reluctant to return. I began to realize my heart wasn't in the type of job a former Legat might take. I had already heard from a few former Legats who had taken corporate jobs that nothing in the private sector compares with what they did in the FBI. I knew I could not tolerate a position that would feel like a step down. I had already made that mistake by returning to the San Francisco office.

During my job search, someone commented to me that it must be hard no longer having the power I once had as an FBI agent. It struck me as an odd observation, one I had never considered because I never perceived myself as having power. My job as a Special Agent for the FBI was just that: my job. Any power I possessed came from my perception that I wasn't weak and helpless; not from carrying a gun, but because I knew I was strong, physically and mentally. My role models were other women I worked with, strong personalities, strong bodies, and strong convictions, who knew they could do the same job as a man. Did they join the FBI with the hope they would attain power for themselves? I don't think so. I believe their power came from within, from belief in their own abilities to follow their own paths, their own roads less traveled.

So, what is power? Did I ever have it? It has taken me this long to realize there is a difference between "power" and "empowerment." Most women, like my mother, don't choose a path of helplessness, powerlessness, or subordination. I had to learn that I was warring against the powerlessness I saw in my mom, when she lost battles against my dad. The only way I could avoid a similar fate was to leave and find an empowerment that could shield me; my own personal Stargate shield.

Men in the FBI, I believe, have a tough time letting go of their perceived power. Carrying around a badge and a gun perhaps gives them a false sense of their own security and power. Without these accoutrements, they may feel powerless. Without the gun and badge they might not know who they are.

I started to look at my female friends who had retired before me. With a few exceptions, female agents I knew rarely took a position in the private sector. Most male agents seem to retire on Friday and start work on Monday with large corporations in positions of security, investigations, or protection, employment similar to their jobs in the FBI. Many of those jobs allow them to carry guns.

A lot of women tend to do something creative after the FBI. I have friends who have chosen to go back to school for landscape design, open their own business, purchase a plant nursery, earn a real estate license, become editors, potters, and career coaches. At first, I thought female agents moved in a different direction because they wanted to step outside the protective shadow of an internationally revered organization and become someone separate, someone whose identity isn't tied to a gun and a badge and a legend. Now I believe it is because those women were tired of playing the game, not wanting to put up with the shit anymore. They focus their desires on something that doesn't feel like a battle in a war they'll never win.

What I learned in the course of my own job search was the same lesson I should have remembered from my time in the FBI, particularly the last few years of my career. The "good old boys club" simply moved from within the circle of the FBI to an outer circle, still comprised those guys who will only help guys, leaving the women outside the door where they will never be admitted. I like to believe that women can throw off the yoke of the FBI more easily than men. Women agents often have a more challenging trajectory in their careers. We recognize the bullshit. Leaving it behind isn't all that difficult.

In my search for the next phase of my life, post-FBI, I was fortunate enough to attend a writing retreat in northern California. There I met two women who ran the retreat, each bringing her own special gifts and unique insight to the group, which was made up of all women, with the exception of two men. They knew I struggled with being there, with what the FBI had meant to me and how it had changed me, morphed me into the person I had become over the course of twenty-six years. These two women took me aside one evening and handed me a small piece of paper on which was written the question, "Who do you want to be now that your life is your own?"

PART SEVEN

CHOICES AND CHANGES

ABOVE: At the Great Wall during former Attorney General Eric Holder's visit to Beijing; with the ALAT Brenan Despain and Analyst Len Pi. BELOW: At a meeting with Chinese counterparts during one of former FBI Director Robert Mueller's visits to Beijing; Former Ambassador to the People's Republic of China Jon Hunstman, Jr. is to the Director's left.

ABOVE: Kathy and former Secretary of State Hillary Clinton during her visit to the US Embassy Beijing. The *Chargé d'affaires* brought her over to introduce her to me because I was the only female head of agency in the embassy at that time. BELOW: On the firearms range with two other female Special Agent trainees at the FBI Academy, Quantico.

ABOVE: Beijing Legal Attache office personnel with former FBI Director Robert Mueller at the US Embassy Beijing. With me are ALAT Brenan Despain, LOS Debra Kwasney, and Analyst/Translator Len Pi. BELOW: At an international conference in Beijing, China, where presentations were given in multiple languages throughout the day.

Kathy received her FBI badge and credentials upon graduating from the FBI Academy at Quantico.

Kathy holding evidence in Colombo, Sri Lanka. The weapons would be used in a terrorism investigation in the United States.

Kathy in Male, Maldives at the going away party hosted by the Maldives Police Service.

ABOVE: Kathy with former Deputy Inspector General, Kesh Shahi, of the Nepal Police, in Kathmandu, Nepal. BELOW: Kathy on the firearms range with a classmate during New Agent's Training at the FBI Academy in Quantico, Virginia.

ABOVE: Kathy and Keith at "Night Under the Stars," an outdoor event in New Delhi, India. The event was attended by US Embassy New Delhi personnel and everyone was expected to wear traditional Indian clothing. BELOW: Kathy with classmates during a training course on the Marine Corps Base, Quantico, Virginia, while attending the FBI Training Academy.

CHAPTER FORTY-SIX

TO ALL WOMEN

★ ★ ★

The longings of women;
butterflies beating against
ceilings painted blue like the sky;
flies buzzing and thumping their heads
against the pane to get out.
They die and are swept off
in a feather duster.
—Marge Piercy, *The Longings of Women*

I've subconsciously, and sometimes consciously, held myself to a higher standard than other women. I always thought I was stronger, could hold my shit
together tighter, not allowing masculine negativity and energy to penetrate
the Stargate shield I put on every day before I walked out the door. Now I
feel like that shield is a hair shirt, a penance I wore over my true self, atoning
for sins I didn't commit. I am so ready to toss it aside.

When I was still in the FBI, I gave little thought to what other women
dealt with, at least other women who didn't work in a man's world. My "suck
it up and move the fuck on" attitude sufficed for every person with a vagina,
as far as I was concerned. It wasn't until the latter years of my career that I

started to feel a tectonic shift in my way of thinking. It all really started when I lived overseas.

There I saw women who were poverty stricken, dirty, living on streets and under bridges, begging for food for themselves, begging for food for their children that they had no choice but to bear as a result of an unwanted marriage, a wanted marriage, and sometimes likely, physical and sexual abuse.

In other countries, 99 percent of the time, I was, inevitably, the only female in the room. If another woman was present, she would be serving me tea, always quietly, moving slowly as if what she really wanted more than anything was to fade into the woodwork. Whenever a "she" appeared over my shoulder to pour me a cup, I would look her full in the face, acknowledge that she existed, and say thank you. Nine times out of ten, this acknowledgment resulted in a startled response, a deer caught in headlights. Sometimes I would see a tiny smile curl one side of her lips. Then she would scurry away to stand in the corner once again. I can only imagine the mental, and yes, physical abuse some of these women dealt with on a regular basis.

I have rarely experienced this type of physical abuse from men I work with. I cannot say what it's like, nor will I insult those who do know. I will say that I've been five-foot-nine since I was eleven, so I've learned to carry myself differently. My aura, I am told, is not a lovely amber, or lavender, or cool blue. Rather, my aura is a stormy "I will fuck you up if you mess with me." Maybe those men who prey upon women have passed me by, muttering to themselves, "She's too much trouble, I'll move on to another target." Men who perpetrate these crimes are bullies and cowards, after all. Their need for power and control feeds their hatred of the feminine.

Trying to understand the fear of so many women around the world and the fact that their bodies and their lives don't belong to them has stopped me in my tracks. My experiences, the atrocities I learned of through my job, became the genesis of my rabid desire to support women's rights and to become an advocate however and wherever I could.

When I was Legat Beijing, I received a request from an FBI office in the United States. A young woman, Jane, traveling alone, had crossed the border from Nepal into Tibet on a trek popular with hikers. According to the request, hikers must sign a book when crossing the international border into Tibet, which is controlled by China. All visitors must be accounted for. The name listed just beneath Jane's was a man from the United States, John. According to Jane's family, John was unknown to her. John was currently residing in southern China, teaching English as a second language. My office was asked to obtain permission from the Chinese government to interview him to find out if he knew the whereabouts of Jane. She had disappeared, the family hadn't heard from her in weeks, and she was presumed dead.

Surprisingly, the Chinese government gave permission to interview John, so I sent my ALAT to southern China to talk to him. Upon returning to Beijing, the ALAT said John had been extremely nervous during the interview, which was not surprising considering he was talking to the FBI in a foreign country. John had admitted he had met Jane but had lost her along the trail as they hiked into Tibet. He said he couldn't provide any further details. In his case, maybe he wouldn't. Without a confession or a body, we could do nothing. Appeals to the Chinese government came to naught. What's another lost woman in the world?

When I lived in India, I never feared to go out by myself. I was tall and strong, and I made sure to go only to those places I knew well. There were places, however, I warned other women to never go alone, to go in pairs or even groups of three or four. Old Delhi was one of those places. An ancient warren of narrow alleyways, darkened doorways leading to more narrow alleyways and dead ends. Most everyone I knew obtained the services of a guide when venturing into the maze. Each time I went, men would brush up against me, rub their arms on my breasts; I could feel hands grazing my hips and thighs. I found myself lashing out, arms thrashing, yelling at them. "Stop! Fucking! Touching! Me!" In India, this kind of behavior by men is called "Eve teasing" and, amongst women less aggressive or strong, is most likely just a precursor to rape and assault, or worse, murder.

Not too long ago I was sharing a story with another American woman. We were discussing women's rights and the state of our country, which, up until recently, was headed by a self-proclaimed sexual predator. I had told her that while working overseas, 99 percent of the time I was the only woman in the room, sometimes the only Caucasian, and oftentimes, the only non-Muslim. I delineated these details simply to illustrate that women still rarely have a place at the table. Her only response was "Weren't you afraid they would rape you?"

In all the times I have worked solely with men, both in the United States and overseas, it never once occurred to me that the men around me would try to rape me. *Weren't you afraid they would rape you?* was a litany that kept repeating itself inside my head. Her comment spoke volumes about her own reality. I have been fortunate to have never experienced that kind of brutal assault. Perhaps she wasn't so lucky.

Women through the ages have been sexually assaulted; in some cultures, women are only a vessel. Females, young and old, have been kidnapped and forced into sexual slavery since time immemorial, the shame and toil of one of the oldest professions foisted upon their broken souls. Yet, women bear the brunt of the blame—you shouldn't have gone there; what were you wearing; you asked for it; maybe you should have stayed in your place.

The day after Donald Trump was elected President, I commented to Keith that I was afraid this single event would perpetuate the beginning of one specific action—increased violence against women. If a man who laughs and sneers at women, obviously holding no respect for all things feminine, can be elected to the highest office in our land, and arguably, the world, what's going to happen to us? If the words, "grab their pussy" becomes part of the normal conversational lexicon of the President of the United States, women everywhere are doomed to retreat into a past from which we have fought so hard to pull ourselves out.

Are we seeing more violence against women now? Or are we just more aware of it? Are men who have harbored feelings of their own inadequacies, long held resentments that women are no longer in their "place," rising up en masse to take charge of our bodies, our rights, our freedom to see the world, and ultimately our lives? The United States leads the way and is a guiding light to most of the world. This I have seen from my time working overseas. So, have we, the United States, given the men of the world who feel this way, permission to act on their basest of natures?

I have always been on the side of women and I had and still have many female friends in the FBI with whom I commiserated on the status of all the eye-rolling and dick-measuring trials and tribulations we dealt with on the job. But it wasn't until I moved back to the US and spent more time with my mom that my tectonic shift started to shudder into a full-blown earthquake. She made me aware of what I hadn't bothered to see.

In the last couple of years of her life, I asked her questions my younger self would never have dared, seeking answers my younger self would have deigned unimportant, even nonexistent. Not just things like, "What do you think of the weather today, Mom?" but questions about her; what dreams she had that were never realized; did she ever love my dad; when was the happiest time of her life. She started telling me stories in a voice rusty with disuse. No one had ever been interested enough to realize she was a fully formed human being with hopes and dreams, shattered in the reality that she was born in a time before there were choices.

Each time I prepared to leave after coming home for a visit, my dad never said, "I'll miss you." His only response to my leaving was "Well, I might be dead when you get back." I had become accustomed to his litany; he had been saying it for decades.

My mom, on the other hand, always told me she would miss me, but she never begged me to stay. She would take my photo just before I left, chronicling, as she always did, our lives in frozen moments, sending me on my journey with her words, "Be careful. I love you." But I only saw what I didn't have—the love of my dad.

On one of my visits home from overseas, I had been browsing the old encyclopedias I had so loved as a child. They had been a magical world I could step into, glossy color photos of places I longed to see, birds I wanted to hear, snakes I desperately wanted to avoid. As I browsed, I noticed numerous pages had bits and pieces of napkin and snatches of paper tucked into the bindings. I then realized that each time Mom had asked me questions about where I lived, which countries I had visited, the cultures I had encountered, she had gone to her own trusted source—the encyclopedias—and explored for herself all those places I had seen that she had not. Finding those scraps of paper had cracked my heart wide open. Now, I believe in not begging me to stay, in not making me feel guilty about leaving, my mom had given me the untethered life I was meant to live. Maybe she wished she could leave, too.

Maybe I needed the space of years, the space of miles, but now I can look back and see my mom in moments frozen in amber. I see her life, I see what she didn't have, what she had long ago stopped longing for herself. She had built a box around herself, shoving her disappointments and her lack of choice behind the tyrannical running of our household, never a hug or a kiss, never a minute to listen to our fears or our happiness. I once resented her for it, was angry at her rigid self-control. I dismissed her pain. But I had learned from her and I surrounded myself with my own protection, my own shield.

I've come to learn all women have protective shields. Underneath, we wear a resilience of strength that, in Asian symbolism, is like the willow branch, swaying and thrashing against the harsh winds of life, bending, but never breaking.

My mother taught me, with her voice that was not a voice, a voice she had but didn't know was hers because she thought she didn't deserve it. She taught me, with my view of her life, that I would not and could not be the kind of woman who remained silent. She taught me that I didn't have to change myself, but it was a lesson that was years in the understanding.

The evolution of my feminine self I found through my job, ironically, in a man's world. My years with the FBI brought me to this place where I can truly see myself, my mother, my female friends, those women who came before me, the women who will come after me.

Judith Ortiz Cofer says in her essay "The Woman Who Slept with One Eye Open" that women can have macho, a quality that men in certain countries consider a male prerogative. She goes on to say that the term "macho," when divested of gender, can simply mean the arrogance to assume that you belong where you choose to stand, that you are inferior to no one, and that you will defend your domain at whatever cost. I took on my own mantle of macho in the FBI, sometimes with grace, sometimes not.

Women are expected to be feminine, not raise their voices, and not show anger. These things are not supposed to come naturally to our so-called nurturing gender. If we raise our voices, we run the risk of being called a bitch, a harpy, taking on those masculine traits that label us man-haters. Society remains constant, so therefore we have to change, we have to adapt, find ways to couch our opinions and remain quiet in the face of harassment and unwanted advances. If not, we leave ourselves vulnerable, at the mercy of public opinion. Or, as is the case of most women around the world, at the mercy of a patriarchal society.

Do I expect women to go to the extremes in behavior and personality I felt necessary in order to survive a male-oriented, chauvinistic job? No. But maybe we should scream and curse and raise our voices until we are heard. Maybe we should choose a place to stand, make it our own, and defend it at all costs until society starts to change, and we can remain constant, valuing who we are as women, inferior to no one.

CHAPTER FORTY-SEVEN

STAY OUT OF MY UTERUS

★★★

My decision to not have children was rooted long ago. It began with my steadfast promise to myself that no man would ever hold dominion over me because I was unable to set myself free. I vowed to never have children because I didn't want to be like my mother. She took every care for us, fed us, clothed us, sacrificed for us. But in my heart, I knew she didn't want us.

Before she died, she told me that before she married my dad, he said to her that he didn't want any kids, to which she replied, "Well, I don't want any either."

"Well, Mom, I'm glad that worked out for the both of you," I said, softening my sarcasm with a smile.

"I know what you're saying, but I loved you all. I really did. I only regret I didn't have the time to spend with all you kids. I was always working, and I was always tired. I never got enough sleep."

Yes, my mother loved us, but loving us out of obligation and wanting us seemed very different things. I didn't want to love out of obligation. I wanted to love another person because they gave me something I wanted in my own life.

I didn't blame my mom for her feelings. Somehow, instinctively I understood her. She didn't have the choice of birth control and abortion and career. She would not have been the first woman throughout the ages to be frustrated with her lot in life. Nonetheless, I disdained other women who made the choice to have children. Why, I would ask myself, would you have children when you could make the choice to be free of an obligation that would last a lifetime? I thought those women must be trying to fill a child-sized void in their hearts. I scorned women who made the choice to be housewives. I was stronger, more independent, and in my arrogance, completely ignored that some women just don't have a choice.

I never voiced my lack of enthusiasm for kids. Not because I felt I was wrong or that something was wrong *with* me for thinking the way I did. I just never gave it any thought. No one ever asked—especially my mom—so the topic never came up. I knew what I didn't want children and that was that. It felt totally unnecessary to say anything, until I met Keith.

The night I told Keith I didn't want children was on a New Year's Eve. We had been dating for only a couple of months, but I knew I loved him. We had known the minute we laid eyes on each other. On that night, we had started to talk about a future together. Telling Keith I didn't want children for the first time was pivotal. It wasn't a turning point in my life, but it might have been. He would either walk away, both of us feeling bereft at losing something that had just been found. Or we would reach out to each other, continuing down a path wide enough for only two people to navigate.

I told Keith I did not want children, that I had *never* wanted children, words once spoken, never to be retrieved. My resolve slowed my speech, but I knew the words needed to be said, sooner rather than later. If I had to let him go, it must be now, absolve him of any need to stay. I told him if he wanted children, he should find another woman to spend his life with. I could not and would not ever change my mind and if at some point down the road he thought he would be able to convince me otherwise, he was seriously mistaken. He let me finish, my measured words dwindling to an end, both question and statement hanging in the air. While I had talked, he had continued to look into my face, the tiniest of smiles curving one side of his lips as if he knew what I was going to say. Pulling me against him, solid and matter of fact, he said, "I don't particularly want kids either, so it will never be a problem."

Years followed, we married, I never gave another thought to my decision. Every now and then something would happen like witnessing an adolescent meltdown or hearing a teenager talk back to a parent and we would look at each other and say, "I'm so glad we didn't have kids." We would then laugh and move forward into a life of adventure, happy and fulfilling, stressful and busy, the question of our decision never blighting our day-to-day existence.

My contented, childfree existence was only ever marred by the judgment of others. Other women, that is. I would stand mute, as women I knew, even in the FBI, would tell me I was selfish to not have children. I would stand mute as women would say there's something wrong with me, there's a piece of me missing, I will regret it someday. I would stand mute in the face of their disdain, their conviction that *I* was the one lacking, my uterus held hostage by my own unadulterated narcissism and self-indulgence.

I became accustomed to questions from female strangers I met along the way, particularly overseas, where children are ubiquitous and the societal notion of a woman's worth stands firm on the issue of child-bearing. The inevitable question would come: "How many children do you have?" The question "Do you *have* children?" was never entertained as it was universally assumed, I most certainly *did* have children, my female characteristics being self-evident.

"I don't have children" was followed by a look of pity, and empathy would soften their features. "Oh, you can't have children?"—a statement and a question at the same time.

"No," I would answer, "I don't want children," which would be followed by a long pause, their merciless gaze never leaving mine, an undisguised veil of aversion and repugnance reducing their lips to a harsh slash. This was never more evident than in China, where the one-child policy had held women hostage since 1979. How dare I, a woman who could have as many children as I wanted, reduce their forced fruitlessness to a mockery with my childfree existence? Women in China had only one choice, you get one child, no more. If you got pregnant a second time, you had to have an abortion. The family tradition of having the son take care of his elders became a factor in women's lives and women caught on fast to a system that gave them no choice. Ultrasounds proved to be their friend; a female fetus was aborted, a male fetus was fed and nourished, the parents' futures guaranteed into their old age.

Sometimes if I really liked and respected the woman who had just trampled my personal choice with her high heel, I would walk away feeling less than, my womanhood diminished, the question of my perceived emotional damage bouncing around in my head like one of those little red rubber balls I used to play jacks with. Most times, I would just walk away irked, fuming, cursing under my breath, but never retaliating. "Shake it off," I would say to myself. "It's just not worth it."

As my fecundity in the eyes of other women began to fade in measured pace with my age, questions of impending motherhood became fewer and fewer. I became adept at responding to children inquiries forcefully enough that the questioner would tiptoe away, no doubt thinking society was a better place from my lack of offspring let loose to wreak havoc in the world.

Only recently has the question of my childless existence once again raised its annoying and ugly head, like one of the toothless cobras I used to see in India . . . imprisoned in a wicker basket by beggars at street corners, rising reluctantly from their sleepy existence, their bite ineffectual but still intimidating enough to make you pay attention.

I've learned to anticipate what will come next when I say, "I don't have children. I didn't want any." The look is always judgmental, never more so than one day when a woman landed a comment about my childfree choice, "There's a special place in hell for you." Given the circumstances surrounding the comment, I like to think it was made in jest. But it hurt, nonetheless, and then pissed me off more.

I relayed to Keith my frustration while he listened with sympathy and understanding, having witnessed my frustration over the years. He had been told by members of his own family that there was something wrong with me for not wanting children, the fault being all mine, of course, because what normal woman does not want children? Finally, tired of hearing my own voice, I shrugged my shoulders and said, "Oh well, I'm used to it by now."

Why should I have to say, "Oh well, I'm used to it?" Haven't women been saying this about men for decades, even hundreds of years? "Oh, that's just men, we put up with their verbal comments, their gestures of superiority, their self-anointed place at the top of the sexual food chain." Women are finally standing up with the #MeToo movement and saying, "I've had enough."

I, too, have had enough. There is nothing wrong with me. Just because I chose to not have children does not mean I don't like children or even understand them. It does not mean I have no empathy for children.

When I lived in India, I had children come to the windows of my car begging for money every day. They were dirty and skinny and hungry. I saw women with children trudging along behind them digging in garbage dumps, searching for something to eat or something they could sell in exchange for food. Education and health care existed in a stratosphere far from the rumble of their hunger pangs. This was humanity at its most heinous. And these were children brought into the world of women with no choice.

I have many nieces and nephews; I have mentored them and talked them through things they couldn't or didn't want to address with their parents. I have guided young women I've met throughout my life into their ambitions, their hopes, their dreams, their careers. I have helped young women obtain much needed and desired abortions and I have bought *Playgirl* magazines so I could teach young women about the male anatomy—expectations deflated, of course—and what to expect during their first sexual encounter. Would their parents have done these things for them? Perhaps not, which is why they looked to someone else.

I've taken a poll of my closest childfree girlfriends, and there are more than a few. Without exception, they realized they didn't want to have children early in life. They are also, overwhelmingly and without exception, brilliant, independent, unselfish, and giving people. They have given back to our society in ways most people will never know about, especially those friends who worked in the FBI, CIA, and other government agencies. I also have friends with children who have said to me in voices faint with guilt, "I love my children, but I think I would have been just as happy without them." Did they make a truly informed decision, or did they cave in the forceful wave of pressure flung at them from every corner of our society: schools, church, government, workplace, men . . . other women?

Hillary Clinton has said that a lot of people recoil from an angry woman. Why is this true when angry men are viewed as strong and righteous? Whereas women who are angry are simply viewed as unhinged, one cat-spitting scream away from the nuthouse. I've always thought Mrs. Rochester, of *Jane Eyre* fame, was a misunderstood character. Maybe Mr. Rochester just stuck her in the attic because he wanted a younger version. Or maybe he just stuck her up there because she told him she didn't want to birth a snot-nosed, screaming brat every year of her life until her sanity disappeared along with her hair, her teeth, and any semblance of bladder control she ever possessed.

Women should stop pressuring and ostracizing other women just because they didn't make the same choice. Women should be more cognizant of what they say and how they say it. Women should stop demonizing those of us who made an informed decision to not bring children into this world. In the words of one of my best childless-by-choice friends, "Stay out of my uterus."

Be happy for all of us that we have the freedom to make this choice, at least for now. Women who choose to have children have made those decisions—hopefully—of their own free will. We should all be allowed the same courtesy.

I'm going to go out on a limb here and speak for *most* women. I feel *our* path of choices is becoming more and more narrow. I personally feel the walls of choice and freedom are closing in and although there's still more than a pinpoint of light at the end of this particular tunnel, I'm terrified and appalled and full of grief and loss that the glimmer just might blink out and that we, the feminine, will be shunted aside before we can ever realize our full potential.

I'm angry at a society that still feels the need to control women and what we do with our bodies. I'm angry at a backward religious society that seems to have gained a stronger toehold in our personal lives. My most fervent wish is that women join me in rejoicing in the fact that we still have the choice to birth or not birth future generations. Let's fight for choice before the word is no longer allowed in the vernacular amongst women.

CHAPTER FORTY-EIGHT

MY MOTHER'S GIFT

★★★

My mother is my mirror, and I am hers . . .
This body is your body, ashes now
and roses, but alive in my eyes, my breasts,
my throat, my thighs. You run in me
a tang of salt in the creek waters of my blood,
you sing in my mind like wine. What you
didn't dare in your life you dare in mine.
—Marge Piercy, *"My Mother's Body"*

When my mom became ill in the last months of her life, I bathed her. She would stand on shaking legs in front of me, docile in her determination to stand on her own two feet rather than sit in the plastic and metal chair brought by the home health care nurse.

I felt her sigh, a deep breath, held and released. As her shoulders relaxed, her head drooped forward, her neck a tender stalk, vulnerable. Her hair was soft and white. Wispy tufts light as a dandelion, its feathery seeds ready to take to the wind in a single, warm breath; her pink scalp laid bare through the sparse strands.

She bent her head in supplication and trust, allowing me to gently clean her with a washcloth worn to a transparent softness. My hands slid against her skin with the soap I had gotten for her from Lush, the scent she loved, roses and springtime flowers, heavy in the humid air of the bathroom.

As I touched her, I never failed to be amazed by the skin on her back.

My mom had always favored sleeveless or short-sleeved shirts when she worked outside or in her garden, shorts and white Keds completing her ensemble. I remember when I was really small, she worked in a dress, tight around the waist, usually covered by an apron or towel, full skirt allowing her freedom of movement, an earlier iteration of the white Keds, sometimes with holes where her toes had worn through the thick, canvas fabric.

Her body now bore witness to the mark of the burning sun. Her arms and legs, no longer softly tanned by days and hours of exposure, were now flecked with brown spots, skin wrinkled as delicately as a wind caressing the sands of a desert. But the skin of her back was creamy white, flawless, no moles, sunspots, or age spots marred the milky surface.

As I smoothed the soap over her skin, I marveled at its suppleness, her flesh as yielding to my touch as that of a young girl's. This skin had never seen the sun, never been exposed to the harsh nature of my mother's daily work. Did she know how young and beautiful this skin on her back was? Had she protected this one place on her body that had never been violated with the harshness of her life? Had this unblemished place ever been touched with tenderness and love, stroked in admiration?

My father had only used my mother for one thing. Well, two really. Sex and work. Once when Mom and I were sitting at the kitchen table talking about my dad, which we often did after his death, her voice became tremulous, thick with tears I knew she would never shed. "Your dad only wanted one thing from me." And in strangled articulation, using words I did not know my mom knew, words I cannot repeat even now, she described how my father had used her body, time and time and time again. Years earlier, my brother-in-law, the surgeon, told me my mother had been exhausted by having so many children. Although emotionally strong, she was a tiny woman, and multiple births had slowly leached the life from muscle and bone. He had put her on birth control pills after the birth of my little sister because he knew my father would never resort to any responsibility himself.

Maybe the skin on my mother's back knew that it had the most difficult, essential burden of all. For it protected the backbone of this woman, the strongest person I've ever known, the strongest person I will ever likely know.

This may be why this creamy expanse of skin remained so fresh. Perhaps it sheltered the strength my mother hid so well, the strength to keep moving forward, while pushing deep down inside herself, her own dreams, her own disappointments.

Did she believe herself unloved? Did she believe herself to be undeserving of love?

As I stroked my mother's skin, tears rolled down my face. I had not always been a good daughter. I had not always understood the depth of her hurt and disappointment and frustration. My tears bore witness to my own shame and I bowed my head, my supplication mirroring hers, knowing I could never take away the years of not comprehending, the years of not seeing her for who she was.

Was I the only one to touch this skin with love, tenderness? Was the softness of her sighs as she bent her head, a surrender to a touch she had never known, wanted without the knowing?

I have been loved by a man who has touched me with tenderness and respect and awe. The hollows and contours of my body have known what this feels like. But, I know, deep in my soul, there is and will always remain a secret part of myself, the part that gives me the strength to stand guard over my hurts and my disappointments.

Will someone someday in the near or distant future find a secret hidden place on my body, the one place that protected that strongest part of me? Will they marvel that the body of an aged woman could harbor such a secret, protected by the satiny, lithe flesh of the young girl I once was?

I gently dried my mom's skin with the softest towel I could find, warmed by the heat of the bathroom. I watched her flesh ripple across her fragile bones as she raised her head, the expanse of her back falling into soft folds across her ribs, one after the other until she stood straight, her arthritic hands gripping the bathroom sink in front of her. She had given me a glimpse of her secret, the place of strength she had hidden from me all along. Will she know I will carry it with me for the rest of my life, this image of her vulnerability? I hope she knows, as she watches over me now, this last glimpse of her has been the seed that planted itself many years ago in the soil of my own strength, the strength to live in my own age, my own time, where I could be who I wanted to be, and never have to suffer the disappointment of my lost dreams. Her strength has been her gift to me.

As I slid her flannel nightgown over her head, I spread my palms across her warm flesh one last time. I know now the most vulnerable part of her, and I know we have come full circle. She had touched my little girl skin, always rubbing lotion into it, perhaps hoping I would never endure what she has endured, that it would provide a bulwark against my own hurts and regrets. And as she brought the circle of her life to a close, she also moved toward her next beginning, where her skin can become new again, yielding and resilient, readying herself for her return to the time in between, where she will be pure light once again.

THE GREAT DIVIDE

★★★

Who will provide the grand design; what
is yours and what is mine?
'Cause there is no more new frontier;
we have got to make it here.
We satisfy our endless needs and justify our bloody deed;
In the name of destiny and in the name of God.
—The Eagles, "The Last Resort"

One short year after I last saw Sri Lanka, the civil war that had ravaged the country for twenty-six years finally ended. I know the FBI had some small part in bringing it to a close. I feel grateful that I had the opportunity to work with some of the friendliest people I have ever met. Sri Lanka is an incredibly lush and beautiful country with an ancient and intricate history. I have often thought I could move there and finish out my days in this breathtaking country that had finally found peace.

On April 21, 2019, Easter morning, that peace was shattered. When I read the news, my heart broke for this country I had come to love, one that sang its siren song to me. I want you to know this place, understand its beauty, so that you will understand its loss.

These are my memories, and my own imaginings, as to how the Cinnamon Grand Hotel must have looked in the aftermath of the tragic bombing.

Sunlight

The Taprobane Restaurant was in full swing. The air hummed with the lift and lilt of conversations in English and Tamil and Hindi, a myriad of accents from around the world, faces both white and brown. Early morning greetings merged with the hushed voices of the waitstaff, the swish and susurration of their skirts moving from table to table, "More tea, madam?" "More coffee, sir?" "How are you today?" "What are your plans for the day?" I loved this fresh time of morning at the Cinnamon Grand Hotel in Colombo, Sri Lanka—generous, wide welcoming smiles of the people added to the sweetness of my first taste of tea grown on an estate not a hundred miles from where I was sitting. A soothing and familiar buzz of activity surrounded me—the musical chime of silverware on china, the soft whoosh of steam as buffet lids were raised for a quick inspection of the contents, the animated conversation between the egg popper chef and an inquiring guest. I always looked forward to eavesdropping on an exchange between the egg popper chef and a newcomer. The conversation usually involved the level of spice placed between the crepe and the egg. My own experience had taught me that what is considered "not very spicy" in Sri Lanka hovers somewhere around the Naga Viper chili on the Scoville heat scale. My first encounter with spicy foods here had ended with a face numb from chin to hairline, tears blending with the snot that poured out of my nose; the hotel staff ran to and fro trying to locate cool yogurt or a glass of milk to put out the fire in my mouth. From that point on, all foods consumed in Sri Lanka were ordered with a firm, "Not too spicy, please."

Despite the lively chatter, and the bellowing clamor for yogurt as another unsuspecting foreigner consumed the local spice, I felt at peace. This place, the Cinnamon Grand, was my home away from home in India.

My four-hour flights from Delhi to Colombo always left in the late evening and landed after midnight. The hour-long slow and undulating weave through traffic on crooked, randomly paved roads from the airport always left me exhausted. I usually didn't get to sleep until after 2:00, sometimes 3:00 in the morning. So, the Taprobane restaurant became a welcome interlude before my 8:00 A.M. in-brief with the ambassador at the US Embassy. Later, meetings with my Sri Lankan government counterparts would take me into the heat of the day.

My morning here became a time to reconnect. I would spend at least an hour chatting with the staff I had gotten to know, staring out the windows at the lushness of the garden, following the goldfish in their lily covered pond, the lazy circuits of their confined space, comforting and meditative. I cannot help but recall this scene as I imagine the room exploding.

Shadow

The large windows overlooking the garden from the Taprobane are now gone. All that remains are jagged teeth along the frames, bits of cloth and food and blood clinging to the sharp edges.

Floating on the surface of the goldfish pond, just beyond the now absent windows of the restaurant, is ash; splintered glints of shattered glass compete with the metallic gold and orange scales of lifeless fish, floating atop the debris and soot-stained water.

Quiet blankets the dense soup of air, layered with smoke and dust, which will fall softly on the faces of the dead. The egg popper chef is slumped against the wall, his jaunty white hat fallen down across his face, covered in dark red smears, a combination of his notoriously spicy sauces and his own blood.

Dishes, teacups, and silverware are pulverized and bent amid tables, blown away from the center of the restaurant, buffet lids twisted, covered in bits of egg and bacon and bread.

Here lies an arm, there a leg, twisted and ragged, grotesque in their contortions. There lies a young woman, one of the staff, the concussion of the blow leaving her face intact, peaceful in its repose.

The center of the storm leaves very little of the person who perpetuated this atrocity. His body is almost obliterated, the backpack carrying his judgment now in fragments. These minuscule bits will be pored over and questioned. Where did you come from? Why did you come here? Why, always why?

The screams and cries of those who still live have receded. Their loss of what was meant to be a joyful sunny morning of celebration had yet to find lodging in their circumscribed world.

Birdsong

After a day filled with meetings at the US Embassy and later with Sri Lankan counterparts or officials, I would have a few quiet hours to call my own in the late afternoons. Dinner was frequently an official function. At other times, I would meet embassy personnel at a casual, local restaurant. During those stolen hours, I could often be found in the Cinnamon Grand's tropical garden. Just beyond the Taprobane restaurant, a swimming pool with turquoise blue tiles glinted in the late afternoon sun. Just to the left of the pool was a large pavilion with several casual sitting areas, teak and cane plantation chairs scattered around in casual disarray, a carved teak bar, its bartenders particularly adept at fashioning a mouthwatering tropical iced cocktail to quench the thirst of a hot and humid afternoon.

After exchanging my business suit for a salwar-kameez, the loose gauzy pant and tunic sets I had gotten into the habit of wearing off-duty in India, I would race down to the garden and curl up in one of the spacious chairs. Legs tucked under me, my hand clutching a sweating mix of tart and sweet tropical juices, I could finally relax. The warmth enveloped me, and my muscles would loosen, pulling away from my bones as my skin became damp in my cotton clothes. When I lifted my hair from the nape of my neck, I felt the breeze across my damp skin. I never minded that I would need to take my second shower of the day before dinner.

Most of the other guests preferred to stay in their confined air-conditioned spaces during the late afternoon heat of the day. These hours under the pavilion became mine alone. I could empty my mind and listen to the rustling of the coconut palms, dry fronds rustling in the sea breeze that carried the fragrance of salt and fish, frangipani and lilies. Flowers I couldn't name, waxy and lush with their plate-sized blossoms, were tucked amongst the cashew and banana trees. Lime trees, heavy with bright green fruit, marched along the walls of the garden. Giant elephant ear plants waved to me as a breath of air lifted their heart-shaped faces, the sun shining through their transparent skin; chartreuse against gold, veins outlined in emerald.

The train that ran along the tracks skirting the edge of the Arabian Sea would rumble in the near distance, sailing past the windows of the US Embassy that stood just above the water's edge. I remember commenting to the Ambassador that although his office afforded him a magnificent view, he was seated in one of the most vulnerable addresses in the entire country. One train car of explosives would be the end of the American embassy. I don't think he appreciated my observation.

Silence

I imagine my pavilion must be quiet now, although not with the stillness of tranquility. There is no soft slap-slap of water against the pool tiles; no one is swimming on this day. The bright blue of the tile is dimmed by leaves and blossoms, torn and ragged and brown, floating on the still surface. The pathways once carpeted with carefully tended and manicured grass are now flattened, clods of dirt kicked up under the chaos of hundreds of feet fleeing the carnage, herded away from the fear of imminent danger.

The mouthwatering odors no longer waft from the open-air kitchen of the Lagoon Restaurant. The lingering aromas of spice and the sea are masked by smoke and fire. There are no customers inspecting the varieties of fresh fish laid on beds of shaved ice, their scales wetly gleaming and iridescent. The blackboard announcing the specials of the day in white chalk, now a cloudy smear.

The trilling song of the parakeets and the soft whistles of the parrots that once serenaded my hours of solitude can no longer be heard. I hope they have flown in the face of the slaughter.

The sweetness of tropical blooms has been obscured by the omnipresent odor of underlying decay that is typical of all tropical climates. On this day, decay has triumphed.

Repose

I would like to believe the birds of my garden sanctuary have escaped to the cool mountains of the central highlands, the earthly Garden of Eden of this island paradise. Here, the air is not raging and feverish with the tension of humans. Perhaps they will ride on a warm thermal, sent to comfort them by an ocean breeze. Then they will look down on the tea bushes that cover the hills like a tapestry, threaded through the weft and weave with the colorful clothing of the tea pickers.

And when they see this island from their bird's-eye view, they will lament that death has come once again to this place of incredible beauty. They will know in the instinct of their bones that the balm of peace has lasted only ten short years. The hate and discord of decades of civil war is once again sown on the wind.

They will know what we will never see; each mountain, one after the other, is connected through the greens and browns of the valleys; streams flow into creeks, and creeks flow into rivers, all merging into vast oceans. And they will know what we do not. We do not have to kill each other in the names of our gods. We can find peace and commonality. We can all live within the embrace of the one that sustains us and gives us life, Mother Earth. For she can give, and she can take away. And if she tires of our unwillingness to end our own self-destruction, then perhaps she will shake us all off, as easily as fleas falling from a dog's back.

MY FBI

★ ★ ★

After I retired from the FBI, I mourned my job; I missed the people I worked with, I longed to be overseas, I missed feeling like I was making a difference. I watched the news and every time something happened around the world, I wished I could be there to help, to once again be a part of something that dominated my life for almost three decades.

After Donald Trump was elected to our highest office, and arguably, at one point, the most important and powerful position in the world, I watched, along with the rest of the country, as the FBI's reputation was sullied and dulled through the machinations of poor leadership and a preposterously sycophantic Congress.

In 2019, I watched as Robert Mueller testified to this same Congress, attempting to say something loud and clear to those of us who have worked in counterintelligence, but which fell on the deaf ears of those who simply want to tear down a man who has dedicated his entire life to public service, beginning with his voluntary two tours of duty in the extremely unpopular Vietnam War.

As I watched him stumble over his words, hesitate in a way I had never witnessed, I realized how exhausted he must be. I wanted to lash out at those who continued to pepper him with questions, not hearing what he was saying, beneath all the words he was speaking. The indignity with which Robert Mueller was treated by Congress and the media not only made me angry, it frightened me.

I see the same pattern being played out in the media, and the news, and on the internet. They say law enforcement, and by extension, the FBI, should no longer exist, defunded and disassembled. Someone said to me not too long ago, "I think there should be no FBI. All you do is spy on us." Although I wanted to shout a diatribe of four-letter words at this person, I took a deep breath and said, "Close your eyes."

Of course, when you ask someone to close their eyes after they have admitted to an FBI agent that the FBI should no longer exist, the last thing they're going to want to do is commit such an act of vulnerability. So, I persisted.

"Please, just close your eyes and listen to me."

"Imagine the person you love most in the world. Don't tell me who he or she is, just picture them in your mind. Now imagine that person kidnapped or abducted from your grocery store parking lot or taken off the street in the dark. Now imagine that the person who has taken the one you love is a known murderer, rapist, serial killer . . . you name it, it doesn't matter. It is someone who wants to harm your loved one. You desperately want that person back home, safe. Right? Who are you going to call to get him or her back? If there is no FBI and there is no law enforcement and you think you're going to get that person back all on your own, then think again."

I cannot know if my example moved the person to whom I was talking. I got no response except for a shrug of shoulders and a contorted quirk of lips. I have since used that same example when I hear the latest call to defund and do away with law enforcement across the country.

In this day and age of the internet, Facebook, Instagram, and Twitter, society can distance itself from the front lines without having to be present; thus, it's easy to judge an organization such as the FBI. Those who stare at their phones and computers all day and say what they want from a distance—knowing there will be no repercussions—live their lives behind a lens of safety and security while the FBI is out there fighting all over the world. The public will never know all the FBI's successes. Most are kept quiet, so the rest of the country can sleep at night. Their failures, however, are aired for the world to see, each word culled, and every action sifted until only detritus remains. There is no understanding that important decisions are not made in a vacuum; decisions that can impact our entire population are made with the best of intentions, and oftentimes with less-than-ideal intelligence and circumstances.

The FBI has flaws in its organizational structure and in the people who work along the rungs and strictures of its very rigid procedures and regulations. It is an agency staffed with humans. Humans are flawed. People have opinions, and prejudices, and core beliefs, some embedded since childhood, some discarded after a life of learning, others gained along their paths of discovery. But I can say with some assurance, looking back on my years as a Special Agent, the majority of those humans who joined the FBI did so with the intention to do good, to make our country a better place, and to make a difference, if only on a microlevel, one life at a time. The FBI is best when dealing with a crisis; that is when the organization truly comes together, working as a unit of one team, one message, one goal: to do what is right.

Gandhi said, "You must not lose faith in humanity. Humanity is an ocean; if a few drops of the ocean are dirty, the ocean does not become dirty."

I hope my country doesn't lose faith in the FBI.

Kentucky Windage, noun.
1. An adjustment made by a shooter to correct for wind (or motion of the target) by aiming at a point horizontal to the target's position in the sight rather than by adjusting the sight to compensate.
2. Adjusting your aim to compensate for the circumstances.

ACKNOWLEDGMENTS

★★★

My deepest love and gratitude go to the women of the FBI who were first colleagues and eventually lifelong friends.

To J.T.B, my best friend, thank you for all the years of love, laughter, support, and encouragement. You are the sister of my heart.

To the incomparable women who were by my side during my years overseas: Debbie K. and Lisa G. in China, my gratitude for your dedication to the job knows no bounds. You made me look good as a Legat, and as much as I value your work ethic, I value your friendship most of all.

To Garnet W. and Karen K. in India, thank you for helping a new Legat learn to navigate the field of landmines known as the International Operations Division.

To Ang H., you stand on solid ground, you are Mother Earth, my friend. Thank you for your friendship through all the years and for sharing your own struggles. And thank you for your patience when I asked you to read my first drafts.

To Ebet W., thank you for allowing me to see through your eyes that women of the FBI have a unique humor that can never be understood by the outside world. Thank you for the years of laughter. There's more to come.

To Andi C., Sylvia H., and Mary Lou F., thank you for helping save my life. I will always be in your debt and you will always be my friends.

To Laura B., my fellow China explorer, thank you for helping me navigate the labyrinth called FBI Headquarters. But most of all, thanks for being my friend.

To Tao A., thank you for all the years of support in IOD. And thank you for sharing your stories of China with me.

To the mentors of my early years, Deb P. and Lynne H., my younger self did not take the opportunity to tell you how much your encouragement and your example allowed me to become the agent I grew into. I thank you now for showing me the way.

To Maria P., beautiful inside and beautiful outside, thank you for helping me survive the NYC years and for teaching me all things Italian.

To the incomparable Kimberly Crum of the Shape and Flow writing studio, your words, "You have a story, and you can write it," set my feet firmly on the path to writing this book. Your knowledge, encouragement, and confidence in my ability to make a dream come true will never be forgotten.

To my literary agent, Alice Speilburg, of Speilburg Literary Agency, thank you for the hard work you have put into this book. You believed in it even when I, at times, stopped believing in it myself. I hope I have written a story you are proud to represent.

To my circle of trust, my fellow writers from the Shape and Flow workshop: Anne W., Harriette F., and Nancy B., thank you for reading, editing, and listening to endless iterations of my writing with your kind words of insight and gentle critique. You have held me up and carried me to this place. Your own words and stories have been my inspiration.

To Kathleen R., thank you for being a beta reader on my early chapters. Your insight into the life of a fellow Kentucky girl allowed me to see what I needed to share, albeit reluctantly.

To the Pegasus Books team, thank you for choosing my story, out of all the stories that come your way every day. Thanks to Jessica Case, my editor, for explaining things to me, ad nauseam, so that I wouldn't tumble over a cliff. And thanks to Jen Rivera, publicist, for helping me carry this book into the world.

I would be remiss in not saying thank you to the men I've mentioned in this book, and a few others who helped me at various times in my FBI career. This is a heartfelt shout-out to those men who were honorable and supportive and encouraging.

To Larry, who literally ran the extra miles to help me through my two mile runs at Quantico, thank you for your generosity of spirit, and your dedication to the team. You know who you are.

To Gene, who sat by my side and stood behind my shoulder counting every bullet, thank you for your humor and constant teasing, and that suitcase of beer you smuggled into our dorm building. You know who you are.

To the FNU LNU (First Name Unknown, Last Name Unknown) DEA agent who gave me that extra point, thank you for recognizing an injustice against a woman. Although I don't recall your name, you have never been forgotten.

To Tom, my first Assistant Director in the Legat program, thank you for giving me the opportunity to serve my country overseas. And thank you for being the one and only lone supervisor who ever said thank you for being Legat in not one, but two difficult areas of the world. You know who you are.

To Cass, the Unit Chief who first believed in my ability to be Legat Delhi, thank you for your email to me, telling me I was your shining star out in Legat land. I still have it. You know who you are.

To former Ambassador to China Jon Huntsman Jr., thank you for your support while I was Legat Beijing. When I first sat in front of you, I said, "I'm not going to tell you what you *want* to hear. I'm not going to blow smoke up your ass. I'm going to tell you what you *need* to hear." At that, you threw back your head and laughed, and said, "Well, that will be refreshing." Thank you for your humor and not kicking me out on my ass for being straightforward and cheeky.

To former FBI Director Robert Mueller, thank you for showing me what leadership looks like, and for giving me the honor of serving my country overseas, an experience that changed my life.

I don't hate men as I have often been accused. I love men, but I have learned it takes a very special man to respect and appreciate a strong, willful, assertive woman. In my experience, those men are few. Which brings me to the man who is last on the page, but always first in my heart . . . one of the few.

To Keith, nothing is real until I share it with you. Every word, every sentence, every story in this book I began sharing with you from the first night we met. Now it is real.